COMMODITY FUTURES

COMMODITY FUTURES
Markets, Methods of Analysis, and Management of Risk

ANTHONY F. HERBST
Roy E. Crummer Graduate School of Business
Rollins College
Winter Park, Florida

JOHN WILEY & SONS
New York • Chichester • Brisbane • Toronto • Singapore

Library of Congress Cataloging in Publication Data:

Herbst, Anthony F., 1941–
  Commodity futures.

  Includes index.
  1. Commodity exchanges. I. Title.

HG6046.H47   1986   332.64′4   85-31503
ISBN 0-471-09769-1

Printed in the United States of America

10 9 8 7 6 5 4 3 2 1

Preface

It was in 1976 that I first became interested in futures trading. With the upheavals in raw materials prices, especially petroleum, and in the financial markets, it became increasingly apparent that futures trading would become more important. As managers became aware of the risk management potential of futures in operations outside of agriculture, a traditional user of futures, growth exploded. On the other side, speculators found increasing opportunities for testing their skills and luck.

The contents of this book are arranged to provide a logical progression from fundamental knowledge to specific and in some cases rather technical information. The organization reflects what I found to be effective in teaching a graduate level finance course on futures (risk management and speculative markets) at the University of Texas at Arlington. Also of influence on contents and organization was the nearly 20/20 hindsight obtained by actually trading in a number of futures markets covering a broad range of different contracts including currencies, precious metals, meats, grains and soybeans, interest rate, and stock index futures. In writing this book I posed two questions to myself: What have I learned that would have been useful had I known it before starting to trade futures? and How can I best convey this information to others?

This book is written primarily for persons who may be unfamiliar with the futures markets. Included in this group are stock market investors, speculators, and executives of organizations contemplating development of a hedging program. It is intended as an easy-to-read, yet technically sound, comprehensive treatment of futures. Although not intended as a textbook, it can be used in courses covering futures markets, as a supplement to the highly technical journal articles assigned, by providing important background information. After reading this book, the readers will be prepared to approach the trading of futures and options on a rational basis, either as hedgers or as speculators. And those with a background in economics and statistics will be well prepared to read critically the technical articles concerned with futures and options that appear in the academic journals.

Books of this type are seldom written without the aid and encouragement of many persons. This book is no exception. My special thanks go to my wife, Betty, and to our children, Mya and Geoff, for their encouragement and forebearance. I am also indebted in various ways to the following persons who contributed to the completion of this book directly or indirectly, tangibly or otherwise: David Borowski (Commodity Futures Trading Commission), Galen Burkhardt (Chicago Mercantile Exchange), Roger Dickenson (University of Texas at Arlington), Bruce Dresner (formerly of Shearson Lehman/American Express), Rob Frenzel (Nowlin Mortgage Company), Milo Hamilton (Uncle Ben's, Inc.), William Jiler (Commodity Research Bureau), Mark Jenkins (M.W. Jenkins and Company), Albert Kalinich, Norman Mains (Drexel Burnham Lambert), William Melms (A.G. Edwards), Kim Rupert (Money Market Services), Gertrude Shirk (Foundation for the Study of Cycles), Joseph S. K. Wu (Taiship Company, Ltd.), and my students and colleagues at the University of Texas at Arlington. Separate acknowledgment is warranted for Stephen Kippur and Nettie Bleich, both of John Wiley & Sons, Publishers, for their patience and encouragement in completing this work.

Any errors that remain are my responsibility.

ANTHONY F. HERBST

Winter Park, Florida
April 1986

Contents

14   Metals   221

15   Tropical Products   243

16   Other Physical Commodities   259

COMMODITY FUTURES

1
Introduction

Seldom has the U.S. financial scene undergone such a wave of innovations as we find occurred in the futures markets in the 1970s. And in the 1980s there is little reason to believe that the situation will soon change. In fact, as more business managers learn of the risk-reduction opportunities available to hedgers in futures markets, and as disillusioned stock market investors and speculators turn to the futures markets, we might predict that these markets will grow in economic importance. Availability of additional futures contracts, in different underlying commodities,[1] will contribute to industry growth through market segmentation; that is, by providing more diversity to appeal to a larger number of potential participants in the markets.

Up to the present, futures trading has been overwhelmingly an American and British phenomenon, though markets do exist elsewhere. Innovation of contracts in financial futures, however, has been almost exclusively in the United States. As recognition of the advantages to be gained from these markets spreads, we might reasonably expect not only further growth in the United States but imitation elsewhere.

Volatility and uncertainty in recent years, coupled with chronic inflation, have led many business managers to use futures markets to reduce their firms' risk exposures by hedging.[2] The main impediment to hedging by nonagricultural firms has been, and continues to be, a severe shortage of personnel who understand how futures markets may be used to reduce risk and, at the same time, misconceptions and ignorance at the policy-making level of many enterprises that prevent them from either hiring knowledgeable persons or training individuals already in the organization. If top management either does not understand futures markets or, worse yet, thinks it understands but has incorrect or outdated perceptions that stand in the way of policies allowing or requiring hedging, it is unlikely the organization will use them.

The small margin requirements (generally around 10 percent of the contract value, give or take a few percentage points) provide exciting opportunities for leveraged profits (and losses) to speculators. Those who have come around to realizing that the stock market cannot always provide a positive return after adjustment for inflation and taxes can find futures either an interesting alternative to a dull stock market or, more prudently, a useful adjunct as part of an overall portfolio. Futures need be no more risky than stocks or bonds; by putting up the same margin as on stock purchases, the risk per dollar of equity should on average be no more.

HISTORY OF FUTURES EXCHANGES

The origins of futures trading have been ascribed to various past cultures and economies. A plausible case can be made that the first system of trading for futures delivery recognizably similar to modern exchanges was developed in Japan in the seventeenth century.[3] Rents collected by feudal landlords from their tenants were in the form of a share of the year's rice harvest. Transition to a money economy from an agrarian economy required that the nobility have money available at all times. Surplus rice was shipped to Osaka and Edo for storage. There it provided the liquidity the landlords needed; it could be sold for cash in those cities. When cash was needed quickly they began selling warehouse receipts for the rice that was in storage to merchants who bought in advance of their requirements.[4] Before long the sale of warehouse receipts on rice in storage evolved into sale of futures contracts (and only futures contracts) on the Dojima rice market.[5]

In the Western world, "to arrive" contracts of sale date from 1780 in the Liverpool cotton trade and may have existed earlier.[6] In the United States the Chicago Board of Trade was formed in 1848, and by 1860 contracts in quantity were being made for futures delivery of specified amounts of grain at a particular location.[7]

According to one authority on futures markets:

> We need look no further back than the frontier of the U.S. in the mid-19th century for the origin of modern commodity futures trading. The essential ingredients of mercantile law, warrants for interchangable units, futurity of contracts, and price speculation were already developed and present in U.S. commerce. The circumstances of the frontier, particularly in the grain trade, were the catalyzing agent out of which futures trading grew.[8]

Whatever the earliest futures trading date and place may be, there are few who would take exception to the view that the City of Chicago has been the focal point of futures market trading in both volume of contracts traded and the dollar value of those contracts. London can claim a similar distinction for Europe. Though there have been, and continue to be, commodities exchanges in other cities, they have until recently tended to specialize in one (or few) commodities of local or regional interest. A notable exception is New York, which recently has mounted a challenge to Chicago in the arena of financial futures contracts. Time will tell whether or not New York, the traditional U.S. financial center and home of the two largest organized stock exchanges, will be able to compete effectively with Chicago's financial futures, which have the advantage of several years' head start.

FUTURES CONTRACTS AND FORWARD CONTRACTS

Forward contracting is common in merchandise trade. Without it, business trade and planning would be greatly hindered. If a small baking company could not order flour in advance of its immediate needs, for example, it would have to buy large quantities at the prevailing price and store it until needed. There would be uncertainty about what the price would be when the next order would be placed. The miller would have a more difficult task in planning how much flour to produce without orders in hand, and shortages would be more likely to occur.

Forward contracting is widely used in international trade to hedge trans-actions risk in currency exchange. The exporter may be paid in a currency other than his or her own when the export goods are delivered weeks or months into the future. Or, the importer may have to pay in a currency other than his or her own when the goods arrive. In such situations either the exporter or the importer will engage in forward contracting for currency through a bank.[9] The exporter, if paid in a foreign currency, would sell the foreign funds for the domestic currency. The sale price (exchange rate) is set not at the rate actually prevailing at the future date, but at the forward rate quoted today. The exporter then knows *today* exactly how many units of domestic currency he or she will receive when the goods are paid for at a later date. If it is the importer who must pay at a later date in a foreign currency, then the cost of the foreign funds can be set today in terms of the domestic currency. Currency forward quotes are made for 1, 3, 6, and 12 months into the future.

Forward contracting is typically done directly between individual entities. Forward contracts can therefore be tailored to the specific needs of the contracting parties. There is no standard contract size and no intermediary between buyer and seller. There is no central market place where forward contracts are traded or concluded. Generally no money is exchanged or deposited until the agreed upon delivery date; that is, there is no margin deposit. Because forward contracts are directly between the contracting parties, if there is default on the contract it is up to the individual entities to seek compensation.

Futures contracts are traded by delivery month.[10] In agricultural commodities delivery months reflect trade interest preferences related to harvest, storage, and custom. In other commodity futures (e.g., silver), there are contracts for delivery in virtually every calendar month out to some 18 months in the future. Still, certain months are heavily traded while others have little activity. Contracts are standardized by size (quantity in each contract) and by grade (quality). However, generally higher or lower grades may be delivered at a specified premium or discount from the standard grade. Delivery may only be made at certain locations specified by the exchange. Margin money is required as a performance guaranty from both buyers and sellers. Additional money is required when equity adjustments resulting from price changes bring the margin below the maintenance level. Equity is adjusted daily.

One of the most important features of the U.S. futures exchanges is that the exchanges guaranty contract performance: The exchange takes the opposite side in all trades. It is a buyer to all sellers and a seller to all buyers. Seldom has there been a serious problem regarding futures contract performance.[11] Another important feature of most futures markets is liquidity. Contracts may be bought and sold quickly during trading hours, and an existing contract may be liquidated simply by taking an offsetting position.

FUTURES TRADING AND SECURITIES TRADING

In the purchase of common and preferred stock shares, bonds and other financial securities, the buyer owns the securities. However, if they are bought through a margin account on credit they will be held by the broker carrying the account.

Securities held by the purchaser's broker in "street name," that is, in the broker's name, are held for the customer. Dividends and capital gains and losses are attributed to the customer, though collected by the brokerage firm. With voting shares it is the buyer who is entitled to cast the votes or assign the proxies.

When securities are sold "short" it is actual shares that are sold. What this means, in practice, is that the shares are borrowed from another customer's account with the same brokerage firm or from another firm's customer's account. This means that share owners who keep shares with their brokers in street name contribute to selling. To the extent that selling, and short selling in particular, contributes to downward pressure on price it is difficult to see the advantage in it for the shareholder. In opening a margin account the customer is required to sign a form permitting his or her broker to loan shares held in the account.

Short sales are always done through a margin account. Short sellers of securities are responsible for paying dividends on the borrowed shares they sell. Also, they must provide the same margin to their brokers as would have been required if they had bought instead of sold. The short seller does not receive the proceeds on the short sale; these are held by the broker. Nor does the short seller receive interest on the proceeds.

Existence of short selling along with the sale of owned shares may help to facilitate a smoother adjustment of prices than would otherwise be possible. It is clear that it does allow those who view a particular security's price appreciation prospects negatively (referred to as "bearish" on the market) equal opportunity to participate in the market with those who hold the opposite view (referred to as "bullish" or optimistic). Without short selling it is likely that trading would be much thinner in many issues. Thinly traded issues tend to have more volatile price movements than actively traded issues and they usually lack liquidity: It may not be possible to buy or sell without affecting the market price.

No particular dollar amount is required to open a cash account for securities purchases. Some stockbrokerages are happy to open small accounts, anticipating that they will become larger. Other firm's don't care to be bothered. Yet even if the firm is willing to take on small accounts, the particular account representative who has the initial contact with the prospective customer may not be interested, especially if it means diverting time and attention from larger accounts.

A margin account for securities currently requires $2000 to open. The current margin requirement is 50 percent, which means that the customer must pay half the cost of the securities he or she buys, with the broker loaning the balance. Since the 1930s the margin requirement has ranged between 40 and 100 percent (no loans from brokers). The interest charged on margin loans has generally been 1.5 to 2 percent over the bank prime rate.

Maintenance margin for securities is currently 25 percent. Brokers generally add another 5 percent to this, so that the customer has a 30 percent maintenance margin. What this means is that the customer will have to put up additional funds if equity falls to 30 percent of the account. When share prices decline it is the customer who absorbs the loss, not the broker. Therefore, the margin loan does not deline, while the cutomer's equity does. If the customer cannot or will not pay, securities will be sold to meet the margin requirement.

In securities trading commissions are paid both when initiating a position and when terminating it. Commissions may be several percent at each end of the transaction, depending on the size of the transaction and other factors. Though "round lots" are generally 100 shares and 5 bonds, it is possible to buy any whole number of shares from one upward. Commissions, however, are less on a per-unit basis when round lots are transacted.

Securities markets are regulated at the federal level by the Securities Exchange Commission (SEC), and the Federal Reserve (FED).

On the New York and American stock exchanges there are "specialists" who deal in the stocks of particular firms. They are analogous to shopkeepers who buy for inventory at the "bid" price and sell from inventory for the "ask" price. They take limit and stop orders from brokers and place them in the "book" for later execution. The function of specialists is said to be that of providing "orderly" markets. Some have charged that the existence of specialists leads to price movements other than what would be determined strictly by market supply and demand; and if the specialists can make the markets orderly, they can use the same techniques to move the market in their favor.

COMMODITIES

Commodity accounts generally require a minimum of $5000 to open. Some brokers may impose additional requirements, such as minimum net worth of a specified amount. Accounts, once they are opened, must contain a specified minimum equity for trading to be permitted.

Each commodity futures trade requires a buyer (who is "long") and a seller (who is "short"). Each outstanding pair of long and short positions creates one contract of "open interest." Open interest declines when positions are offset: existing shorts buying and longs selling.

A futures contract is precisely that, an agreement to either deliver or take delivery at a later date, at a price determined today. Most contracts are settled not by delivery but by offsetting open positions before the delivery month. Gains and losses accrue to long and short open positions as the per-unit contract price in the market rises or declines after the position is entered into. Gains or losses are fixed when a position is offset.

Unlike securities transactions, futures contracts are always for a specified number of units of the underlying item. For example, a contract for wheat on the Chicago Board of Trade is always 5000 bushels, never less.[12] More than one contract can be traded, but each is for 5000 bushels. On the Mid-America Exchange the wheat contract is always 1000 bushels.

Since the underlying commodity itself does not change ownership unless and until the contract is held to delivery (the underlying commodity may not yet even exist in some cases), interest is not charged on the difference between the customer's margin deposit and the value of the contract. The margin itself is not a downpayment or partial payment, it is a good faith deposit, or performance guaranty.

Commodity futures margins are specified in dollars and generally found to be around 10 percent of contract value. Initial margins are changed infrequently by the exchanges. When a market is quiet (i.e., volatility is relatively low) initial margin may be less than 10 percent. In volatile markets it may be substantially more. Maintenance margins are normally around 70 percent of the initial margin. For example, if the initial margin on a contract is $3000 the price of the underlying commodity could decline to produce a loss of about $900 before there would be a margin call, and additional funds would have to be deposited or the contract sold.

Commissions on futures contracts are normally less than one percent of the contract value. This is paid only when the position is offset and is thus a

TABLE 1.1. SUMMARY COMPARISON OF FUTURES WITH SECURITIES TRADING

	Securities	Futures
Initial margin	50% of value (20% for nonconvertible bonds)	Approximately 10%
Maintenance margin	30% of account	75% of initial dollar margin
Interest	Prime rate +	Nil
Commission	Generally over 1% on both buy and sell sides	Under 1% roundturn

round-turn commission. For example, a $65 commission on a 5000 bushel contract of wheat when the price per bushel is $4.35, is only 3/10 percent of the contract value of $21,750 (5000 × $4.35). Table 1.1 summarizes the differences between securities and futures contracts.

A comparison of price volatility between common stocks and commodity futures suggests that futures per se are no more risky than stocks. However, the low margin requirements for futures provide substantially more leverage, which can cause swings in equity to be greater. Those who would prefer less risk may still trade commodities, but with more than minimum margin. However, this may not be the best policy to follow, as will become clear in chapter 7.

Notes

[1] The word "commodity" will be used to refer to any item for delivery against an expiring futures contract. This term, therefore, will include financial securities as well as agricultural products, metals, and other physical commodities.

[2] Hedging is described in detail later. For now let us define a hedge as a means of reducing risk by taking a position in a futures market that is opposite to a cash position. For example, a copper fabricator, who makes electrical wire for sale, may buy futures contracts in copper to provide protection against a price increase in raw copper that the firm will need to buy at a later date. A copper smelting firm, having a large inventory, may sell futures contracts to gain protection against a price decline in copper's price.

[3] Henry H. Bakken, "Futures Trading—Origin, Development and Present Economic Status." *Futures Trading Seminar* **2** (1953): 9.

[4] *Ibid.,* p. 10.

[5] *Ibid.,* p. 11.

[6] *Commodity Futures Course* (New York: The Futures Industry Association, 1977), p. I–1.

[7] *Ibid.,* p. I–1.

[8] Thomas A. Hieronymus, *Economics of Futures Trading* (New York: Commodity Research Bureau, 1971), p. 72.

[9] In recent years it has been possible to use the futures contracts in some currencies as an alternative.

[10] Except for some London contracts, which are traded spot (cash) and three months into the future from the spot date.

[11] A notable exception is in round white potatoes in 1979, when 49 out of 57 deliveries on the March contract did not meet grade specifications in New York. See Jack D. Schwager, "A Trader's Guide to Analyzing the Potato Futures Market." *Commodity Year Book 1981* (New York: Commodity Research Bureau, 1981), p. 7.

[12] In most commodities minor variations are allowed for those contracts on which shorts make delivery.

2

The Economic Role
of Futures Markets

Futures markets in the United States have been at the center of controversy for well over a century. Opponents contend that futures trading is a destructive influence on the cash markets for the same commodities, causing increased volatility and price distortions. At the core of their contention is the view that speculators dominate the futures markets, and that their influence is to the detriment of producers and, presumably, hedgers. Supporters of futures trading assert that speculation is necessary to the smooth functioning of futures markets and provides liquidity that is crucial to the viability and usefulness of these markets. They further contend that the factual evidence does not support the charges of opponents regarding increased price volatility. In fact, they go further than denying that increased volatility results from futures trading: They argue that the evidence supports the view that futures trading tends to reduce price volatility.

Theoretical considerations suggest that futures markets provide useful functions that should result in lower prices than would be possible in the absence of such markets. By hedging cash positions with futures positions, it is possible for producers and industrial consumers of commodities to reduce their risk. In practical terms, such risk reduction means less volatility in material costs or net revenues. This should translate into lower end-product prices to consumers as savings are passed on in competitive markets.

Futures markets in principle provide two useful functions: (1) unbiased estimates of future cash prices,[1] and thus price discovery, and (2) the opportunity for producers and consumers to fix today the prices they will pay or receive at a future date. Futures prices must represent present expectations about supply and demand or else arbitrage profit opportunities would exist, and as arbitrageurs entered the markets, prices would adjust. For example, if the price of soybeans for delivery six months hence were greater than the current cash price plus carrying charges, arbitrageurs could make risk free profits by purchasing cash soybeans today, storing them for six months, and then tendering for delivery against a short futures position also entered into today.

EFFECT ON PRICE

The effect of futures trading on the price of the cash commodity must be distinguished from volatility *within* the futures price. It is possible to have a higher level of price volatility within futures prices for a commodity than the cash price exhibits, without the volatility being transmitted to the spot market. Futures prices move to reflect changes in expectations about supply and demand very quickly. Even during a single trading day the price range can be great. In September 1983 the November 1983 soybean contract on the Chicago Board of Trade moved *twice* through its 30 cent limit above and below the previous day's close: Limit up to to limit down; to limit up; to close limit down! The spot market in contrast was much less volatile. It is not conducive to doing business in the spot market to make frequent intraday changes in the cash price. Furthermore, major cash market participants have hedged their positions and find less reason to try to make sudden and frequent changes in the cash price.

In order to validate the assertion that futures trading causes increased cash market price volatility, one would have to show a clear cause and effect relationship, with the chain of causality pointing from futures to spot prices. Simultaneous price volatility in both markets could be due to a common influence, such as a crop report for agricultural commodities, or a money supply announcement by the Fed for interest rate futures.[2]

If one were to find that the futures prices led the spot price (i.e., moved first) that would still not be sufficient to attribute causality. A greater ability to quickly reflect new information—a greater sensitivity to changed expectations—is not in itself proof of causality. In the case of stock index futures, the futures index often leads the spot index. This is a result of the "wait to be traded" phenomenon identified by Zeckhauser and Neiderhoffer,[3] the fact that the spot index reacts only as its individual component issues are traded. With broad based indices in particular, such as the Value Line, some issues will not trade for some time.

Most of the research to date on the relationship of futures trading to spot market volatility has examined spot market price variability during time spans in which there was futures trading and comparing with periods in which there was no futures trading. The erstwhile onion futures market has been a popular choice for such research. A more recent approach has been to try to fit a transfer function model between futures and spot prices in financial futures.

In the following, some studies that may be considered representative are discussed. Numerous other studies have been published and research on the subject continues. Omission of a study should not, therefore, suggest anything other than this writer's preferences, and not a judgment about the quality of the works cited or those omitted.

ONION FUTURES

More studies have been done on futures and spot price volatility in onions than in any other commodity. This may seem strange because onions are not what most people think of when futures markets are mentioned. However, onions are unique in that futures trading in onions was outlawed by Congress because of allegations that futures trading was harmful. This provides researchers with a clear line of demarcation between periods with and without futures trading—which is the apparent reason for the popularity of onions as a vehicle for research.[4] While onions have received most of the attention by researchers interested in a possible linkage between futures and spot price volatility, studies have been performed on other commodities also. Roger W. Gray (1973) examined similar questions for Maine potatoes, which share many characteristics with onions. Gregory S. Taylor and Raymond M. Leuthold (1974) studied the cattle market. Both these studies concluded that futures trading was beneficial to the trade and not a source of cash market price distortion. More recently, nonagricultural futures have received similar attention. W. Gary Simpson and Timothy C. Ireland (1982), for example, investigated the effect of futures trading on the cash market for Government National Mortgage Association (GNMAs), using a transfer function model. This will be discussed in the next section. Now, on to onions!

Trading in onion futures began in 1940. Prior to 1948 most trading appears to have been by onion farmers and others who were in the market for hedging purposes. In 1955 trading in onion futures was brought under the regulatory authority of the Commodity Exchange Authority (CEA). In the latter half of the 1950s political pressure mounted for abolition of trading in onion futures, and in July 1958, Senator Lyndon B. Johnson of Texas (soon to become Vice-President and then President of the United States) introduced a bill to outlaw trading in onion futures.

Despite opposition from such influential persons as Senator Jacob Javits of New York, who saw in the banning of futures trade in onions a dangerous precedent for other commodities, the bill became law and futures trading in the commodity was halted in 1959.

Opponents of futures trading in onions were able to marshal convincing evidence to the effect that 89.6 percent of all traders were speculators,[5] with half of the contracts held by hedgers being in the hands of onion brokers. And, it was asserted that less than 5 percent of trading was for true hedging—130,000 carloads of onions were traded in futures contracts, but only 1300 carloads were actually delivered in one season.[6] This information, combined with large price fluctuations in 1958 and the CEA associating these with speculative market participation, helped pave the way for passage of the trading ban.

While it would not necessarily have halted passage of the Johnson bill, Aaron C. Johnson (1973) disclosed that the 1958 onion crop was unusual. The per-capita production was one of the smallest during a 20-year period, and this set the stage for the rapid increase in prices.

Perhaps as much as the evidence introduced in support of a trading ban, the opposition to futures trading from large growers and shippers helped assure the bill's passage. After all, it could be reasoned, if those who stood to benefit most from having a futures market to hedge in were opposed to it, why should they be forced to endure the continued existence of such an apparently dysfunctional market? It is interesting to examine the industry structure to gain insight on this question.

Richard S. Higgins and Randall G. Holcombe (1980), citing Donald Comin's *Onion Production* (1946), provide interesting observations on the onion industry. Control of temperature and humidity controlled storage facilities was concentrated in the hands of a few large firms. Smaller growers, who had no adequate storage facilities, would sell their late crop on the spot market. On the buying side were the large growers who stood to profit by storing the crop for later sale. The relative bargaining strength of the large growers enabled them to purchase at favorable prices from small producers. According to Higgins and Holcomb:

> With the establishment of widespread trading in onion futures, the smaller producers gained an alternative to selling to the larger producers. They could keep their crop at harvest and at the same time sell a futures contract to hedge. The advantage of the futures market was due not so much to the fact that smaller producers did transact in the market but rather that they had the alternative to do so if they did not receive favorable spot prices from the larger producers in the fall.[7]

It is understandable that the large growers would be opposed to futures trading if it would undermine their control of the industry. Smaller producers found in futures prices a reference for use in bargaining with the large growers. If the small producers could be kept ignorant of such information through a ban on futures trading, the bargaining position of the large growers would be restored. Given the stakes involved, and the concentration of market power, it is not difficult to speculate on why the large growers lobbied to gain passage of a ban on trading in onion futures.

Having examined the background of the industry, and obtained a perspective on the circumstances favoring passage of the Johnson bill, let us now consider some of the research that has focused on the question of whether or not futures trading led to greater price variability.

Roger W. Gray (1963)[8] examined index numbers of marketing season prices received by farmers for onions. He compared four periods: 1922 to 1941; 1942 to 1949; 1949 to 1958; and 1958 to 1962. The visual evidence provided by graphing the index numbers for these periods suggests that the period over which there was significant futures trading (1949–1958) was different than the other time periods. The marketing season index numbers were confined to a markedly narrower range for this span, indicating less seasonality existed when there was futures trading.

Aaron C. Johnson (1973)[9] reconsidered Gray's study a decade later, using new data that had accumulated in the interim. Johnson points out that between 1958 and 1962, onion prices tended to rise seasonally at about double the rate they exhibited during the period of substantial hedging.

However, for the crop years of 1962 to 1968, Johnson observed that the seasonal price pattern of onion prices was very similar to the prevailing pattern over the period of substantial hedging activity. Because 1958 was an unusual year, it seems that Gray's results were distorted by its influence. According to Johnson:[10]

> With the exception of one year [1958], the seasonal pattern in the farm price of onions remained relatively stable for 20 years; a period characterized by 9 years of substantial hedging and 10 years with no hedging. . . . The 1958 crop year was somewhat unique for at least two reasons. First, it was . . . a year of little hedging. . . . Second, . . . the per capita production of . . . late summer onions was the third smallest during the 20-year period.

In conclusion, Johnson states:[11]

> it is not at all clear that the presence of the futures market in onions had any perceptible impact on the seasonal pattern in cash onion prices. The data . . . strongly suggest it had none.

Richard S. Higgens and Randall G. Holcombe (1980)[12] took a different approach to earlier researchers. Following a test used by C. Cox (1976),[13] based on an examination of the price variance of onions during periods with futures trading and those without, Higgens and Holcombe test whether or not futures trading increased onion price volatility.

Higgens and Holcombe begin with the proposition that, on average, the expected future price equals the actual future price. Formally, this is expressed in the equation

$$P_t^a = P_t^e + \varepsilon_t \tag{1}$$

where ε is normally distributed with zero mean and variance σ_t^2 and Cov(ε_t, ε_{t+1}) = 0 for all t. As Higgens and Holcombe (hereafter H and H) point out, Equation (1) expresses a weak form of the rational expectations hypothesis because the equation assumes that the expected probability distributions are realized.

The idea expressed by Equation (1) is that on average the market's anticipated future prices will be realized, and the forecast errors will be normally distributed around actual future cash values. The normality assumption implies there is neither an upward nor downward bias in price expectations.

H and H test the null hypothesis that $\sigma_t^2 = \sigma^2$ for all t. Theory suggests that volatility will be less in the presence of futures trading (i.e., $\sigma_1^2 < \sigma_2^2$, where subscripts denote preabolishment and postabolishment). Rejection of null hypothesis, coupled with $\sigma_1^2 < \sigma_2^2$, would support the contention that futures trading reduced price volatility in onions.

Published monthly growers' prices were used to measure the cash price. Because the expected prices could not be directly observed in the absence of futures trading, H and H used the following model to estimate them:

$$P_t^e = \sum_{i=1}^{3} \alpha_i X_i^e + \sum_{j=1}^{n} \rho_j P_{t-j}^a \qquad (2)$$

where nominal gross national product is used for X_1 to measure expected change in demand, the consumer price index is used for X_2, and an agricultural crop price index is used for X_3. The second summation reflects use of past, lagged onion prices.

Equation (2) was estimated twice, first for the period in which there was trading in onion futures, and then for the period after trading was abolished. The summary statistics for the two periods are:

	Preabolishment	Postabolishment
R^2	0.65	0.80
N of obvs.	129	189
F	32.45	106.44
Sum of squares	101.95	330.84
Durbin-Watson	2.00	1.96

The value of the F-statistic used to test the null hypothesis, $F(189,129)$, was $S_2^2/S_1^2 = 3.24$, and the null hypothesis is rejected in favor of the alternative at the 1-percent level. The authors conclude that "Price variability is lower with a futures market than without."[14] However, they caution that "A test of the differences of the simple variances of mean prices before and after is obviously not well specified. It is the variance of the price adjusted for price level and income differences that is the relevant measure of price variability."[15]

H and H point out that it is interesting that none of the X_i^e's coefficients are significant at the 0.05 level over the period of futures trading while all become significant after futures trading in onions was abolished. They suggest that this may be due to the greater ease of conducting intertemporal arbitrage with futures markets then without. Without futures markets other factors become more important and intertemporal arbitrage more profitable.

Roger D. Congelton (1981),[16] in a critique of the article by H and H, suggests an alternative interpretation of their findings. He suggests that Equation (1) indicates H and H are more concerned with price predictability than with price variability. Additionally, he raises the question of whether formal futures markets are necessarily more efficient than "informal futures markets", but does not indicate how one would recognize such an informal market. Perhaps he meant forward markets when writing of informal futures markets.

Noting that both the R-square and F-statistic values are greater in the postabolishment period, Congleton concludes that onion prices were relatively more predictable after cessation of futures trading, even though macroeconomic factors became more important. He does not directly dispute the main conclusion of H and H regarding the comparison of variances in the preabolition and postabolition periods. However, in his remarks he states:

> And thus, the evidence provided by HH may be used to support the contention that informal futures markets outperformed their formal counterparts and did so in more demanding circumstances.[17]

If one accepts that the onion industry is dominated by a few large firms, then it should not be surprising that prices would be more predictable in the absence of a formal futures market. Economic self-interest would suggest that these firms might act to harmonize the price of onions with macroeconomic variables, thus making prices more predictable. One might well question, however, whether the postabolishment period provided "more demanding circumstances" for those who would gain by managing onion prices.

FINANCIAL FUTURES

Using a technique that allows for testing the influence of futures price volatility on cash price volatility over "before" and "after" time spans, Simpson and Ireland examined the case of GNMA securities.[18] Their study is interesting both because of the subject markets examined and because of the statistical methodology employed. Fewer studies have been done on the still relatively new financial futures than on the agricultural markets, and the methodology of early studies was not able to draw upon potentially more powerful statistical techniques.

Simpson and Ireland employ regression analysis with dummy variables[19] and a multivariate time series (transfer function) model with an intervention term corresponding to initiation of futures trading in GNMAs. The null hypothesis regarding a structural change in market volatility could not be rejected in all but one of several alternative equations tested.

The interpretation that Simpson and Ireland place on their regression results is that they:

> *Suggest that no change occurred in the spread between the volatility of the GNMA certificate rate and the control variable rate or the relative volatility of the GNMA certificate rate and the control rate as a result of the initiation of trading in GNMA futures. . . . Chow test results also indicated that neither the slope nor the intercept terms changed in the period after trading began in GNMA futures.[20]*

In their transfer function modeling of the relationship between futures and spot GNMAs, the intervention parameter for the change in cash GNMA volatility induced by initiation of futures trading was not significant. That is, the null hypothesis that the term was zero could not be rejected. The authors interpret this to mean "that the intervention event, the trading of financial futures, did not produce a response or alternation of the output series, the weekly or daily volatility of GNMA certificate rates."[21]

Simpson and Ireland conclude that GNMA futures trading had no influence on cash prices, either daily or weekly. They caution, however, that their measure of volatility was the amplitude of short-run price movements, and not their frequency or direction. They also do not rule out that futures market speculation may cause isolated distortions of spot market prices, even though the evidence suggests that on average futures trading does not affect cash prices.

CONCLUSION

The results of research into the question of whether and to what extent futures trading may influence cash market prices are not one-sided. However, on balance they tend to support the view that futures trading does not cause distortion of or increased volatility in cash prices.

Although research published to date has not ruled out the possibility of occasional, isolated distortions of cash prices, it appears that there exists no pattern of influence upon the cash market from futures trading.

A potentially troublesome conceptual problem exists with studies designed to divulge a causal linkage from futures prices to cash prices. This problem is that if the futures markets properly and quickly adjust to changing market fundamentals, and do so more rapidly than cash prices, then it would appear that futures price changes induce spot price changes. Researchers must be careful not to attribute causality solely on the basis of futures price reactions occurring before cash price changes when both change in response to the same factors. There are institutional considerations that suggest cash prices will be somewhat less subject to frequent or rapid adjustment as futures prices, and thus would tend to lag somewhat.

The studies cited in this chapter were selected as representative of research to date on the subject. Numerous other studies have been performed, but time and space do not allow each to be discussed.

Notes

[1] Unbiased estimates of future prices can be stated precisely as follows. Let P_o^F be today's price of a futures contract maturing at time F. Let P_F^C be the cash price at time F. Then $n = (P_o^F - P_F^C)$ is normally distributed with zero expected value. That is, $n \sim N(O,v)$ if futures prices are unbiased estimators.

[2] It is interesting to note that, since the cash markets are open after the close of futures trading and after the Friday afternoon release by the Fed of the prior week's change in money supply, the cash price reacts on Friday afternoon and futures cannot catch up until Monday morning. Thus, the chain of causality would seem to point from cash to futures!

[3] Richard Zeckhauser and Victor Niederhoffer, "The Performance of Market Index Futures Contracts." *Financial Analysts Journal* (January–February 1983): 59–65.

[4] It is somewhat puzzling that researchers have tended to focus on onions, for which trading was outlawed, for their before versus after comparisons. Reason would suggest that perhaps equally fertile territory for research could be found in those futures for which futures trading has suddenly been authorized, with no prior history of such trading.

[5] One should make note of the fact that a majority of traders might hold far less than a majority of open contracts. Thus, while speculators might outnumber hedgers, the number of contracts they hold might be no more than the number held by large hedgers.

[6] This would be neither surprising nor alarming to those familiar with futures markets and hedging. It is typical for less than 2 percent of contracts to be consummated by delivery, most are liquidated by offsetting transactions.

[7] Richard S. Higgens and Randall G. Holcombe, "The Effect of Futures Trading on Price Variability in the Market for Onions." *Atlantic Economic Journal* 8 no. 2 (July 1980): 50–51.

[8] Roger W. Gray, "Onions Revisited." *Journal of Farm Economics* 45, no. 2 (May 1963).

[9] Aaron C. Johnson, *Effects of Futures Trading on Price Performance in the Cash Onion Market, 1930–1968* (U.S. Dept. Agr. ERS Tech. Bull. 1470, Feb. 1973). Reprinted in A. E. Peck, *Selected Writings on Futures Markets,* Vol. II (Chicago: Chicago Board of Trade, 1977), pp. 329–336.

[10] *Ibid.,* p. 331.

[11] *Ibid.,* p. 336.

[12] *Ibid.,* p. 336.

[13] C. Cox, "Future Trading and Market Information." *Journal of Political Economy* (December 1976): 1215–1237.

[14] Higgens and Holcombe, "Price Variability," p. 49.

[15] *Ibid.,* p. 49.

[16] Roger D. Congleton, "The Price Variability of Onions: A Matter of Interpretation," *Atlantic Economic Journal* 9 p. 86–87.

[17] *Ibid.,* p. 87.

[18] W. Gary Simpson and Timothy C. Ireland, "The Effect of Futures Trading on the Price Volatility of GNMA Securities." *The Journal of Futures Markets* 2, no. 4 (Winter 1982): 357–366.

[19] A dummy variable has a value of 1 or 0, representing the truth value of a condition.

[20] Simpson and Ireland *Effect of Futures Trading,* p. 364.

[21] *Ibid.*

3
Market Efficiency
and Commodity Price Behavior

The behavior of securities and commodities prices has long been a matter of controversy. Differences of opinion have been polarized into two main camps: those who believe the markets are efficient, and those who believe the markets are not so efficient that analysis cannot lead to larger returns than a naive "buy and hold" strategy. The latter group is further divided into: those who advocate technical analysis, those who advocate fundamental analysis, and those who believe both approaches have merit and should be used together.

The feelings that the advocates of fundamental analysis and technical analysis have for one another can be likened to two groups within a family who are not on speaking terms. Those using both approaches correspond to the family members who get along with both factions. And, as in family feuds, the apparent hostility between the technical and fundamental factions often seems to surpass that between those who believe in market efficiency and those who do not.

RANDOM WALK

A price series that follows a random walk is one that is modeled by the equation

$$P_{t+1} = a + bP_t + e_t \qquad (1)$$

where P denotes price, the subscript the time period, and e a stochastic error term often assumed to be normally distributed with zero expected value. The a term represents "drift" in the random walk and b represents a coefficient of correspondence between today's price and tomorrow's. In a trendless market with the a term equal to zero, one would expect the b term to be 1.0. That is, tomorrow's price would differ from today's by a purely random amount, e_t.

In more formal terms, if commodity prices follow a random walk model, then the best time series forecasting model will be a first-order autoregression model (in the terminology of Box-Jenkins methodology[1]). Such a model is represented in Equation (1). If this model represents the price time series, then none of the autocorrelations or partial autocorrelations will be found to be statistically significant. Use of time series models in forecasting is covered in Chapter 9, and therefore will not be repeated here.

The implication of random walk for commodity traders is this: If commodity prices follow a random walk, then no method of forecasting can improve upon Equation (1), and therefore both technical and fundamental analysis are futile efforts to catch a will-'o-the-wisp.

MARKET EFFICIENCY

If a market is perfectly efficient the price of the commodity will follow a random walk. However, there may be different degrees of market efficiency. In an efficient market, price at any time fully reflects the consensus of value determined by buyers and sellers acting upon their assessment of all pertinent information. If this is the case, then any new information (i.e., unexpected news) will cause price to change until a new consensus of value is reached. Unanticipated events tend to occur randomly, and to be as often bullish as they are bearish. Thus, price changes are as likely to be positive as they are to be negative.

Surprises are what move prices significantly from an equilibrium range in large, actively traded markets. Formal confirmation of expectations seldom cause prices to move in the direction that the uninitiated would expect. For example, the U.S. Department of Agriculture (USDA) crop reports have little influence on price *unless* they surprise traders with significant differences from what was expected prior to the announcement. If widespread drought and hot weather in the central United States have damaged the corn crop, that information will be impounded in the market price of corn. Confirmation of the crop damage will not, therefore, elicit a large, predictable price change. However, if the USDA announcement reports that the damage was much more extensive than had been thought, the price will rise from the current level for cash corn and many futures months.

Forms of Market Efficiency

Researchers have labeled three forms of market efficiency: weak, semistrong, and strong. This categorization has been useful for facilitating empirical

testing of market efficiency. Each form of market efficiency has its own implications for technical or fundamental analysis.

Weak form market efficiency exists in a market if price follows a random
walk. Weak form efficiency implies that it is not possible to accurately forecast
tomorrow's price using only the historical series of prices extending through
today's price. In other words, knowledge of past prices is of no help in predicting whether tomorrow's price will be higher or lower than today's.

If a market is weak form efficient, it implies that technical analysis of price
charts and price series will be of no help in predicting future prices. Traditional and popular technical analysis based on charting would be of no value in
predicting tomorrow's price or any other future price if the market is weak
form efficient. Weak form efficiency, however, does not in itself imply that
fundamental analysis may not be worthwhile.

Semistrong form market efficiency is stated in the proposition that no
publicly available information will enable one to predict tomorrow's price.[2] If
true, this means that fundamental analysis will be no more useful than technical analysis in the effort to trade commodities profitably. If a market is semistrong form efficient, this means that price fully reflects not only its history but
also all other public domain information. Selecting commodity trades by acting
upon articles in *The Wall Street Journal,* or a television news story about
drought in the corn belt, or civil war in a copper exporting nation will already
be reflected in the price by the time the public gets the news.

The fact that a market may test out to be semistrong efficient does not
preclude the possibility that the particular model that was tested was misspe-
cified. The possibility remains that another model, perhaps using different
variables, or the same variables in different ways, may prove useful in predicting future prices. For an analogy, if life is not discovered on Mars or Venus,
that does not rule out the possibility that life will be found on another planet,
perhaps in another solar system.

In contrast to testing for semistrong form efficiency, the tests for weak
form efficiency are much less complex because they may concentrate only on
price, and perhaps a limited number of variables closely related to price, such
as volume of trading and open interest. However, most of the testing on weak
form efficiency has used techniques that are not capable of pattern recognition
unless such patterns constantly repeat within the same data series without
much variation.

Strong-form market efficiency holds if even "insider" information cannot
enable its possessor to "beat the market." That such information can indeed be
useful is not seriously questioned. However, there is a question of the degree to
which different types of inside information are useful in forecasting the direction prices are likely to take. For example, there would seem to be strong a
priori rationale to assume that a U.S. Weather Service forecast of an exceptionally hot summer in the central United States would elicit market reaction
different in degree, if not direction, from the information on the poor Soviet

Union wheat harvests in 1974 and 1979. Initially, such information is known only to a few "insiders." In the case of the Soviet crop failures, orders were placed before the public became aware of the situation, and at prices far lower than they would have been otherwise.[3]

Where the potential exists for insiders to profit from special knowledge at the expense of the public, special measures are sometimes employed. For example, the USDA takes security measures designed to prevent anyone being tipped off about its crop reports prior to the formal press release. To implement this security, anyone entering beyond a certain time past a certain location point within the USDA offices is not allowed to leave until after the report is released. And, to prevent anyone inside signaling to a confederate on the outside, the blinds on all windows in the office preparing the report are drawn.

Market efficiency implies that "beating the market," earning an excess return over and above that of a simple buy-and-hold strategy will be at best a difficult undertaking. At worst, it will be impossible. Examination of some specific empirical studies may shed some light on the question of market efficiency.

EMPIRICAL STUDIES

Since the advent of the random walk–efficient markets hypothesis, countless studies have been performed to test the propositions that they imply. Of necessity only a few of the multitude of studies are discussed here. The choices reflect this author's preferences; others may have selected differently.

Empirical studies have generally followed one of two methodological paths: application of serial correlation and related tests, or testing of various "filter" rules for buying and selling. Serial correlation tests are based on a calculation of the correlation of a given day's price (or price change) with that of one day earlier, two day's earlier, and so on. If there is a regular and persistent pattern in the data, one or more of these serial correlations will be statistically significant. Filter rules are based on a rigid system of buying after a price change of a given amount or percentage, and selling after a price change of another, perhaps different amount.

Serial Correlation

Serial correlation tests were conducted by Larson[4] on corn futures. He concluded that 81 percent of new information is incorporated into the price within one day. Then, apparently because of a tendency to overreaction, a contrary 8 percent move spread over four days follows. Then, over the next 45 days, the remaining 27 percent of price adjustment occurs, bringing the price to a level appropriate to a new equilibrium. Larson's results are based on averages and data from prior to 1960. Whether or not the conclusions would hold today is an empirical question that we may hope will be addressed by researchers.

Larson's results suggest that the corn market is reasonably efficient, and that a trader would have some difficulty profiting from publicly available information. However, if there is a contrary reaction to new information, followed by further movement of almost 30 percent to a new equilibrium, it would appear that there is hope for a skilled trader to profit in the corn market.

Brinegar,[5] pursuing Working's observation that futures prices react to new information that is randomly as likely to be bullish as bearish, found positive serial correlation in wheat, corn, and rye over periods of 4 to 16 weeks. He concluded that there was a statistically significant tendency for trends to continue, though it was not particularly strong.

A technique related to serial correlation (also called autocorrelation) is that of *spectral analysis*. This technique is based on a decomposition of the autocorrelations of a time series into components in the *frequency* domain. If there is a tendency for cycles to be present in the time series this will show up as a large spectral density or "power" around the appropriate frequency.

Labys and Granger[6] used spectral analysis to study monthly future prices over the period of January 1950 through July 1965. Of the commodities studied, they concluded that only wheat had a significant seasonal. However, it should be noted that monthly data are not especially helpful in identifying the cycles of *less* than a month in period, particularly when only 187 monthly observations are employed.

Filter Studies

Filter studies are based on examining the profit and loss records of different mechanical trading rules, rules that can be implemented easily on a computer without a great deal of programming effort. Because of this, it might be argued that such rules cannot be expected to do as well as a human trader, who is capable of incorporating the subtleties and nuances of the market into his or her decisions. Of course, the filter rule does not suffer from whatever bad decisions might be made as a result of human emotion, providing some counter benefit.

If a mechanical trading system can yield positive returns over long periods of time this would suggest that the market in question is not entirely efficient. And, if a mechanical system can "beat the market" there is hope for traders who are trying to do the same.

Houthakker[7] examined wheat and corn futures using filters based on different stop orders between 0 and 100 percent. His data covered the span of October 1, 1921 to October 1, 1939 and then February 1, 1947 to October 1, 1956. The war years were not included because of the suspension of trading.

Houthakker found that different contract months gave markedly different results with the stop percentages he used. For instance, long positions in May wheat gave consistently good results (except for a 1 percent stop which yielded a small loss of 2 cents per bushel) while September wheat yielded consistent losses. However, for short positions these were reversed.

For corn futures he found that long positions in the December contract yielded consistent large profits, the May contract consistently moderate profits, and the September contract losses for all but a 2 cent gain with a zero stop percentage. For short positions, the results were reversed, though the magnitudes differed. It is also noteworthy that the study showed that December corn gave better results with relatively small stop percentages, while for May corn large stop percentages performed better.

Smidt,[8] using daily price data for May soybeans for 10 consecutive May contracts expiring in 1952 through 1961, used a set of fairly complex filter rules. He examined the results of two systems that would have the trader be either long or short one futures contract once any position had been established. Each contract was assumed to be liquidated 10 days before its expiration.

Smidt's first rule requires the trader to buy (or sell) soybeans is an N-day moving average moves upward (or downward) by K cents. For example, if a 5-day moving average were being used with a K of 3 cents, and the five-day moving average went up by 3 cents or more a long position would be established; if the 5-day average were to fall by 3 or more cents a short position would be established. Smidt tested values for N of 1, 2, 3, 5, and 10 days.

His second trading rule is similar to the first. However, the value of K is not fixed, but rather is based on a proportion of the 10 most recent daily price *ranges*. Smidt used proportions ranging from 0.05 to 0.20.

Results of Smidt's study show that losses are incurred in most years even under the most profitable moving average lengths and action prices or proportions. It is remarkable that if the large profits from the bull markets of 1954, 1956, and 1961 are eliminated, none of the filter rules produced significant profits, and most yielded losses.

Smidt also reversed his decision rules to test the proposition that a contrarian strategy might be more useful. He found that profits were both higher and more evenly spread over time than with the original rules, even if the most profitable year was not included. He concluded that profits could be obtained by selling strength and buying weakness in May soybeans. This suggests some inefficiency in this market and contract.

However, Working[9] observed that Smidt's results could be retabulated to show that Smidt's rule worked well in only half the years examined, with an average gain of only 1.26 cents per bushel. In these years, prices were generally more volatile and at higher levels. In the other years gains and losses were approximately offsetting.

Many more studies have been conducted on the question of market efficiency for common stock shares than for commodity prices, either cash or futures. Most have concluded that filter rules provide consistent profits only to one's broker when transactions costs are taken into account.[10]

Of filter rule studies on commodity prices, one of the more interesting is by Stevenson and Bear.[11] They examined the performances of three trading rules:

1. Buy and hold with a stop loss X percent under the entry price. Sell on last trading day of the contract.

2. After a move of X percent, establish a position in the direction of the market. Place a trailing stop X percent below entry price for a long position, X percent above for a short. The stop is moved if and as the price goes in the trader's direction.

3. When the price changes by X percent, go with the market; that is, go long if the market has risen X percent, short if it has fallen X percent. Hold for an X percent change from the entry price.

Stevenson and Bear simulated the performance of the trading rules with filters of 1.5, 3, and 5 percent. Unlike many other studies, their's included commission costs. They examined two markets over the period of 1957 to 1968 (12 years), corn and soybeans.

Of the trading rules, only the second performed well with both corn and soybeans. The 5 percent filter provided the best profitability, and profitability increased as the filter size was increased over the range they considered. Rules 1 and 3 worked well only with soybeans, and then only with a 5 percent filter. Of the rules, the third gave the poorest results.

Recent Evidence

Although most studies in recent years have concentrated on the stock market, the questions they raise about market efficiency have implications for the commodity markets also.

Black (1973) observed that even when transactions costs were included, the Value Line ranking system showed excess returns, suggesting the market is not, after all, as efficient as most researchers had thought. Jensen (1978) devoted an entire issue of the *Journal of Financial Economics* to evidence contrary to market efficiency.

Holloway (1982) reached similar conclusions to Black's almost a decade later, strengthening the view that the market is not as efficient as had been thought. It is interesting that public knowledge of Black's study had not seriously diminished the usefulness of the Value Line rankings.

Bonin and Moses (1974) and Rozeff and Kinney (1976) found that the stock market had seasonal effects. Other time effects have been identified by Reinganum (1982) and Roll (1982), who found end-of-year effects. Weekend effects were found by French (1980) and day-of-week effects by Gibbons and Hess (1981).

CONCLUSION

The weight of evidence suggests that the question of market efficiency had been laid to rest prematurely by academic researchers. That the markets are less than perfectly efficient will surprise few brokers, speculators, or other practioners, even if many academics are chagrined by the revelation.

If markets are *somewhat* inefficient, this should not lull anyone into the error of thinking that profits are easy to achieve. The markets *are* relatively efficient. Thousands of market participants strive with their wits, analytical techniques, and financial resources to make profits in the commodities markets. It would be hazardous to assume that a naive scheme for beating the market, such as one based on filter rules, can offer consistent profits over the long run. The adoption of such a rule by a large number of traders would assure a decline in its usefulness.

One may be able to earn large profits in the commodities markets, but only with difficulty. It should be remembered that in the commodities markets equal amounts are lost as are made by traders. In fact, when commissions are included, trading becomes a negative-sum game.

To profit in the commodities markets one must *anticipate* developments before they occur, and establish positions in the harmony with the market. To do this, one may find contrary opinion useful along with technical analysis, fundamental analysis, and econometric techniques.

Notes

[1] See, for instance, S. Makridakis and S. Wheelwright, eds., *The Handbook of Forecasting: A Manager's Guide* (New York: Wiley, 1982).

[2] One must rule out such cases as new information released *after* the markets close on a given day. Such information may enable one to predict the direction of price movement the following day, but not in such a way as to profit from it; the market will *open* at the appropriate price.

[3] Failure by U.S. agencies to disclose this information could be said to be tantamount to subsidization of grain sales to the Soviet Union by those victimized in the markets at the time.

[4] See Arnold Larson, "Measurement of a Random Process in Futures Prices." *Food Research Institute Studies* **1,** no. 3 (November 1960).

[5] See Claude Brinegar, "A Statistical Analysis of Speculative Price Behavior," *Food Research Institute Studies* **1,** no. 3 (November 1970).

[6] See W. C. Labys and C. W. Granger, *Speculation, Hedging and Commodity Price Forecasts* (Lexington, MA: Heath, 1970).

[7] See H. S. Houthakker, "Systematic and Random Elements in Short-Term Price Movements." *American Economic Review* **51** (1961): 164–172.

[8] See Seymour Smidt, "A Test of the Serial Independence of Price Changes in Soybean Futures." *Food Research Institute Studies* **5,** no. 2 (1965).

[9] See Holbrook Working, "Tests of a Theory Concerning Floor Trading on Commodity Exchanges." *Food Research Institute Studies* (Supp. 7 1967): 5–48.

[10] See Paul Cootner, "Stock Prices: Random vs. Systematic Changes," reprinted in P. Cootner, ed., *The Random Character of Stock Market Prices* (Cambridge, MA: M.I.T. Press, 1964), pp. 231–252.

Or Eugene Fama and Marshall Blume, "Filter Rules and Stock Market Trading." *Journal of Business* **39** (Supp. 1966): 226–241.
[11] See Richard Stevenson and Robert Bear, "Commodity Futures: Trends or Random Walks?," *Journal of Finance* **21**, no. 1 (March 1970): 65–81.

References

1. F. Black, "Yes, Virginia, There Is Hope: Tests of the Value Line Ranking System." *Financial Analysts Journal* (September–October 1973): 10–14.

2. Joseph M. Bonin and Edward A. Moses, "Seasonal Variations in Prices of Individual Dow Jones Industrial Stocks." *Journal of Financial and Quantitative Analysis* **9** (December 1974): 963–991.

3. Claude Brinegar, "A Statistical Analysis of Speculative Price Behavior." *Food Research Institute Studies* **1**, no. 3 (November 1970).

4. Paul Cootner, "Stock Prices: Random vs. Systematic Changes," reprinted in P. Cootner, ed., *The Random Character of Stock Market Prices* (Cambridge, MA: M.I.T. Press, 1964), pp. 231–252.

5. Eugene Fama and Marshall Blume, "Filter Rules and Stock Market Trading." *Journal of Business,* **39,** (Supp. 1966): 226–241.

6. K. French, "Stock Returns and the Weekend Effect." *Journal of Financial Economics* **8** (March 1980): 55–70.

7. M. Gibbons and P. Hess, "Day of the Week Effects and Asset Returns." *Journal of Business* **54** (October 1981): 579–596.

8. Holloway, "A Note on Testing an Aggressive Investment Strategy Using Value Line Ranks." *Journal of Finance* **36** (June 1981): 711–720.

9. H. S. Houthakker, "Can Speculators Forecast Prices?," *Review of Economics and Statistics* **39,** no. 2 (May 1959): 143–151.

10. H. S. Houthakker, "Systematic and Random Elements in Short-Term Price Movements." *American Economic Review* **51** (1961): 164–172.

11. M. Jensen, "Some Anomalous Evidence Regarding Market Efficiency." *Journal of Financial Economics* **6** (July–September 1978): 95–102.

12. W. C. Labys and C. W. J. Granger, *Speculation, Hedging and Commodity Price Forecasts* (Lexington, MA: Heath, 1970).

13. Arnold Larson, "Measurement of a Random Process in Futures Prices," *Food Research Institute Studies* **1**, no. 3 (November 1960).

14. Spyros Makridakis and Steven C. Wheelwright, eds., *The Handbook of Forecasting: A Manager's Guide* (New York: Wiley, 1982).

15. M. Reinganum, "Misspecifications of Capital Asset Pricing: Empirical Anomalies Based on Earnings' Yields and Market Values." *Journal of Financial Economics* **9** (March 1981): 19–46.

16. M. Reinganum, "The Anomalous Stock Market Behavior of Small Firms in January: Empirical Tests for Year End Tax Effects." Unpublished manuscript, University of Southern California, March 1982.

17. Charles Rockwell, "Normal Backwardation, Forecasting and the Returns to Commodity Futures Traders." *Food Research Institute Studies* **7** (Supp. 1967): 107–130.

18. R. Roll, "The Turn-of-the-Year Effect and the Return Premia of Small Firms." Unpublished manuscript, University of California at Los Angeles, March 1982.

19. M. Rozeff and W. Kinney, "Capital Market Seasonality: The Case of Stock Returns." *Journal of Financial Economics* **4** (October 1976): 379–402.

20. Seymour Smidt, "A test of the Serial Independence of Price Changes in Soybean Futures." *Food Research Institute Studies* **5**, no. 2 (1965).

21. Richard Stevenson and Robert Bear, "Commodity Futures: Trends or Random Walks?," *Journal of Finance* **21,** no. 1 (March 1970): 65–81.

22. Norman D. Strahm, "Preference Space Evaluation of Trading System Performance," *The Journal of Futures Markets* **3,** no. 3 (Fall 1983): 259–281.

23. L. G. Telser, "Futures Trading and the Storage of Cotton and Wheat." *Journal of Political Economy* **66,** no. 3 (June 1958): 233–255.

24. Holbrook Working, "Tests of a Theory Concerning Floor Trading on Commodity Exchanges." *Food Research Institute Studies* **7** (Supp. 1967): 5–48.

4

The Basics

In commodities trading, including financial futures, there are a number of fundamentals which one should know. Among them are the types of orders that may be placed, price limits, initial and maintenance margins, and taxes. This chapter attempts to provide basic training so that the reader will be prepared to read with confidence the chapters that follow. We begin with the reading of price quotes.

FUTURES QUOTES

Commodity futures price quotes are similar in many respects to those for stocks. However, there are some crucial differences. Figure 4-1 contains price quotations from *The Wall Street Journal* published on January 25, 1984. The quotations are for January 24, 1984, the previous trading day.

Some commodity futures contracts are traded on more than one exchange. For example, corn is traded on the Chicago Board of Trade (CBT) in a 5000 bushel contract size, and also on the Mid-America Commodity Exchange (MCE) in a 1000 bushel contract. Gold is traded on several exchanges, and there are differences not only in contract size, but also in the delivery months between the exchanges and in the trading hours they are open, due to time zone differences. In the case of gold, it is correctly said today that it trades 24 hours a day because there are exchanges in the United States, England, Singapore, and Hong Kong. A trader can literally buy or sell gold futures at any time of day or night, provided, of course, that his or her broker has someone to answer the telephone and place the order.

Let us first examine CBT corn. Seven contract months are listed from March 1984 through May 1985. Each contract month is a separate trading entity, and may usefully be considered a separate commodity. March 1984 corn is not the same thing as July 1984 corn; deliveries on March corn must be

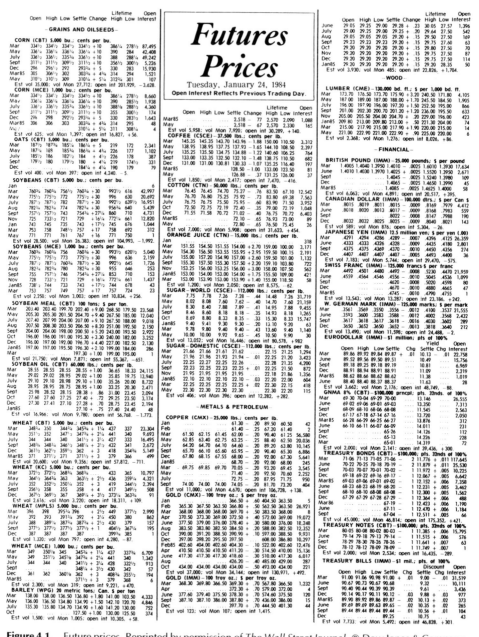

Figure 4.1. Future prices, Reprinted by permission of *The Wall Street Journal,* © Dow Jones & Company, Inc. 1986. All rights reserved. January 25, 1984 p. 44.

Figure 4.1. (Continued)

made long before July. However, one can take delivery of March corn, store it for the intervening months, and then tender it for delivery against a short position in a later month such as July.

The price of March 1984 corn opened at 334 1/2, or $3.345 per bushel. It stayed there all day, in a situation termed "locked limit up." Unlike stocks, commodity prices generally have a maximum allowable price move in a given day, measured from the prior day's settlement price. Such limit moves occur in response to unexpected news. In the case of corn (and also soybeans) a report was released by the USDA, which estimated that corn and soybeans supplies were much smaller than previously indicated. (Only some 10 days earlier another USDA report had indicated supplies were much larger than the earlier estimate, sending prices down their allowable limits!) If prices were to move their allowable limit for several days, the limits are eventually expanded to facilitate reaching a new equilibrium.

In contrast to March 1984 corn, and to the May, July, and September 1984 contracts, the December contract rose only 5 cents on the day. December opened at 298, which also was its highest price for the day. It traded down to 292 1/2, and *settled* at 293 3/4. In commodities the settlement price is based on the prices of the last few trades of the day and the bid-ask spread at the close of trading. It is often different from the price of the actual last trade. The exchange determines what the settlement price will be. In the case of contract months locked up at their daily limit, the settlement and high prices are the same, even though in such cases there may have been no trading at that price.

The reason that the contracts for December and later months had less of a price increase is because they represent a different *crop year*. In agricultural commodities there is often a clear distinction between crop years. In the case of corn, the March, May, and July contracts represent grain that has already been harvested, as does much of the September contract. This is all the corn there will be (barring imports) until the next crop is harvested, and this cannot happen until winter ends, fields are tilled, seed is planted, and so on. In the terminology of economics, the supply curve of the current crop corn is *inelastic*. That is to say the supply will not increase significantly even if the price were to rise appreciably.

The lifetime high and low prices are provided, showing for example, that the March contract corn at one time was as high as $3.8625 per bushel, and as low as $2.7850. The last column of numbers at the right shows the *open interest*. This is something for which there is no counterpart in the stock market.

One unit of open interest is created for every matched buy and sell order by traders who are not offsetting existing positions they hold. For example, in March 1984 corn, there were on the prior day (i.e., January 23) 87,495 contracts to sell (short positions) *and* 87,495 contracts to buy (long positions) 5000 bushels of CBT corn. If all these contracts were to be held, and not liquidated by offset (by canceling with an order to sell if long or buy if short), then delivery would be made on 87,495 contracts. In some cases, open interest may exceed the total available supply of a commodity, but usually this does not create any problems. In all but a few noteworthy, unusual cases it has been uncommon for much more than 2 percent of open contracts to be held to consummation of the transactions in the actual sale or purchase of a commodity.

Besides open interest, the quotations include estimated trading volume for the aggregate of all contract months (figures are not available for volume on individual months) and the actual volume of trading the previous day. And finally, the total open interest is shown, along with the change from the prior day. A change in open interest of −3628 means that 3628 contracts were liquidated by holders of existing positions. Sale of an open long or short position to a new participant merely transfers the position, it does not cancel it.

However, when an existing long position in one contract is sold *and* an existing short position is covered by purchase, open interest falls by one unit.

The more active commodities are afforded full newspaper quotation coverage. Less active contracts are listed by their most active month under the heading "Other Futures Markets." "London Metal Exchange Prices" heads quotes for that exchange.

London Metal Exchange quotes are different from quotes on U.S. exchanges. There is only the spot, or cash price, and the price for delivery 3 months in the future. Both bid and ask prices are shown, indicating the spread. For example, one could sell spot aluminum ("aluminium") for 1099.50 pounds sterling or buy it for 1100.50.

In addition to futures prices, it is important to have quotes for cash, or spot market prices, especially to hedgers who are concerned about the *basis*. The basis is the difference, or spread, between the cash price and the prices of a futures contract. Figure 4-2 shows cash prices for January 24, 1984. Prices for many commodities not traded as futures are included, such as pepper and print cloth. In comparing spot prices to futures, one must make allowance for transportation charges, unless the spot price is for a commodity at an exchange-specified delivery location.

THE EXCHANGE FACILITY

The physical arrangements of the various futures exchanges differ from one another. However, a typical arrangement is for trading to be held in a "pit." A pit is a set of concentric, roughly circular steps, arranged into a pyramid, with similar steps descending on the inside to the floor level. Each step level may have eight sides (i.e., be octagonal) to facilitate identification of a particular side with a particular contract month. Traders stand on the steps of the pit, where they may easily see one another. In some futures trading there is a ring rather than a pit. A large, circular brass rail, raised to a convenient height for leaning is used, and traders face one another across the ring. On some smaller exchanges, where there are few active traders at any one time (and in London precious metals trading), traders sit at tables or desks.

A common and distinguishing feature of commodity futures exchanges is that trading is done by *open outcry*. Trades are offered to others at the pit openly, with hand signals and spoken offers. There are no specialists as there are on the New York and American Stock Exchanges. Private deals are restricted to ensure that the spirit and function of a true auction market is maintained.

Traders may trade for their own accounts or for others. They must own an exchange seat to trade. Those who trade to profit on small price changes and who seldom if ever hold position overnight (i.e., from one day to the next) are

Tuesday, January 24, 1984
(Quotations as of 4 p.m. Eastern time)

	Tues.	Mon.	Yr.Ago
GRAINS AND FEEDS			
Alfalfa Pellets, dehy, Neb., ton	119.00	119.00	97.00
Barley, top-quality Mpls., bu	2.80-2.90	2.80-2.90	2.37½
Bran, (Wheat middling) KC ton ...	114.00	119.00	84.00
Brewer's Grains, Milw. ton	137.00	137.00	108.00
Corn, No. 2 yellow Cent-Ill. bu	bp3.25½	3.16	2.41
Corn Gluten Feed, Chgo., ton	134.00	135.00	111.00
Cottnsd Meal, Clksdle,Miss. ton ..	202.5-205.	200.-202.5	160.00
Flaxseed, Mpls., bu	n7.50	7.50	5.45
Hominy Feed, Ill., ton	113.00	111.00	78.00
Linseed Meal, Mpls., ton	160.00	160.00	135.00
Meat-Bonemeal 50%-pro, Ill. ton .	a230.-235.	225.-230.	231.25
Oats, No. 2 milling, Mpls., bu	1.96-2.02	1.94-2.00	1.67½
Rice, No. 2 milled fob Ark. cwt	18.0-20.0	18.0-20.0	18.25
Rye, No. 2 Mpls., bu	n2.50	2.50	2.52
Sorghum, (Milo) No. 2 Gulf cwt ...	5.92	5.75	5.20
Soybean Meal, Decatur, Ill. ton ...	201.50	192.50	177.50
Soybeans, No. 1 yel Cent.-Ill. bu ...	bp7.51½	7.30	5.64½
Sunflower Seed, No 1 Mpls. cwt ...	n15.05	14.60	9.05
Wheat, Spring 14%-pro Mpls. bu ..	r4.18	4.15½	3.90¼
Wheat, amber durum, Mpls. bu ...	n4.40-5.15	4.40-5.15	4.07½
Wheat, No. 2 sft red, St.Lou. bu	h3.55	3.52	3.21½
Wheat, No. 2 hard KC, bu	r3.78¼	3.78¼	3.98¾
FOODS			
Beef, 700-900 lbs. Mid-U.S.,lb.fob .	1.08	1.09	.93½
Beef, boxed, gross, Mid-US cwt ...	f113.41	114.21	101.14
Broilers, Dressed "A" NY lb	x.6902	.7000	.4631
Butter, AA, Chgo., lb.	1.41	1.41	1.47
Cocoa, Ivory Coast, $metric ton ...	g2.826	2.923	1.823
Coffee, Brazilian, NY lb.	n1.50	1.50	1.32
Eggs, Lge white, Chgo doz.	1.13-1.15	1.13-1.15	.60¾
Flour, hard winter KC cwt	9.25	9.20	10.45
Hams, 17-20 lbs, Mid-US lb fob	.71	.72	.85
Hogs, Iowa-S.Minn. avg. cwt	50.00	50.50	59.00
Hogs, Omaha avg cwt	e50.40	51.00	58.75
Orange Juice, frz con, NY lb.	b1.51	1.50	1.08
Pepper, black, NY lb.	g1.03	1.05	.68
Pork Bellies, 12-14 lbs Mid-US lb ..	.67	.70	.83
Pork Loins, 14-17 lbs. Mid-US lb ...	1.00	1.07	1.18
Potatoes, rnd wht, 50 lb., fob	y3.87½	3.91¼	1.25
Steers, Omaha choice avg cwt	69.44	69.50	59.50
Steers, Tex.-Okla. ch avg cwt	e70.13	70.50	62.00
Steers, Feeder, Okl Cty, av cwt ...	68.00	68.25	69.25
Sugar, beet, ref. Chgo-Wst lb fob ..	.3110	.3110	.2890
Sugar, cane, raw NY lb. del.	.2161	.2148	.2160
Sugar, cane, raw, world, lb. fob ...	.0682	.0725	.0630
Sugar, cane, ref NY lb. fob	.3260	.3260	.3310
FATS AND OILS			
Coconut Oil, crd, N. Orleans cif ...	a.50¼	.50½	.20
Corn Oil, crd wet mill, Chgo. lb. ...	n.26½-.27	.26½-.27	.22
Corn Oil, crd dry mill, Chgo. lb.	n.26¾-.27½	.26¾-.27½	.22¾
Cottonseed Oil, crd Miss Vly lb. ...	b.30	.29	.16¼
Grease, choice white, Chgo lb.	b.18¾	.18¾	.14⅜
Lard, Chgo lb.	.30	.27	.16½
Linseed Oil, raw Mpls lb.	.32	.32	.25
Palm Oil, ref. bl. deod. N.Orl. cif .	n.50¾	.49⅝	.19½
Peanut Oil, crd, Southeast lb.	.47	.47	.25½
Soybean Oil, crd, Decatur, lb.	.2875	.2775	.1656
Tallow, bleachable, Chgo lb.	.19½	.19¾	.14¾
Tallow, bleachable, Mo. River lb.	b.19	.18¾	.13⅞
Tallow, edible, Chgo lb.	.30	.28	.16¼
FIBERS AND TEXTILES			
Burlap, 10 oz. 40-in. NY yd	n.3055	.3055	.2300
Cotton 1 1/16 in str lw-md Mphs lb	.7027	.7103	.6012
Print Cloth, cotton, 48-in NY yd ...	s.85	.85	.61
Print Cloth, pol/cot 48-in NY yd ...	t.54	.54	.47½
Satin Acetate, NY yd	.70½	.70½	.61½
Sheetings, 60x60 48-in. NY yd	.82½	.82½	.72½
Wool, fine staple terr. Boston lb ...	2.27	2.27	2.13
METALS			
Aluminum ingot lb	p.815	.815	.76
Cobalt cathodes 99.9% NY lb.	ip-6.95	6.95	5.15
Copper cathodes lb	p.64½-.65	.64½-.65	.77½
Copper Scrap, No 2 wire NY lb	k.48½	.49	.56
Lead, lb.	p.24-.28	.24-.28	.21¼
Mercury 76 lb. flask NY	308.00	312.00	350.00
Nickel plating grade lb	p3.29	3.29	3.29
Steel Scrap 1 hvy mlt Chgo ton	105.00	105.00	65.00
Tin Metals Week composite lb.	6.2273	6.2298	6.2670
Zinc High grade lb	p.51	.51	.40
MISCELLANEOUS			
Hides, hvy native strs lb fob	.55	.55	.37
Newspapers, old No. 1 Chgo ton ...	50.00-55.0	50.00-55.0	37.50
Rubber, smoked sheets, NY lb.	n.58	.58	.45
PRECIOUS METALS			
Gold, troy oz			
Engelhard indust bullion	365.50	371.75	488.75
Engelhard fabric prods	383.78	390.34	513.19
Handy & Harman base price	365.10	371.35	488.75
London fixing AM 365.20 PM ...	365.10	371.35	488.75
Krugerrand, whol	a378.50	378.50	500.00
Platinum, troy ounce	475.00	475.00	475.00
Silver, troy ounce			
Engelhard indust bullion	7.985	8.305	12.920
Engelhard fabric prods	8.544	8.886	13.867
Handy & Harman base price	8.025	8.26	12.960
London Fixing (in pounds)			
Spot (U.S. equiv. $7.977)	5.6980	5.8755	8.3130
3 months	5.8280	6.0085	8.5410
6 months	5.9775	6.1555	8.7410
1 year	6.2650	6.4445	8.2195
Coins, whol $1,000 face val	a7,055	6,990	9,355

a-Asked. b-Bid. bp-Country elevator bids to producers. h-Terminal elevator truck bids to producers. c-Corrected. d-Dealer market. e-Estimated. f-Carcass equiv. value. g-Main crop, ex-dock, warehouses, Eastern Seaboard, north of Hatteras. i.-f.o.b. warehouse. k-Dealer selling prices in lots of 40,000 pounds or more, f.o.b. buyer's works. n-Nominal. p-Producer price. r-Rail bids. s-Thread count 78x76. t-Thread count 78x54. x-Less than truckloads. y-Maine origin; varies seasonally. z-Not quoted.

Figure 4.2. Cash price quote. Source: Reprinted by permission of *The Wall Street Journal,* © Dow Jones & Company, Inc. 1986. All rights reserved. January 25, 1984 p. 44.

called "scalpers." "Pit traders" generally take on larger positions and hold them longer. "Floor traders" are professional speculators, often carrying large positions and constantly studying the action in the pit and the comments of other traders. While the foregoing generally trade for their own accounts, "brokers"—the largest category in most futures markets—execute orders for others, for which they receive a fee for each trade. They also trade for their own accounts.

Orders are wired from brokerage houses to their respective order desks on the floors of the exchanges. Runners take the orders to the pit where they are filled. Brokers working for the various firms can be found quickly by the distinctive, sometimes brightly colored jackets they wear. Market orders are filled as soon as possible. Limit and stop orders are held in the "book" until they can be filled. Once an order is filled, the slip is marked to indicate the price, number of contracts, time, and broker having the opposite side of the transaction. Then the slip is handed to a runner, or dropped on the floor where the floor trader stands. It remains a mystery how, at the end of each trading day, trades are matched and differences reconciled. Yet they are.

OPENING AN ACCOUNT

Commodity brokerage firms, and this includes most stock brokerage firms, that also maintain commodities operations, generally require a client to deposit at least $5000 to open a commodity trading account. In addition, the prospective client must pass a "suitability" screening. This means that the prospective client be qualified for commodity trading in the sense that he or she has been appraised of the inherent risks, has sufficient financial resources to allow trading, and is not disqualified by reason of mental illness or legal constraint. In practice, one finds that few mature persons who have financial resources beyond the immediate security needs of themselves and their families are turned down as being unsuitable. Suitability does not mean that the prospective client has demonstrated any indications of market or trading knowledge likely to lead to profitable trading.

Once the account has been opened, the trader must maintain an equity balance of at least $2000 in order to trade for other than liquidation of open positions. Thus, if losses accumulate to $3000 or more, the trader must either put additional funds into the account or else be content to do no more than close currently open positions.

Most brokerage firms now offer money market funds. Therefore many persons open commodity and money market accounts at the same time. Funds are transferred to the commodity account as required. As long as the funds remain in the money market account they draw interest. Excess commodity account funds may be moved to the money market account. This arrangement has the advantage of allowing the trader to meet initial margin and margin calls by a simple transfer initiated by his or her broker. It has the disadvantage of allowing losses to accumulate without attention being called to them because the broker typically does not notify the client of the transfer of funds to the commodity account. Thus, the client may have an unpleasant surprise when the monthly statement arrives, or when there is a margin call for which insufficient funds remain in the money market account. In this latter event, the client must inject fresh funds or have positions liquidated to meet the margin call.

Once the account has been opened and the client has identified the trade he or she wishes to make (and that need not be done right away!), there are several types of orders that the trader should be knowledgeable about.

TYPES OF ORDERS

There are several dimensions to types of orders. One is the time dimension and another is the price dimension. Of time orders, the shortest lived is the *Fill-Or-Kill* (FOK) order. If an FOK order cannot be filled when it arrives at the trading pit on the exchange floor, it is canceled. A day order is the next longer lived order normally encountered. A day order expires at the end of the trading day if it is not filled before then. A *Good-Thru-Week* (GTW) order expires at the close of trading on Friday if it has not been filled before then.

The longest lived order is the *Good-'Til-Canceled* (GTC) order. Such orders can lie dormant indefinitely, then be filled long after the client forgot about them and long after he or she had any desire to have the trade executed. These orders share some characteristics with a land mine that, once placed during a war, lies forgotten, only to explode under an unfortunate farmer long after the war has ended.

Because of the tendency to forget about GTC orders, only to have them cause undesired effects, many brokers send weekly reminders; that is, confirmation of the standing order. Other brokers do not enter true GTC orders. Instead, they enter orders good through end-of-month. It is then the client's responsibility to reenter the order for the next month if that is desired.

Market-on-open or *market-on-close* orders are to be executed only during the formal opening or closing periods. These orders can play an important role in the trading strategies and tactics of some market participants.

In addition to the foregoing time orders, a trader can ask his or her broker to pull (i.e., cancel) an order after a certain hour of the day or a certain date. If the request is straightforward, most brokers will be accommodative. However, such variations tend to impose additional responsibility upon one's broker (i.e., the customer representative the trader speaks with). If the responsibility becomes too great, with increased probability of errors, the broker can (and should) try to convince the client to use an alternative strategy for market entry or exit.

Outside of the time dimension, in that of price, there is another rich set of different types of orders.

A *market order* is to be executed "at-the-market," meaning at whatever price the trade can be executed when the order gets to the trading pit on the exchange floor. That price may be substantially different from the price quoted to the customer when he or she entered the order in a volatile market.

To ensure that no more than a certain price is paid to establish a long position, and no less for a short position, a *limit-order* is used. This is typically stated as: "Buy 5000 bushels May Chicago Wheat at $3.97 or better." The "or better" phrase allows the order to be filled at the limit price of $3.97 per bushel, yet does not prevent filling the order at a price more favorable to the trader.

In order to protect a profit, or limit a loss in the event a trade does not turn out as anticipated, a *stop-order,* also referred to as a *stop-loss-order,* is used. A stop-order becomes a market order (or limit order) if the price falls to that level for a sale, or rises to that level for a purchase. A similar order is a *market-if-touched* (MIT) order, not as often used. An MIT order also is triggered if a certain price level is reached. However, an MIT order is used to sell at a higher price or buy at a lower price, whereas a stop order is just the reverse: that is, a stop is used to sell at a lower price or buy at a higher price—just what a trader would do to try to limit a loss, hence the term "stop loss."

Contingent orders, such as *one-cancels-other* (OCO) orders, are seldom encountered because of the burden placed on the broker to see that the order is executed, and the increased risk of errors with such orders. The resistance to formal contingent orders can often be circumvented by working with an individual customer representative (i.e., "broker") who will enter such orders on a best efforts basis.

Take-your-time and *not-held* orders allow the floor brokers in the pit to use their judgment and discretion in filling an order. A small trader would generally be well advised to use a limit order, although this is not a true substitute. These orders are well suited to large traders who may not want a large number of contracts to trade at one time, especially in a commodity where trading volume is thin, because of the possible influence on price.

For the trader who is interested in price relationships between commodities, there are spreads or straddles. Nowadays, the two terms are used interchangeably, with "spread" generally more popular. Spreads are based on being long one contract, short the other, with profit or loss determined not on absolute price level, but rather on the difference in price between the long and short contracts.

Spreads may involve different contract months of one commodity (termed an *intracommodity* spread) or different commodities without regard to the contract months (*intercommodity* spread). From the broker's perspective, intracommodity spreads present fewer difficulties with regard to order execution because both sides of the spread may be filled in the same trading pit. In contrast, intercommodity spreads can present logistical problems ranging from virtually none to significant. For recognized intercommodity spreads (read "for commonly entered spreads based on some logical connection between the commodities") brokers have become adept at filling them, and indeed there are spread brokers who specialize in filling these orders.

Spreads may be entered by "legging into" them one side at a time or by doing both sides simultaneously. A spread order thus may be written up either as two separate orders or as one spread order. Figure 4-3 contains an order ticket. Note that there are rows for both spread side buy and spread side sell. Although an intercommodity spread may actually be filled by legging in, it may nevertheless be written up as a spread order on the same ticket.

Spread orders typically include a statement of the premium, which acts much as a limit order. A typical spread order would be expressed by a trader as "Buy one March Sugar, sell one July Sugar, 50 points premium July." This means that the July contract price must be at least 50 points above the March for the order to be filled. The order could be placed without specifying the premium, but that would leave the trader vulnerable to fills that are less than satisfactory.

MARGIN

The respective exchanges establish the margin requirements for their futures contracts. In the case of commodities, margin is not a partial payment on the commodity; rather, it serves the function of a surety bond, or a good faith deposit. The futures contract is not itself a purchase or sale of a commodity; it is a contract to conclude a purchase or sale in the delivery month. Ownership of the commodity does not change hands unless and until delivery is arranged after cessation of futures trading. Generally less than 2 percent of futures contracts are carried to delivery. The futures contract confers both the right and the obligation to take delivery in the case of a long position, or to make delivery if one is short. This means that price changes result in gains or losses just as if the trader owned the underlying commodity.

Gains and losses are realized when a futures contract is offset with an opposite transaction or when delivery is made. However, to ensure performance, it is necessary to require a good-faith or margin deposit. The margin provides a buffer to absorb any losses the trader may suffer, so that they do not become the brokerage house's losses. If the trader's equity falls below a certain level he or she will receive a margin call and will then have to deposit more funds or else positions will be liquidated to free up funds.

It should be understood that while the purpose of margin is to provide some assurance of financial capability by the trader and a buffer to absorb losses, the trader is nevertheless liable for any losses over and above the margin deposit. Normally this does not pose a problem. However, in a rapidly moving market, where there are several days of limit moves, it can happen that the trader's

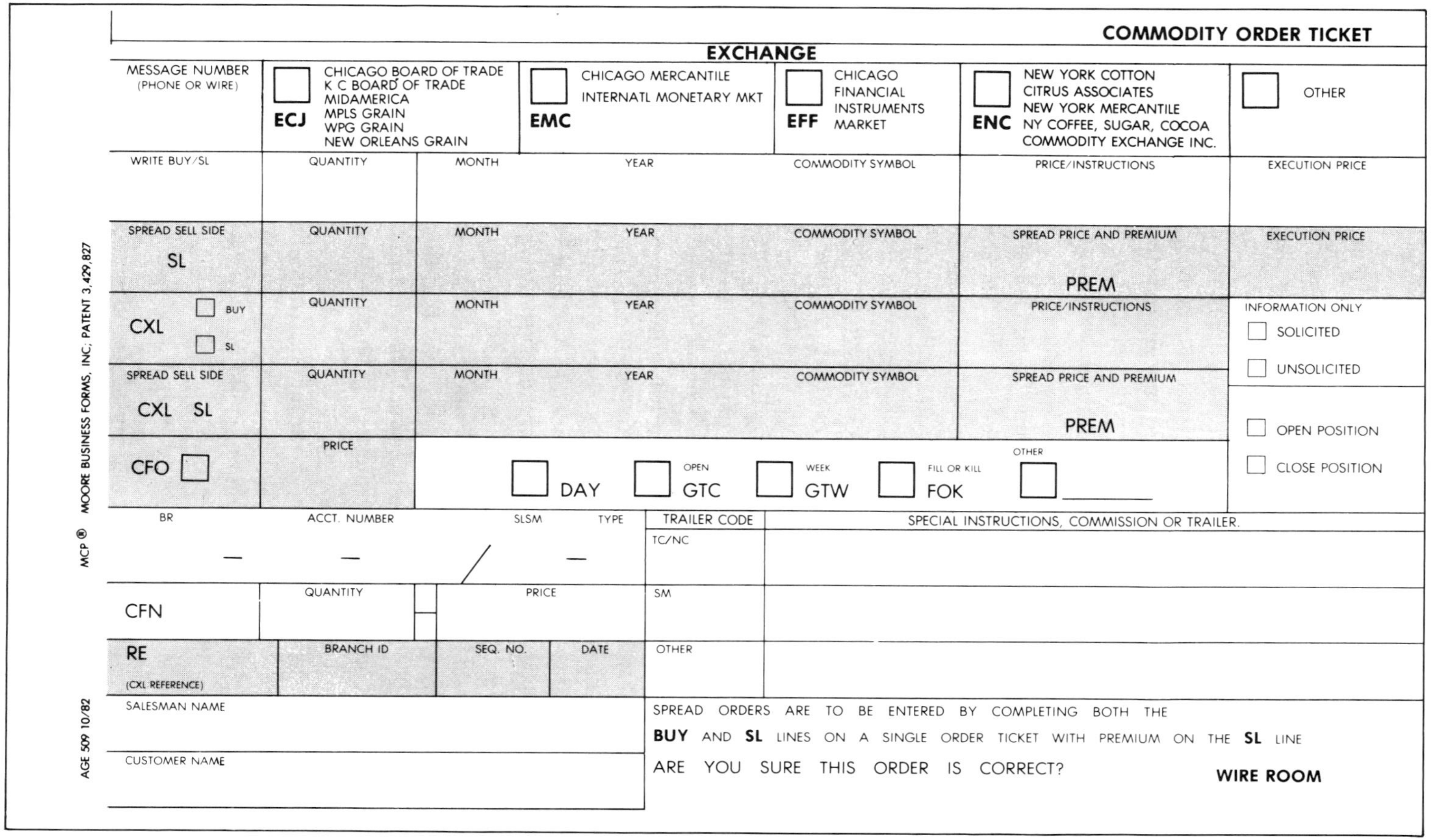

COMMODITY ORDER TICKET

EXCHANGE

MESSAGE NUMBER (PHONE OR WIRE)

ECJ — CHICAGO BOARD OF TRADE / K C BOARD OF TRADE / MIDAMERICA / MPLS GRAIN / WPG GRAIN / NEW ORLEANS GRAIN

EMC — CHICAGO MERCANTILE / INTERNATL MONETARY MKT

EFF — CHICAGO FINANCIAL INSTRUMENTS MARKET

ENC — NEW YORK COTTON / CITRUS ASSOCIATES / NEW YORK MERCANTILE / NY COFFEE, SUGAR, COCOA / COMMODITY EXCHANGE INC.

OTHER

WRITE BUY/SL — QUANTITY — MONTH — YEAR — COMMODITY SYMBOL — PRICE/INSTRUCTIONS — EXECUTION PRICE

SL / SPREAD SELL SIDE — QUANTITY — MONTH — YEAR — COMMODITY SYMBOL — SPREAD PRICE AND PREMIUM — EXECUTION PRICE

PREM

INFORMATION ONLY
SOLICITED
UNSOLICITED

CXL — BUY — SL

SPREAD SELL SIDE — QUANTITY — MONTH — YEAR — COMMODITY SYMBOL — PRICE/INSTRUCTIONS

CXL SL — QUANTITY — MONTH — YEAR — COMMODITY SYMBOL — SPREAD PRICE AND PREMIUM

PREM

OPEN POSITION
CLOSE POSITION

CFO — PRICE — PRICE

DAY / SL,SM — OPEN GTC — WEEK GTW — FILL OR KILL FOK — OTHER

BR — ACCT. NUMBER — TYPE — TRAILER CODE — SPECIAL INSTRUCTIONS, COMMISSION OR TRAILER

TC/NC

CFN — QUANTITY — PRICE — SM

RE — BRANCH ID — SEQ. NO. — DATE — OTHER

(CXL REFERENCE)

SALESMAN NAME — SPREAD ORDERS ARE TO BE ENTERED BY COMPLETING BOTH THE BUY AND SL LINES ON A SINGLE ORDER TICKET WITH PREMIUM ON THE SL LINE

CUSTOMER NAME — ARE YOU SURE THIS ORDER IS CORRECT? WIRE ROOM

MCP® MOORE BUSINESS FORMS, INC; PATENT 3,429,827

AGE 509 10/82

Figure 4.3. Commodity order ticket. Courtesy of Moore Business Forms & Systems Division.

losses exceed the account equity. The trader is legally obligated to make good on the difference.

Initial margin is the amount of the trader's money that must be paid to the broker when a purchase or sale is first made. Initial margin may be satisfied by the deposit of U.S. Treasury bills. For most commodities, initial margin is in the range of 5 to 10 percent of the total contract value, rounded to an even hundred dollars. For financial futures, the percentage may be much less: A million dollar Treasury bill futures contract may be bought or sold for margin of less than 1 percent. When establishing margin requirements the exchanges take volatility into account, and try to set the requirement high enough so that the amount serves its buffering function well, yet not so high that it discourages trading.

Maintenance margin is usually around 75 percent of initial margin. When account margin falls to the maintenance level the trader will receive a margin call from his or her broker and must deposit additional money. In the case of a trader with one open position, this is clear. For a trader with positions in several different commodities, it is a little more complicated. When there are multiple open positions, the total equity is compared to the total required maintenance margin. If equity is too low, there will be a margin call.

Margin calls must be met promptly—the same day or the following day. Brokers may allow their customers to mail a check at their discretion. However, margin calls require urgent and immediate attention. A trader who does not meet a margin call must expect to have some of his or her contracts liquidated to free up funds in his or her account.

Some traders will prefer to meet any margin calls and deposit initial margin by writing checks, or by having their banks wire-transfer funds to their brokers. Others may prefer the convenience provided by having a separate money market account with the same broker so that their customer representative can simply transfer funds as may be required. Those who choose the latter course would be well advised to request their brokers to inform them of all such transfers. Otherwise, one day they may find that they have incurred far larger losses than they had imagined possible, and that they money market account is a frail shadow of its former self. The advantage offered by keeping reserve funds outside the brokerage firm is that margin calls provide reminders to the trader, regarding performance, that are not easily ignored. Also, a losing trade can be obscured by the favorable performance of others, so the trader must pay close attention to not only the overall account but to each individual open position.

TAXES (AND TAX STRADDLES)

Until the Economic Recovery Tax Act of 1981 commodity futures could be used by individuals with large federal income tax liability to defer the tax to the next year. This involved the use of *tax straddles,* simple in principle but often complex in implementation.

In its simplest form, a tax straddle could be based on simultaneous purchase and sale of two different delivery months in the next calendar year. Silver was especially popular for this purpose because it had no "crop year" effects to contend with and the price of distant months reflected carrying charges, mainly interest rates. Another important factor is that the price of silver tends to be volatile, so that by year's end one contract would likely show a profit, the other a loss. The trader would offset the losing contract, establishing a *realized* loss which would match much or all of the taxable income the trader wished to defer paying taxes on. At the same time the losing contract was liquidated another delivery month would be entered, either long or short as the original position had been, thus keeping the trader in the straddle. Since the price spread between different months reflected mainly interest costs, over much of the era in which tax straddles were employed, the risk to the trader was small.

An example may serve to clarify the principle involved in a tax straddle. Assume that a person had taxable ordinary income of $100,000 on which she would have a large tax liability. To defer the tax liability into the next year she would need a matching loss. Let us assume she was advised by a broker in October 1978 to sell 20 March silver contracts, each for 5000 ounces, and simultaneously to buy 20 May silver contracts. By the end of December the price of silver had changed significantly. Her broker advised offsetting the March short positions by purchase of 20 contracts, with simultaneous sale of 20 July contracts. Table 4-1 illustrates what happened in this hypothetical case.

TABLE 4.1.   HYPOTHETICAL TAX STRADDLE—SIMPLE CASE

October 31, 1978		
Sell 20 March 1979 Silver at	$5.00	
Buy 20 May 1979 Silver at	5.20	
Spread	$ .20	
December 23, 1978		
Buy 20 March 1979 Silver at	$6.00	
Sell 20 July 1979 Silver at	6.45	
Hold 20 May 1979 Silver at	6.22	
Realized loss on March 1979 Contract (20 × 5,000 × $1.00)	= $100,000	
Unrealized Gain on May 1979 Contract (20 × 5,000 × $1.02)	= $102,000	
Net Gain or Loss		$2,000
Position as of December 23		
Long 20 May Silver at	$6.22	
Short 20 July Silver at	6.45	
Spread	$ .23	

Note that the *realized* loss on the March contracts exactly offset the $100,000 of ordinary income on which the trader wished to defer the income tax. (In examples, things almost always work out propitiously due to a sort of poetic license.) Although the trader had a loss for tax purposes, her commodity account equity actually improved marginally because the May rose at a somewhat faster rate than the March over the span from October to December. One could not, however, have relied on such serendipity. If the price of silver had fallen rather than risen, or if interest rates had fallen, there could just as well have been a loss of similar magnitude.

In this simple example, there is also the problem of what would happen to the price spread if interest rates were to change. Everything else held constant, if interest rates rise then carrying charges also rise. This would cause the spread to widen. A fall in rates would cause the spread to narrow.

The following discussion is about an advanced tax straddle strategy known as a *butterfly spread* (see Figure 4-4). These spreads had the potential not only to defer tax on gains but to convert gains from short term to long term, thus subjecting them to the lower tax prevailing on long-term capital gains.

COMMODITIES TAXATION SINCE 1981

It has been said that all good things must eventually come to an end. So it was with commodity tax straddles. The Economic Recovery Tax Act of 1981 brought tax straddles to an abrupt end. It also established a precedent for taxing unrealized gains and allowing deduction of unrealized losses. Investors may find that it will not be long before the precedent is extended to stock shares and perhaps other assets eventually.

Taxes on commodities currently are figured as follows:

Gain and loss from "regulated commodity futures contracts" must now be reported on an annual basis under a mark-to-market rule, i.e., treated as if they were sold for fair market value on the last business day of the taxable year. Any capital gain or loss on a regulated futures contract which is marked-to-market or recognized is treated as 40% short-term and 60% long-term capital gain or loss. Thus, the maximum effective tax rate on these gains cannot exceed 32%.[1]

For those having losses on mark-to-market special rules apply. The mark-to-market requires that gain or loss on contracts held from one year into the next must be adjusted to take the mark-to-market gain or loss into account.

Hedgers were not affected by the change in rules, provided that the hedge is for bona fide business reasons. Special rules apply to such things as straddles other than in commodity futures contracts and stock, disposition of commodity related properties, cash-and-carry, and certain other transactions.

Whether the Economic Recovery Tax Act of 1981 will be changed to permit the use of tax straddles again is debatable, but the "smart money" will proba-

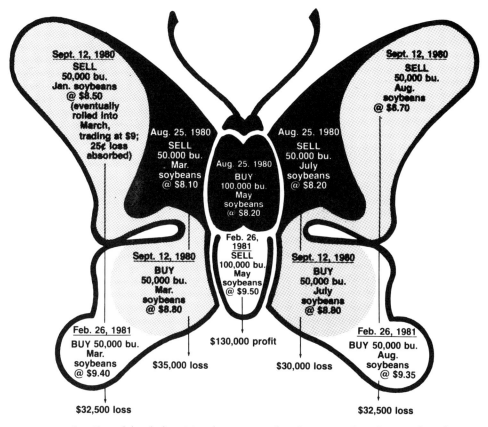

Sept. 12, 1980
SELL
50,000 bu.
Jan. soybeans
@ $8.50
(eventually
rolled into
March,
trading at $9;
25¢ loss
absorbed)

Aug. 25, 1980
SELL
50,000 bu.
Mar.
soybeans
@ $8.10

Aug. 25, 1980
BUY
100,000 bu.
May
soybeans
@ $8.20

Aug. 25, 1980
SELL
50,000 bu.
July
soybeans
@ $8.20

Sept. 12, 1980
SELL
50,000 bu.
Aug.
soybeans
@ $8.70

Feb. 26,
1981
SELL
100,000 bu.
May
soybeans
@ $9.50

Sept. 12, 1980
BUY
50,000 bu.
Mar.
soybeans
@ $8.80

Sept. 12, 1980
BUY
50,000 bu.
July
soybeans
@ $8.80

Feb. 26, 1981
BUY 50,000 bu.
Mar.
soybeans
@ $9.40

$130,000 profit

$35,000 loss

$30,000 loss

Feb. 26, 1981
BUY 50,000 bu.
Aug.
soybeans
@ $9.35

$32,500 loss

$32,500 loss

Since the silver debacle last March, some traders have sought other markets for deferring certain income taxes. No matter what market, the Internal Revenue Service examines such transactions on an individual basis.

By Dan Manternach, contributing editor

A wise man once said the only sure things in life are death and taxes. And as long as there are taxes, there will be attempts to limit or avoid them. Nothing wrong with that; it's just good business as long as what you call "avoiding" isn't called "evading" by the IRS.

Years ago, sharp commodity traders learned that one method of shielding capital gains income was to "roll" it into the next tax year through use of commodity spreads.

Silver quickly became the commodity most often chosen for the technique.

It was a high-value commodity, closely associated with money itself. Most importantly, silver was recognized as having the least "spread-risk" between the various contract months. In fact, the term "silver straddle" almost became synonymous with "tax straddle."

Eventually, traders found that when properly executed, the tax straddle could convert short-term capital gains, taxed as ordinary income, to long-term capital gains, only 40% of which is taxed.

That secondary advantage was a little trickier to gain, of course. Because

long-term capital gains can be claimed only on long futures positions, the spread had to be placed in a commodity where the "loss" leg would most likely occur in the short position. Furthermore, long positions have to be held at least six-months-and-a-day for capital gains treatment.

That latter requirement intensified one big risk in such straddles: Losses from change in the spread between long and short positions would wipe out or even exceed the tax savings. Traders quickly latched onto silver as
continued

Figure 4.4. Using butterflies to spread soybeans, Reprinted from *Commodities* (now *Futures*) Magazine, 219 Parkade, Cedar Falls, Iowa 50613, November 1980.

the best commodity for limiting such risk.

The spread between various contract months in silver primarily is a function of value and interest rate (cost of holding inventory). From mid-1974 until late in 1978, both were very stable.

To limit spread risk even further, traders invented a cute little creature called the "butterfly spread." Unlike a simple spread (short one contract month, but long another) the butterfly has a "body" position, and two "wing" positions on either side of the contract month chosen for the body. The wing positions each are equal to one-half the number of contracts involved in the body position.

By 1979, silver's lure of stability was gone due to exploding prices and interest rates. Traders also were tired of continual IRS challenges.

What commodity is most popular now? Broker Dan Basse of Commodity Hedgers and Traders in Cedar Falls, Iowa, likes soybeans because they meet all his criteria for a good tax straddle: heavily traded, thus liquid; volatile enough to offer good opportunities for taking a strategic loss; and freedom from harassment and challenge by IRS.

Perfect butterfly

The butterfly diagram shown is a "perfect" butterfly spread, where everything goes as planned.

But for an example, suppose it was mid-August 1980 and you had $65,000 in short-term capital gain you wanted to roll into 1981. You're especially interested in converting short-term gain in 1980 to long-term gain for 1981. Since you only can do that by holding a long position for six months or more, it's obvious you need to choose a spread where you'll most likely lift the short position to take the loss for 1980.

The six-month holding requirement also means you must retain the option to have the "left wing" of your spread as far out as March. You also must be careful that the "right wing" of the spread does not fall into the 1981 crop year (beginning with the September contract).

Also, it's an extra safety feature if the two wings of the spread are equidistant from the body. Through this thought process, you've narrowed the options for the central (body) position to the May contract.

The remaining question is whether to make the body the short position, with the wings long, or vice-versa. Because you are a bull on beans, and May has a history of seasonal strength, you choose to make the body the long position by buying 100,000 bu. of May beans on **Aug.** 25, the day that contract broke out of a bullish pennant formation on the charts. The price: $8.20 per bu. That same day you sell 50,000 bu. of March beans at $8.10, and 50,000 bu. of July beans at $8.20.

In this hypothetical situation, you didn't have to wait long to accumulate the desired $65,000 loss. On Sept. 12, soybean futures made key reversal tops on the charts. You buy back the March and July contracts at $8.80, taking losses of $35,000 and $30,000, respectively. Immediately, you re-sell 50,000 bu. of January beans and 50,000 bu. of August beans to maintain the butterfly spread.

You successfully had canceled out the $65,000 in gain accumulated prior to placing the spread. But because you immediately reassumed a spread position by selling January and August beans, the offsetting profit in the long May position was secure. Because your goal is to hold the long May position for at least six-months-and-a-day (until Feb. 26), you would have to roll that short January position into March as the delivery period for January approached. But if you're lucky, the extra $550 investment in brokerage commissions will help convert the profit from the long position to long-term capital gain, isolating 60% from taxes altogether!

In the real world, there are several things that could go wrong with a butterfly spread. Carrying charges and premiums don't always expand and contract evenly.

Dead wrong

Another obvious possibility is that a market will peak before you've held your long position six months. As markets decline, the portion of your profit in your long position (eligible for long-term capital gains treatment) gets smaller and smaller, while it accumulates in your short position (taxed as ordinary income).

You also must consider the possibility that you're dead wrong on market direction altogether, and that you wind up lifting your long position to take your loss in the initial tax year. That eliminates all possibility of converting short-term gain to long-term gain.

The brokerage commissions on this fairly complicated example would run anywhere from $3,300 to $3,850 (depending on whether you rolled the January position into March). But for those in high tax brackets, commission costs involved in shrewd use of a butterfly spread can look like pin money compared to potential tax savings. □

Figure 4.4. (Continued)

44

bly bet against such change. The alarming deficits in the federal budget in the 1980s, and consequently the seemingly insatiable appetite for more taxes, suggest that rather than relax the rules for commodity futures, it is likely that there will be an attempt to apply the mark-to-market principle to other investments.

Note

[1] *An Analysis: 1981 Tax Legislation* (Coopers & Lybrand, U.S.A., 1981), pp. 4–5.

HEDGE: *To secure oneself against a loss on (a bet or other speculation) by making transactions on the other side so as to compensate more or less for possible loss on the first.*

THE COMPACT EDITION OF
THE OXFORD ENGLISH DICTIONARY

5

Hedging

The quotation which opens this chapter defines hedging as it is normally considered. Over the years the process of hedging has typically been described by writers who have offered hypothetical examples in which futures contracts are used to obtain "transactions on the other side" of a cash position. The idea of hedging expressed in most such examples is that of hedging to "insure" against losses arising from adverse price movements in the cash position side of the hedge.

The main economic justification for futures trading is to allow hedging. Hedging provides for risk reduction, and thus lower production costs for those who are able to use them.[1] No futures market has survived for long that has not been supported by hedgers.

Modern portfolio theory applies to hedging as it does to investments. Just as individual securities must be considered within the context of the overall investment portfolio, so too must hedging be viewed within the overall objectives, goals, and philosophy of the firm. While an integration of futures trading and portfolio theory is still to be developed, we may nevertheless hypothesize that ways will be found to use futures to reduce both the company specific risk (i.e., alpha risk) and also the portfolio (beta) risk compared to what it would be in an all-stock and bond portfolio.[2]

To complete our definition of hedging, let us adopt that of Thomas Hieronymous, a leading authority on commodity markets:

> *Hedging was defined . . . as the assumption of a position in futures equal and opposite to an already existing or immediately anticipated cash position. This is a definition descriptive of the process. We now add a second definition: to hedge is to insulate one's business activities from price level speculation while retaining the opportunity to speculate in basis variation. This definition takes hedging out of the academic context of risk shifting and puts it in the business context of trying to make a profit.*[3]

The basis variation to which he refers is the essence of hedging. Businesses, by hedging, avoid risks associated with *price level speculation*. However, the *basis risk,* the risk arising from differences in price relationships between cash and futures, is *not* eliminated by hedging. Hedging thus is speculation in price relationships, or basis, as a preferred alternative to speculating in price level. Since basis tends to be far less volatile than either cash or futures prices, hedging reduces risk. But, because there is some volatility in the basis, hedging does not eliminate risk. Hedging involves the substitution of lesser risk for greater risk, of manageable risk for risk that in some cases could ruin the firm.

Basis is the difference between the cash price of a commodity at a particular delivery point and the futures price of that commodity, using the nearby or dominant contract. For a given hedger and hedging transaction, his or her basis may be defined as the difference between the cash price at the local delivery location and the futures price (of the contract which expires when, or after, the cash position is liquidated). There are two fundamental types of hedges, the long hedge and the short hedge.

THE LONG OR BUYING HEDGE

The long hedge is used by those who are short the cash commodity—those who do not have the cash commodity at present and will have to buy it at a later date. Since hedging involves opposite positions in cash and futures (though, as we shall see later, not necessarily equal positions), a firm that is short the cash commodity takes a long position in the appropriate futures contract by buying it, hence the name.

Schematically, Figure 5-1 displays what is involved in a long hedge.

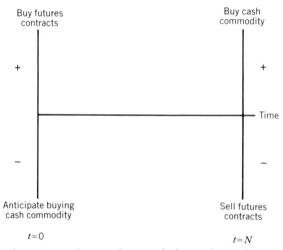

Figure 5.1. Schematic diagram of a long or buying hedge.

THEORETICAL CONSIDERATIONS

In this section we examine the effects of hedging when cash and futures prices converge (i.e., the basis narrows to zero) at time $t = N$, when the hedge is lifted. Two basic cases may be considered: a normal or carrying charge market and an inverted market in which the cash price is higher than the futures price. We discuss three possible situations for a normal market: (1) cash and futures prices both rise, (2) cash price rises and futures falls, and (3) both cash and futures prices fall. Since in most respects the results from an inverted market are the inverse of those in a normal market they will not be discussed separately here.

HEDGING IN A NORMAL MARKET

In a normal, or carrying charge market, the cash price is lower than futures prices.[4] This reflects the fact that many commodities can be stored for delivery later to satisfy open futures contract positions. If the futures price of a deliverable commodity were to exceed the cash price by a significant amount, arbitrageurs would buy the cash commodity while simultaneously selling futures contracts. As long as the futures price exceeds the cash price plus carrying charges (for deliverable commodity meeting contract specifications) arbitrage will be profitable. However, such easy profits will not last for long. The buying by arbitrageurs will tend to cause the cash price to rise while, at the same time, their selling will tend to cause the futures price to decline. Eventually futures prices will reflect the storage, insurance, and related charges stemming from carrying the cash commodity forward and delivering it to satisfy an open short futures contract.

Figure 5-2 depicts the results of perfect hedges in normal markets. They are perfect in the sense that at time $t = N$ the cash price equals the futures price; that is, the basis is zero. It is important to note that this figure is a schematic diagram in which the price relationships are exaggerated for the sake of clarity and, in practice, the basis seldom will be precisely zero on the day the hedge is lifted. For the purpose of illustration, however, by assuming a zero basis at $t = 0$ the principles involved may be portrayed more clearly.

Case 1: Long Hedge

In this case both cash and futures prices rise over the life of the hedge. Since we are considering a normal market, the cash price rises more than the futures price. A hedger short the cash commodity and long the futures contract has lost money. By hedging the cash price was fixed at the price prevailing at time $t = 0$, C_0. At $t = N$ the cash price $C_N = F_N^N$, the futures price. Consider the relationships between the prices: The long hedger loses $C_N - C_0$ on the cash

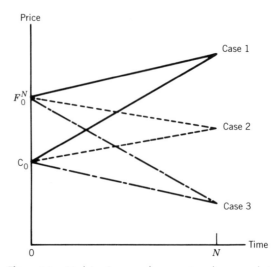

Figure 5.2. Hedging in normal or carrying charge market.

position, but gains $F_N^N - F_0^N$ on the futures position. The difference between these is a net loss (excluding commissions and interest opportunity cost) of $F_0^N - C_0$, which equals the initial basis. In this case a long or buying hedge has lost an amount equal to the basis. But that is not as bad as one might think. Without hedging the loss would have been much more: $C_N - C_0$. This hedge has been effective.

Case 1:   Short Hedge

In this same case a hedger long the cash commodity and short futures would have gained amount $C_N - C_0$ on the cash position and lost amount $F_N^N - F_0^N$ on the futures position. The short hedge has gained the basis but lost the opportunity appreciation in futures price. Without the hedge a net gain of $C_N - C_0$ would have been made on the cash commodity position. With the hedge, a portion of the gain equal to $F_N^N - F_0^N$ has been given up. The hedger would have been required to put up additional margin as the futures position went against him. And, unless the hedger actually intends to sell the cash commodity at $t = N$, he or she will have to raise the funds to cover the loss on the futures position beyond what the margin deposited can meet.

The short hedger would have made a clear profit if he or she had not hedged. However, we should *not* conclude that the short hedge should not have been placed: No more than one should argue that automobile insurance should not have been purchased because he or she had no accidents in the past year. The loss of insurance premiums was small compared to the probably much larger loss incurred if in a serious accident without insurance. This hedge is analogous. The opportunity losses when hedges do not work well, as in this case, over the long run should be offset from hedges that work especially well. Unless one can accurately forecast the price trend of a commodity, and thus hedge selectively, losses when they occur should be viewed as the price that must be paid for assurance that large losses do not occur.

Again, it should be noted that Figure 5-2 exaggerates the differences between cash and futures prices for the purpose of illustration. The differences in fact are smaller than the figure suggests, reflecting the carrying costs for storable commodities and the interest rate structure with financial futures contracts.

Case 1: General Observations

From the previous cases we may make some generalizations. Figure 5-3 illustrates the results from this hedge. When the cash and futures prices *both* increase (but the basis narrows to zero) long hedges will lose an amount equal to the basis at $t = 0$. On the other hand short hedges, while not resulting in *net* losses, will result in less gain than if the holder of the long cash position had not hedged.

Case 2: Long Hedge

In this case the cash price rises while the futures price falls. When the hedge is placed the cash price is C_0 and the futures price of the contract maturing at time $t = N$ is F_0^N. When the hedge is lifted at $t = N$ the long hedger loses $C_N - C_0$ on the cash position and loses $F_N^N - F_0^N$ on the futures position.

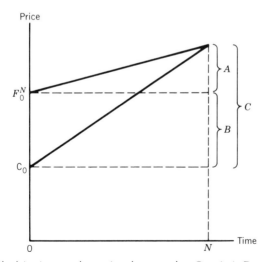

Figure 5.3.   Results of hedging in normal, carrying charge market, Case 1. A: Denotes long hedger's gain (short hedgers loss) on futures position; B: Denotes long hedger's net loss (short hedger's net gain) on the hedge (equals basis change from t = 0 to t = N); C: Denotes long hedger's loss (short hedger's gain) on cash position.

Once again the long hedger has lost an amount exactly equal to the change in the basis, even though in this case the proportions due to cash and futures are different.

Case 2: Short Hedge

The short hedger in this case gains $C_N - C_0$ on his or her long cash position while gaining $F_N^N - F_0^N$ on his futures position. As in Case 1: Short Hedge, the short hedger gains the basis less the costs of hedging: commissions plus opportunity cost on margin deposits.

Even though the proportions of gain due to the decline in futures and the rise in cash price differ from Case 1, the short hedger has gained an amount equal to the basis, less the costs incurred by the hedging operation.

Case 2: General Observations

For Case 2 we may make the following generalizations. The long hedger loses an amount on the hedge that is equal to the basis plus his or her cost of hedging. The short hedger gains an amount equal to the basis on his or her hedge, less applicable costs. Figure 5-4 illustrates the results of this hedge.

Case 3: Long Hedge

Under this scenario the price of the cash commodity (which the hedger is short) and the futures contract price both fall. The futures price falls by more

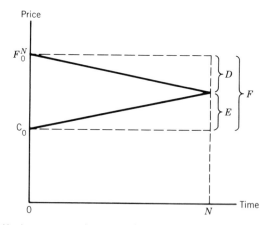

Figure 5.4.   Results of hedging in normal carrying charge market, Case 2. D: Denotes long hedger's loss (short hedger's gain) on futures position; E: Denotes long hedger's loss (short hedger's gain) on cash position; F: Denotes long hedger's total loss (short hedger's total gain) on the gain (equals basis change from $t = 0$ to $t = $ N).

than the cash price. Initially cash is at C_0 and the futures price of the hedging contract maturing at $t = N$ is F_0^N, as in the previous cases. At $t = N$, when the hedge is lifted, the long hedger gains $|C_N - C_0|$ since he or she is short the cash position. But the long hedger loses $|F_N^N - F_0^N|$ on the futures. Because $|F_N^N - F_0^N| > |C_N - C_0|$ this hedge has resulted in a net loss to the long hedger equal to what the basis was at $t = 0$.

The hedger in this case is worse off than one who, in similar circumstances, had not hedged. This is because an unhedged short cash position would have been profitable. As in the Case 1 short hedge, however, we do not conclude that the hedge should not have been placed. Over the long run, losses when the hedges do not work well should be offset by hedges that work especially well. If the price trend could have been forecast the hedge need not have been placed. Again, it should be noted that the diagram in Figure 5-2 exaggerates the difference between cash and futures prices, which generally is limited to carrying charges with storable commodities.

Case 3: Short Hedge

Because the futures price has declined more than the cash price, the short hedger, who is long the cash or spot commodity and short futures, finds the hedge has worked well. Since $|F_N^N - F_0^N| > |C_N - C_0|$ a gain equal to the $t = 0$ basis was realized. If the hedge had not been placed the loss would have been $C_N - C_0$.

In a case such as this, hedging is most clearly shown to be useful. The hedger holds the spot commodity and hedges to protect against a decline in price. The price declines and, because the basis becomes zero, the hedger profits by the amount of the basis at time $t = 0$ ($F_0^N - C_0$) less commissions and opportunity cost on margin deposit.

Case 3: General Observations

Case 3 has effects for the long and the short hedger that are similar to those in Case 1. The results from this hedge are illustrated in Figure 5-5. When both cash and futures prices decline (and the basis narrows to zero) long hedges will lose an amount equal to the basis at $t = 0$. Short hedges, will gain the basis, and avoid the large losses realized by those who are carrying unhedged inventory. The reason the short hedger finds hedging more advantageous in both Cases 1 and 3 is that the futures price is always above the spot price, converging to it at $t = n$ when the hedge is lifted. Such a normal or carrying charge market would seem to favor the short hedger, but we must keep in mind that he or she incurs carrying charges by holding the cash commodity, and that these reduce what would otherwise be a net profit on the hedges.

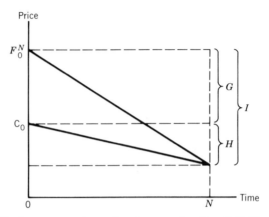

Figure 5.5. Results of hedging in normal, carrying charge market, Case 3. G: Denotes long hedger's net loss (short hedger's net gain) on the gain (equals basis change from $t = 0$ to $t = N$); H: Denotes long hedger's gain (short hedger's loss) on cash position; I: Denotes long hedger's loss (short hedger's gain) on futures position.

GENERALIZATION

In a normal, or carrying charge market, the futures contract price is above the cash price, moving toward the cash price at contract expiration. Losses and gains on hedging transactions are determined by the nature of the hedge (i.e., long or short) and the direction of the price over the period the hedge is in effect. Table 5-1 summarizes the effects of hedging. It is noteworthy that, by hedging, losses and gains are limited to the change in basis over the life of the hedge. This can be seen from examination of the change in prices over the life of the hedge.

In a normal market gains and losses are determined from the relationship

$$F_N^N - F_0^N < C_N - C_0 \tag{1}$$

Rearranging the terms we obtain

$$F_N^N - C_N < F_0^N - C_0 \tag{2}$$

TABLE 5.1. HEDGING GAINS AND LOSSES

	Long Hedge	Short Hedge
Price rises	Loses as much as basis	Gains as much as basis
Price falls	Loses as much as basis	Gains as much as basis

in which the left hand side defines the basis at $t = N$, the right hand side the basis at $t = 0$. Since we have assumed that cash and futures converge we may rewrite this as

$$0 < F_0^N - C_0 \tag{3}$$

Figure 5-6 depicts four outcomes with hedges in a normal market. Figures 5-6a and b represent situations in which hedges provide protection against large losses that would otherwise occur. Figure 5-6c and d represent situations where, if the actual price movement could have been accurately forecast, it would have been better not to have hedged. F_H and F_L define the upper and lower bounds on the futures price over the time interval in which the hedge is placed.

The foregoing examined hedging in isolation. That is, discussion was centered on a single cash position and the futures position which, in combination with it, provided the hedge. In the context of the overall firm a more general treatment may be useful.

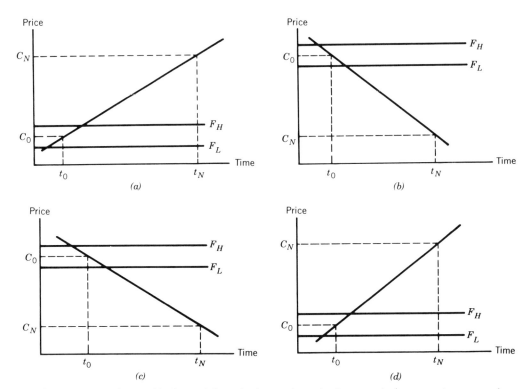

Figure 5.6. Fundamental hedges. (a) Buyer hedges against price increases in future requirements and price *rises*. (b) Seller hedges against price decreases in future cash sales and price *falls*. (c) Buyer hedges against price increases in future requirements and the price *falls*. (d) Seller hedges against price decreases in future cash sales and price *rises*.

HEDGING: THE PORTFOLIO CONCEPT

In this treatment of hedging we begin with an individual or firm with some initial endowment of an asset, either long or short. The hedging process then may be defined as selecting a futures position such that the overall risk is minimized. Following Johnson:

> *Given a position consisting of a number, X_i, of physical units held in market i, a "hedge" is defined as a position in market j of size X_j^* units such that the "price risk" of holding X_i and X_j^* from time t_1 to t_2 is minimized.[5]*

Let us denote the overall return from a portfolio, R, as a weighted average of the returns R_i with weights x_i as

$$R = x_1R_1 + x_2R_2 + \cdots + x_nR_n \tag{4}$$

Each x_i is the proportion of the total invested in that asset. The portfolio return is a random variable because the R_i are random variables. Denoting the expected values of the R_i by μ_i, the variance of asset i by σ_{ii}, and the covariance between the ith and jth assets by σ_{ij}, we obtain:

$$E[R] = x_1\mu_1 + x_2\mu_2 + \cdots + x_n\mu_n \tag{5}$$

$$\begin{aligned}
\text{Var}[R] &= x_1^2\sigma_{11} + x_2^2\sigma_{22} + \cdots + x_n^2\sigma_{nn} \\
&= 2x_1x_2\sigma_{12} + 2x_1x_3\sigma_{13} + \cdots + 2x_1x_n\sigma_{1n} \\
&\quad + 2x_2x_3\sigma_{23} + \cdots + 2x_2x_n\sigma_{2n} + \cdots \\
&= \sum_{i=1}^{n}\sum_{j=1}^{n} x_ix_j\sigma_{ij}
\end{aligned} \tag{6}$$

In the case of a single cash asset, denoted by subscript c, and a futures contract asset denoted by subscript f, we have

$$V[R] = x_c^2\sigma_{cc} + x_f^2\sigma_{ff} + 2x_cx_f\sigma_{cf} \tag{7}$$

Since the correlation between cash and futures is

$$\rho_{cf} = \frac{\sigma_{cf}}{\sigma_c\sigma_f} \tag{8}$$

it follows that

$$\rho_{cf}\sigma_c\sigma_f = \sigma_{cf} \tag{9}$$

Substituting in Equation (7) we get

$$V[R] = x_c^2 \sigma_{cc} + x_f^2 \sigma_{ff} + 2x_c x_f \rho_{cf} \sigma_c \sigma_f \tag{10}$$

Since the cash (or spot) commodity and the futures contract on that same commodity will tend to move in the same direction, the correlation coefficient will be positive, and closer to 1.0 than to 0. By being long in one position and short in the other the effect is to make the term with ρ_{cf} in it *negative,* thus reducing the variance.

To minimize the portfolio risk we must minimize $V[R]$. This can be shown to be[6]

$$x_f^* = -x_c \rho_{cf} \frac{\sigma_c}{\sigma_f} \tag{11}$$

In the case of perfect correlation ($\rho = 1.0$) this reduces to

$$x_f^* = -x_c \tag{12}$$

When the correlation is less than 1.0 the number of units in the cash and futures positions will be different. This may present somewhat of a problem because futures contracts are for a fixed number of units. The hedge may therefore be only approximate. The coefficient of x_c in Equation (11) is called the *hedge ratio.*

CROSS HEDGING

Equation (11) can be especially useful in cases where the cash commodity is not traded as futures contracts. If a futures contract exists on a highly correlated commodity, hedging will still be advantageous. Using futures on a different commodity to hedge a cash commodity position is termed *cross hedging.* In the absence of a futures market in sorghum one might, for example, use corn futures for hedging. Or, one might use U.S. T-bond futures to hedge a corporate bond portfolio.

EXAMPLES

Now that basic principles and theoretical considerations have been discussed it will be useful to examine how hedging can be applied. The examples that follow are representative of fundamental hedges. In practice one finds much more complex and sophisticated hedging to deal with specific situations. However, the basic principles illustrated in these examples apply to all hedging and serve as a foundation of learning on which one can build. For simplicity it is assumed that the optimal hedge ratios are 1:0.

PHYSICAL COMMODITY: BUYING OR LONG HEDGE. Arlingtown Builders is a large construction firm engaged in building individual housing. In order to buy lumber at minimum price and assure its supplies, Arlingtown buys in carload quantities directly from the mill.

It is now January, and Arlingtown expects it will need to purchase 650,000 board feet in May. Management feels that lumber prices will rise more than is currently expected by the market, and wants to be protected. Arlingtown sells houses in advance for fixed prices; an increase in raw materials costs could wipe out its expected profits.

The price per M (i.e., 1000) board feet (MBF) is $145 for the May futures contract. The current cash price is $130/MBF, FOB (free on board) supplier's mill. The *basis* is thus $15 *under*: $145 − $130.

Arlingtown Builders decides to hedge its May purchases, and buys five contracts, each for 130 MBF, on January 7. For each contract the required margin deposit is $900 for a bona fide hedger. Thus, the total margin deposit is $4500. Arlingtown Builders could earn interest at a 12 percent annual rate on this money if it were not tied up in margin. The round-turn commission is $60 per contract, for a total of $300 on the hedge, paid on liquidation of the futures side.

The company is long the basis: short cash lumber and long futures contracts. The cash price and the futures price should converge in the delivery month. In other words, the basis for the May contract should move toward zero by mid-May, because trading ceases after the last business day preceding the 16th of the month.

On the May 12, Arlingtown Builders makes a cash purchase of 650 MBF of lumber, and lifts the hedge by selling five futures contracts at the same time. The cash price is $180/MBF and the May futures contract price is $182. The May contract basis has thus narrowed to $2 under. Let us examine Table 5-2 and see what Arlingtown Builders has accomplished.

At first glance it would appear that this hedge has not worked well. However, if Arlingtown Builders had not hedged its lumber requirements it would have lost $50/MBF, or $32,500 as the cash price went from $130/MBF to $180. Even though the company does not buy its cash lumber until May, it has built $130/MBF into its house prices. In a very real sense the company is short the cash commodity since it has committed to deliver lumber (in the finished houses it builds) at $130/MBF.

With the price going up, as Arlingtown expected, it has cut its losses from $32,500 to $8930, a net gain (i.e., loss reduction) of $23,570 over the unhedged alternative. But what if Arlingtown's price forecast was wrong? What if prices

TABLE 5.2. RESULTS OF ARLINGTOWN BUILDERS' HEDGE

	Cash	Futures
January 7	Short 650 MBF at $130/MBF	Buy five contracts at $145/MBF
May 12	Buy 650 MBF at $180/MBF	Sell five contracts at $182/MBF
	Loss: $50/MBF	Gain: $37/MBF
Loss:	$13/MBF × 650 =	$−8,450
Less:	Commission	$300
	Interest opportunity cost on margin	180
Net Loss:		−480
		$−8,930

declined instead? Let us assume that on May 12 the cash price is $120/MBF and the futures price $121. Table 5-3 summarizes what has been accomplished.

In this case the company lost $9580 by being hedged. If it had not been hedged it would have been $6500 better off ($10 × 650). However, the company sacrificed the chance to profit on a price decline in order to have a large measure of protection if the price went up. The idea is to confine possible gains and losses to a narrower range than would hold without hedging. The essence of risk reduction is to reduce the dispersion of possible outcomes.

If reliable forecasts were available to the firm it might decide to hedge only when prices were forecast to be higher. This would produce much better re-

TABLE 5.3. ARLINGTOWN BUILDERS' HEDGE, ALTERNATIVE RESULTS

	Cash	Futures
January 7	Short 650 MBF at $130/MBF	Buy five contracts at $145/MBF
May 12	Buy 650 MBF at $120/MBF	Sell five contracts at $121/MBF
	Gain: $10/MBF	Loss: $24/MBF
Loss:	$14/MBF × 650 =	$−9,100
Less:	Commissions	$300
	Interest opportunity cost on margin	180
		−480
Net loss:		$−9,580

turns than hedging, regardless of likely market direction. It is obvious that reliable forecasts can be valuable to hedgers. However, since the market price of a futures contract contains a consensus forecast of prices, to be useful to the company an independent forecast would have to forecast future prices more accurately and reliably than the market itself does.

PHYSICAL COMMODITY: BUYING OR LONG HEDGE. It is June, and the management of Polar Heights Manufacturing Company has just reviewed its expenditures for heating oil the past winter. The company used 200,000 gallons, at an average price of $1.20/gallon. The company uses No. 2 Heating Oil because the less expensive grades are not available through local suppliers. Management has ruled out buying from outside the area in tank car quantities because that would require investment in storage facilities in order to be feasible.

The directors would like to see the company reduce the risk of a major price increase in heating oil because the firm's profit margin has declined due to competitive pressures, and a major increase could result in operating losses.

The company expects to use fuel according to the pattern that it has experienced over the past five years, which averages out to

Month	Gallons
November	20,000
December	40,000
January	60,000
February	60,000
March	20,000

Usage in October and April is low enough that management feels it can be ignored for hedging purposes. Since the contract specification for No. 2 heating oil calls for 42,000 gallons the company will be able to hedge only approximately.

In December the anticipated usage matches the futures contract specification very well, differing by only 2000 gallons. However, November and March usage are only about half the futures contract size, while January and February are about 1.5 times as much as the futures contract. Let us draw a time diagram for the company's fuel oil usage:

20,000	40,000	60,000	60,000	20,000
Nov	Dec	Jan	Feb	Mar	Apr

If we assume uniform usage over each month, and 30 days per month, we can easily convert the usage into gallons per day and determine when, on average, 42,000 gallons have been used. The idea is to match futures contracts to usage as closely as possible.

42,000	42,000	42,000	42,000	32,000

| Nov 1 | Dec 16 | Jan 12 | Feb 3 | Feb 24 | Apr 1 |

There are many different hedging strategies the company could adopt, each of which is likely to have somewhat different performance characteristics. This underscores the complex nature of hedging. It is not simply a purchase of "insurance" against price increases.

As one of many variations, Polar Heights Manufacturing Company could buy one October futures contact (to cover requirements through December 16), one December contract (to cover usage from December 17 through January 12), one January contract, and two February contracts. Whenever the company buys spot (i.e., cash) heating oil it will buy 42,000 gallons and at the same time offset the corresponding futures contract. For example, 42,000 gallons would be purchased at the end of September, on the same day that the October futures contract is sold. Since first notice day is the first business day of the contract month, if the company does not want to take delivery, with problems of resale, it must offset its position on the last business day of the prior month.

Now, on June 15, the local cash price for No. 2 Heating Oil is 120 cents/gallon. The New York Harbor barge price is 90 cents/gallon, and the October futures price is 94.05 cents/gallon. The July futures price is 91.14 cents/gallon. *The* New York basis is thus 1.14 cents under (i.e., 90.00 cents − 91.14 cents). *The* local basis is 21.86 cents *over* (i.e., 120 cents − 91.14 cents).

Because the focus on the company's attention is on October, we are more concerned about the October basis than *the* basis. The New York October basis on June 15 is 4.05 cents *under* (i.e., 90 cents − 94.05 cents). The local basis is 25.95 cents *over* (i.e., 120 cents − 94.05 cents). Figure 5-7 illustrates what the

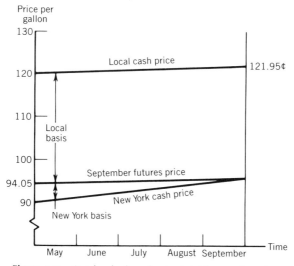

Figure 5.7. October hedge of polar heights manufacturing.

company expects of the October hedge. We assume that on the day the hedge is lifted, September 30, the cash price and futures price are both 95.50 cents/gallon[7] in New York, and the local price is 121.95 cents/gallon.

The local price increased by 1.95 cents, or $819 on 42,000 gallons. However, the futures price has increased by 1.45 cents, or $609 on 42,000 gallons. By hedging the company has saved $609 (less commission and opportunity cost on the small margin deposit). Its effective price increase is $210 (less commission and cost of maintaining the required margin) rather than $819.

Now what about the other hedging contracts? The futures prices on June 15 and the last business day of the month prior to the delivery were as shown in Table 5-4. The company in this example reduced its costs by $3507 less commissions on five contracts (about $300) and the opportunity cost of tying up the funds required for margin (even at 20 percent annual interest, under $800); a minimum cost reduction of some $2400.

In this example the hedge did not provide "insurance" against price increase. In fact, it did not work particularly well compared to the perfect hedges traditionally used for illustration. Nevertheless, the company is still some $2400 better off than it would have been without hedging. And, if the annual interest rate faced by the firm were to have been 20 percent, then buying all requirements in June would not have improved matters a great deal because of the interest expense for carrying the oil inventory from June.

TABLE 5.4. POLAR HEIGHTS' HEDGING RESULTS

Contract	Price ($) June 15	Date of offset	Price when hedge lifted ($)	$ Gain or loss on futures
October	.9405	Sept 30	.9550	$ 609
November	.9535	Oct 30	.9960	1785
December	.9655	Nov 30	1.0100	1869
January (×2)	.9800	Dec 31	.9710	−756
				$ 3507

Contract	Local cash price June 15 ($)	Local cash price when hedge lifted ($)	$ Gain or loss on cash
October	1.2000	1.2195	$ −819
November	—	1.2450	−1890
December	—	1.2625	−2625
January (×2)	—	1.2475	−3990
			$−9324

Net gain or loss $−5817

There are several possible reasons why this hedge did not work as well as we might have expected. The company, as a matter of policy, is committed to making purchases locally; it could bargain for better prices if it were willing to purchase from distant suppliers when the differential made it worthwhile. The local price seems to be somewhat "sticky": It tends to stay at a price that provides a differential of 25 cents/gallon or more over the New York price. In the heating season the local supplier may feel little reason to offer better prices either because of local monopoly or because transportation and storage costs do not allow lower prices to be charged.

If both the cash and the futures prices of No. 2 Heating Oil had risen by just 10 cents/gallon more for each portion of the hedge from June 15, and the local New York differential were the same, the hedge would have been a clear success. The firm would be over $20,000 better off than if it had not hedged at all. And, the experience of the 1970s suggests that a 10 cents/gallon increase is well within the realm of possibility.

FINANCIAL COMMODITY, BUYING OR LONG HEDGE. Sarah Schultz, manager of the Phoenix Pfund, expects to receive $1 million in dividends, interest, and bond redemption payments in three months. It is now December 1. Interest yield to maturity on an 8 percent U.S. T-bond maturing 2005-10[8] is currently 14 percent. Rates have been falling for several weeks, and a consultant who provides forecasts to the fund predicts rates will continue to decline over the coming year.

Schultz decides to lock in the current bond rate by buying March T-bond futures contracts on the CBT. Each futures contract is for $100,000 face value, and can be bought at the moment for 58-07 (i.e., 58 and 7/32), for a yield equivalent of 14.422 percent. Each contract has a dollar value of $58,219 (.58219 × $100,000). To hedge the $1 million that will be received it will be necessary to buy 17 contracts ($1,000,000/$58,219 = 17.18, which we round to the nearest contract.)

This long hedge worked out exceptionally well. Besides protecting fully against the opportunity loss arising by not having the $1 million invested, the hedge earned a profit of almost $25,000 after commissions and the opportunity cost of the margin funds tied up for 3 months (using the 16 percent annual rate applicable to short-term funds). In general it should not be expected that a hedge will yield a profit; hedges that yield small losses should still be considered successful if the hedger would have experienced large losses without hedging. In practice a hedge that exactly protects, yielding neither net gain nor net loss, is rare.

Consider what would have happened if Schultz had not placed the hedge. The $1 million (at market value) of bonds she bought on March 1 would have cost her $168,405 more than on December 1, since the market rate of interest on these bonds fell from 14 percent to 12 percent. Without hedging she would have bought the bonds and earned 12%. By hedging, she in essence locked in a

TABLE 5.5. PHOENIX PFUNDS' HEDGING RESULTS

	Cash	Futures	Basis
December 1	Make decision to buy $1 million of 8% T-bond maturing 2005-10, at price or 60-00, for 14% yield.	Buy 17 CBT T-bond contracts at 58-07 (yield of 14.422%).	+1-25
March 1	Purchase $1 million of cash bonds, at price of 69-29, for yield of 12%.	Sell 17 CBT T-bond contracts at 69-26 (yield of 12.017%).	+0-3
	Opportunity loss: $168,405	Gain: $197,093	1 22/32 (1.6875) stronger

Hedge effectiveness calculation:

Gain:	$197,093
Loss:	168,405

Net before commissions and
    interest on margin $ 28,688   (Also from 17 × 1,000 × 1.6875 basis change)

Less: Commission (17 × $80)   = $1,360
             Interest opportunity
             cost (16% annual rate)[a] = 2,380   3,740

Net gain: $24,948

[a] (17 × $3,500 × .16 × 90/360).

14 percent return *3 months before* the cash was available to invest. The long futures position provided a proxy for the cash bonds, while requiring only $59,500 in margin deposit (17 contracts × $3500/contract), or about 6% of the market value of the contracts.

When March 1 arrives bond yields have declined as forecast. Accordingly, bond prices have risen. With the anticipated $1 million available now to invest the hedge is lifted and cash bonds purchased. Table 5.5 is a summary of what happened.

SUMMARY AND CONCLUSION

Hedging may be defined as speculation on the basis in preference to speculation on the price level. Since basis variation is considerably less than price level variation hedging *reduces* risk. However, hedging does *not* eliminate risk.

In normal "carrying charge" markets, the long hedger generally loses the amount of the basis change as the basis narrows. Only if the futures price declines and the cash price rises over the life of the hedge does the hedger lose less than the basis change. The long hedger, by losing the basis change, is carrying a phantom inventory by being long the futures contract.

The short hedger would appear to do better than the long hedger in a normal market. However, if we factor in the *actual* carrying costs incurred by the short hedger, we see this is not so. The short hedger, who is long the cash commodity, is responsible for financing, storing, and insuring it, and incurs handling costs.

The examples in this chapter suggest that the basis goes to zero when the hedge is lifted. This was useful in explaining the concept of hedging. However, only if the hedge is lifted when the futures contract expires can the basis be expected to be zero. Even then, costs associated with shorts tendering physicals for delivery and longs taking delivery prevent the basis from reaching zero. And, local conditions may cause the local basis to be larger than the basis at futures contract delivery locations.

A complicating consideration in hedging is that of which contract month to use. Unless the hedger plans to make or take delivery of the physical commodity he or she must avoid carrying the hedge into the period in which delivery notices are issued to holders of open futures positions. This is particularly important for those commodities which cannot be retendered. Hedgers not wishing to take either side of delivery of physicals must either use contracts expiring beyond the date the hedge is lifted or risk being unhedged for a period of time when the futures positions are offset.

Modern portfolio theory, and its concept of risk and return have the potential for increasing hedging performance through introduction of a formal rationale that should be especially useful in cross-hedging applications. The key element is found in the variances and covariances between cash price movements in one commodity and futures price movements in the same or a different commodity.

Notes

[1] Other economically desirable consequences stemming from futures markets are price discovery and price forecasting.

[2] In Anthony F. Herbst, "Gold vs. U.S. Common Stocks: Some Evidence on Inflation Performance and Cyclical Behavior." *Financial Analysts Journal* (January/February 1983): 66–74, it has been shown that gold has had negative beta over several spans of years when capital gains were regressed on stock market capital gains. This suggests that gold may be valuable in portfolio diversification. Gold futures may be preferable for this purpose, and other futures contracts may be shown to serve as well or better for reducing portfolio risk.

[3] Thomas A. Hieronymous, *Economics of Futures Trading* (New York: Commodity Research Bureau, 1971), p. 150.

[4] Inverted markets occur because of shortages of deliverable spot commodity, while future supplies are expected to be adequate.

[5] Leland L. Johnson, "The Theory of Hedging and Speculation in Commodity Futures." *Review of Economic Studies* **27,** no. 3 (1960): 139–151.

[6] See Johnson, "Theory of Hedging," pp. 139–151, and also Jerome L. Stein, "The Simultaneous Determination of Spot and Futures Prices." *American Economic Review* **51,** no. 5 (1961): 1012–1025.

[7] Actually, on September 30 the New York cash price was 94.25 cents/gallon, 1.25 cents under the futures price on the last trading day. This reflects the difference between the location of the stocks on which the cash quote is based and the delivery location of the contract specification.

[8] At the time this is written this is a hypothetical issue. However, since the CBT futures contract is predicated on an 8 percent bond not callable nor maturing for at least 15 years, we assume an 8 percent bond is available in order to simplify the example. Formerly the 8 percent T-bond of 1996–01 met the contract specification exactly.

6

Speculation and
Risk Bearing

When one speaks of a person who buys and sells stocks and bonds, whether for the dividends and interest or for an anticipated price appreciation, the term "investor" is generally used. However, a person who buys or sells commodity futures contracts in expectation of profits from correctly forecasting the movement of prices is usually termed a "speculator." Yet what is the difference between an individual who expects the price of a stock to rise, and accordingly purchases shares, and the individual who buys a futures contract because of a similar prognosis about the price?

One must be careful to avoid using the term "investor" to connote socially desirable traits, and the term "speculator" to convey disparagement. The "investor"—that is stock buyer or seller—is in no demonstrable sense morally, socially, or ethically superior to the "speculator" in commodity futures. Buying existing shares or bonds in the secondary market is an exchange of claims and, in itself, does not result in investment in the economic sense; that is, no new productive physical capital is created by the change in stock or bond certificate ownership. This is not to say that active secondary markets in equity and debt instruments are not vital to a modern industrial or postindustrial economy. Such markets provide the liquidity necessary to ensure that firms can raise capital; without active secondary markets it would not be possible to have efficient primary markets. However, it makes no sense to impute moral or ethical superiority to "investors" in stocks or bonds vis-à-vis "speculators" in futures. Speculators are necessary to provide liquidity, and their activities facilitate the process of price adjustment to levels reflecting supply-demand expectations.

How can one distinguish between investing and speculating? Technically, the stock or bond purchaser takes title to the securities purchased. The commodity futures purchaser does not take title unless a long position is held to delivery. Thus, a long futures position is not an ownership, but rather a contract to purchase the underlying commodity at a set price. The holder of a long futures position profits or loses as a result of price movements above or below the price at which the contract was purchased because the futures contract conveys both the right and the obligation to the holder to take delivery if held to maturity. The technicality of when and if title passes to the purchaser would itself provide an insubstantial rationale for distinguishing between an investor and a speculator. If there is a difference, it must be in some other attributes.

WHAT IS SPECULATION?

In futures trading, a speculator is any market participant who is not in the market for the purpose of risk reduction. Thus, speculators are those who are not hedgers.[1]

Compared to stock trading, the normal volatility of commodity prices coupled with the great leverage provided by futures trading provides for proportionately greater volatility in the speculator's account equity. The magnifying effect of leverage increases the price volatility present in commodities: a small price change produces a proportionately much greater change in the speculator's wealth.[2]

IS SPECULATION NECESSARY?

If there were hedgers in the futures markets so that a balance always existed between short and long hedgers, there would be little need for speculators. However, such is not the case. In most markets hedgers tend to be concentrated on one side of the market, either long or short. Because both a long and a short position must exist for every unit of open interest, it is speculators who take up the slack. Without speculators, hedging in most markets would at the very least be difficult, and at the worst impossible. If the amount of copper production hedged by smelters with short futures positions is not equal to the amount hedged by copper fabricators, then speculative positions are necessary for balance.

Besides the balancing effect of speculation, speculative interest provides liquidity. Without speculators standing ready to take positions it would not be possible to buy or sell a futures contract quickly and at a price at, or near, that of the last trade. The greater the speculative interest in a futures market, the greater the liquidity.

The benefits of hedging to reduce the risks faced by producers and consumers of basic commodities are well known. Not only do the hedging enterprises themselves benefit but, because they can pass them on to their customers and shareholders, the advantages gained are widely shared. Hedgers gain protection from adverse price changes in return for relinquishing windfall gains from favorable price changes. Speculators provide hedgers with the opportunity to gain price protection; in return they expect, on average, to make profits for accepting the risk that hedgers want to get rid of. The transfer of risk from hedgers would not be possible without speculation.

COMMODITY VERSUS STOCK SPECULATION

Those who have read the preceeding portions of this chapter may have noted the use of the word speculation applied to both commodities and stocks. This is to put both on the same basis, remove any imputed moral or ethical superiority connoted by the word "investment," and thus facilitate objective comparison. Such comparison is useful because most persons going into commodities have had experience in the stock market.

Leverage

In stock purchases the margin requirement has been 50 percent for more than a decade. The purchaser (or short seller) must put up at least half the cost of the stock bought (or sold short). The broker loans the balance to the customer. On this loan, an interest rate of some 1.5 to 2 percent over the prime, or broker loan rate, is charged. This is quite different from the situation in commodities.

In commodities purchases (and sales) margin requirements are set by the respective exchanges for the commodities they trade. Margin is generally from 5 to 10 percent of contract value. Unlike stocks, where the minimum margin requirement is specified as a percent of value, in commodities trading margin is specified as a dollar amount. Thus the actual percentage of contract value varies with price fluctuations. When there are substantial price changes, margin requirements are changed so that the approximate 5 to 10 percent is restored. In particularly volatile markets the exchanges may raise margin requirements substantially, both to cool off the market and to provide additional safety to the exchange. Margin should be adequate to absorb losses; it is much more difficult to collect additional money from a losing trader than to debit his or her account.

Unlike the situation in stocks, commodities margin is not a down payment but a good faith deposit. And, since ownership is not transferred unless a contract is held to delivery at maturity, there is no borrowed money to accrue interest to be paid to the broker.

With margin in most commodities of roughly 10 percent of contract value, and that for stocks at 50 percent, leverage is much greater in commodities. A two percent change in the price of the underlying commodity will produce a 20 percent change in the trader's equity (assuming initial margin to be the trader's equity). A two percent change in a stock's price will cause only a corresponding four percent change in equity for the stock trader.

The far greater leverage in commodities than stocks provided by the lower minimum margins makes commodities trading seem much more risky. However, if the trader were to use the same margin in commodities there would be no inherent difference in risk. Some commodities positions would be more risky than some stocks, and vice versa. There is nothing to prevent the commodity trader from putting up more than the minimum requirement. However, there is no need to do so because the funds can be placed in an interest earning money market fund and transferred as needed to the commodities account.

The Role of Margin

In stock trading, margin deposit is a down payment, or partial payment, on stock actually bought. The remaining cost is financed with a margin loan from the brokerage firm he or she deals with. The stock bought this way is held by the broker until fully paid for. Thus the broker has both a lien on the shares bought and custody of them.

Margin in commodity trading is not a down payment but a performance deposit or buffer. Margin in commodity trading provides funds to absorb losses that may be incurred by the trader. Without this money the broker would have to make good on the losses and then try to get repaid by the trader afterward. This would be both a nuisance and a difficulty; some traders would delay payment, others might try to refuse paying altogether. When commodities margin falls below approximately 75 percent of the initial requirement the trader receives a margin call, requiring that additional funds be deposited or that some open positions be liquidated. Because margin in commodities is not a down payment or partial payment there is no corresponding margin loan on which interest accrues.

Money Management

According to one authority, "the money management approach is a group of tools and techniques for managing the rewards and costs of trading."[3] These tools, or techniques, are useful within a conceptual framework that treats commodity trading as a business enterprise. And, the enterprise will only succeed over the long term by their application.

In general terms, money management is concerned with minimizing risk for a given expected return (or equivalently, maximizing return for a given level of risk). It is also concerned with avoidance of catastrophic loss (i.e., financial ruin). Money management must relate to the individual trader's circumstances and temperament, or utility. The trader of modest means should not expect to trade in the same manner as one with great financial resources.

Money management encompasses those concepts, techniques, models, and behavioral traits that assist the commodity trader who is in the market to win, to earn profits on money and time invested. Therefore, one who trades commodities for entertainment might not need money management. But one who plays to win, who expects to profit from commodities trading, can hardly expect to do so without sound money management.

Unsound money management in stock market trading may go undetected for a long time, as equity gradually declines. But, in commodity trading unsound money management will quickly be revealed, because the markets are both ruthless and swift in meting out profits or losses.

Trading Costs

Trading futures has associated with it several costs: commissions, information, and opportunity. For traders not temperamentally conditioned for futures trading we may add the physical and emotional costs incurred from the stresses imposed on the trader.

In futures trading commissions are small compared to the value of the contract bought or sold. Unlike stock and bond commissions, futures commissions are "round-turn." Commission is paid only once, on exit from a long or short position. Also, the commission is a flat fee per contract for commodities; it is not figured as a percentage of contract value.[4]

Information costs include all those costs incurred by the trader to obtain information considered necessary to trade profitably. Among these costs are the subscription fees to chart services, newsletters, and telephone "hot-lines." For those who use computers to analyze data, the cost of the computer equipment and supplies must be included.

Opportunity costs are the alternative profits a trader gives up as a result of the decision to trade commodities. For example, if the trader can earn a return of 9 percent per annum on bonds, but sells the bonds to have margin for commodity trading, then the opportunity cost is the foregone interest income.

WHO SHOULD (SHOULD NOT) TRADE?

Whether or not to trade commodity futures, or financial futures, is a question that only the potential trader can answer.[5] Of course, if he or she cannot meet the minimum financial requirements the only possible answer will be in the negative. But what of the person who meets the financial requirements?

Some take the position that futures trading should be undertaken only by those who are well established professionally and financially—by those who can afford the risks involved with what might be considered discretionary funds. Those proffering such a view seldom can provide a satisfactory response to the question of why such a financially well-off individual should wish to trade futures. If one is financially secure then why venture into an unfamiliar and presumably risky new area?

An alternative view is that persons who are willing to face relatively high risk for commensurately high reward should consider trading futures. This view allows for individuals to use futures as a part of their overall wealth-building strategy, rather than something to do after wealth has been accumulated. This alternative view stands up under the illumination provided by modern portfolio theory and other money management principles. The same cannot be said of the view that futures trading should be only for the financially secure.

If futures trading can be considered within the overall financial program, then what remains for the individual to decide is whether or not to do so. The nonfinancial aspects of futures trading may well be decisive for many persons. For an individual to trade futures successfully he or she must be willing to invest the time required to analyze the markets, to plot strategy, to establish and follow tactics based on sound principles of money management. These require not only time, but a large measure of self-discipline. Because of the leverage futures markets provide, traders cannot neglect following market developments unless plans for action are formulated in advance and instructions provided to a reliable broker (i.e., customer representative at the brokerage holding the account).

Once strategy and tactics have been worked out, the futures trader must have the discipline to stay the course. It is often difficult to adhere to a trading plan in the face of market action and the commentary and analysis of others.[6] Work out strategy and tactics carefully, then have faith in your program until facts, not opinions, demonstrate the need for revision. But do keep in mind the principle that it is very difficult to determine where one crosses the line between the "courage of one's convictions" and "bullheaded stubborness" until afterwards.

Finally, the potential futures trader must look inward, into his or her psychological depths, to try to determine whether or not futures trading should be undertaken. If losses will weigh so heavily as to ruin one's disposition, to affect job performance, relations with family and co-workers, and even to affect physical health, then futures trading should be avoided. In some cases a person cannot tell in advance how he or she will handle the adversities that even the most successful traders face from time to time. Thus, it may only become evident after trading for some time that the person involved is ill-suited to it and should quit.

For those who haven't the time or temperament for trading their own commodity account, yet wish to be involved in futures trading, managed commodity funds may be a suitable alternative.

MANAGED COMMODITY FUNDS

The person who wishes to have his or her money managed by professionals in the futures markets has several choices. There are public commodity pools, private commodity pools, and managed accounts, in addition to investment management services that will handle all one's investment funds, not just futures.

Public commodity pools combine the funds of traders into a large single pool. The pool is registered with the SEC. Each individual has a share of the pool in proportion to his or her investment in the pool.

Because commodity pools command larger resources than most individuals possess, they can provide greater diversification. Also, since they are professionally managed, they may be expected to continuously monitor market and economic developments.

The main difference between public and private pools or funds is in registration with the SEC. Private funds, which must start with fewer than 35 investors, are not registered with the SEC. Private pools must also adhere to state restrictions, and cannot offer the fund through public solicitations such as advertising or seminars.

Private commodity pools, because they must start with less than 35 investors, require larger initial commitments of funds than most public funds do. Private funds, because they are not SEC registered, can be established at lower cost and with less delay than public funds.

Managed accounts differ from pools in that the participants' funds are not commingled with those of others. This means that the amount required for a managed account will be larger than that for a pool participation. However, a managed account can be tailored to the overall financial program of the investor, something that a pool cannot do.

Commodity funds and managed accounts offer the advantages of impartial, professional management, and greater potential for diversification. But how have the funds performed? Have managed funds done as well as the investor might reasonably expect? The evidence is not particularly encouraging.

At the end of 1983 there were 73 public fund trading. Of these, only 16 made profits in 1983, and only half of these profitable funds earned more than 10 percent. Almost 80 percent of the funds lost money, with the average return a loss of 9.9 percent. Three funds incurred losses so great that they were liquidated in 1983, and several others had temporarily suspended trading during the year. Altogether, eight funds had losses of more than 30 percent, 17 losses of more than 20 percent and more than half (38 of the 73) had losses of more than 10 percent.[7]

The three best performing funds all earned above 45 percent in 1983, with two of the three earning above 60 percent.[8] The wide distribution of returns from public commodity funds over 1983 suggests the nature of the relationship between risk and expected (not necessarily realized) return: the higher the potential return the greater the associated risk.

Just as one swallow does not make springtime in Capistrano, one year's performance does not tell the whole tale about public pool performance. Table 6-1 displays the lifetime returns of funds started in the years 1978 through 1983. Despite several fund failures, the surviving funds started in 1978 and 1979 have done well compared to those started in later years. The number of strongly trending bull markets in those years compared to the later years may have some connection with this performance.

The year-by-year performance of public commodity funds is shown in Table 6-2. The top-performing Harvest I fund, which has an overall lifetime return of 30.94 percent per annum, has had two losing years (1980 and 1981) but has more than offset this with above average returns in the remaining four years displayed. Remarkably, in 1983 the Harvest I fund had both the largest monthly dollar gain ($2055 in August) and the largest dollar loss ($2941 in February).

Clearly the use of public pools or funds does not provide a smooth road to riches. Yet several funds have done notably well over the long haul, even if overall returns owe much to one or two exceptional years. Now what of private funds?

In 1983 private commodity funds earned a net 2.6 percent. Better than the net loss incurred by the public funds, but far less than the returns on riskless U.S. Treasury bills.[9] Finding a private pool in which to participate may present a problem because of the legal restrictions on advertising and promotion. When considering a private fund the investor would do well to look at how much the pool operators have invested of their own money as a measure of how closely their attention is likely to be focused on the fund's trading activities.

In 1983, although most private commodity funds were diversified, two of the big winners concentrated their trading.[10] Such concentration can produce exceptional gains; it can also produce exceptional losses. However, in a fund that is actively managed by experienced professionals, losses should be cut short while gains are allowed to accumulate. Portfolio theory has not taken such active management into account, but has assumed a passive management policy over the holding period extending from inception to liquidation.

The key to success in funds which concentrate rather than diversify is the fund management. Pick the most capable pool managers and profits should follow. But selecting the best managers may be no easier, in fact may prove more elusive, than picking futures trades oneself. Still, insulation from the stress of making trading decisions and living with the manic-depressive moods that the market can produce may make futures funds attractive to many persons.

If one decides to put money into a futures fund, fees must be examined. Fee structure is not uniform across funds. Some funds charge a flat percentage fee, others a smaller flat percentage coupled with a larger performance incentive

TABLE 6.1. PUBLIC FUND PERFORMANCE OVER THE YEARS*

Fund	Start	1978	1979	Unit Asset Values at End of 1980	1981	1982	1983
Illinois	$1,000 1-78	$812 +18.8%	$1,363 +67.9%	$1,625 +19.2%	$2,584 +75.6%	$2,878 +0.8%	$2,255 -21.7%
Harvest I	$1,000 6-78	$1,543 +54.3%	$4,709 +205.2%	$3,056 -29.8%*	$2,987 -2.3%	$3,784 +33.4%*	$5,040 +38.5%*
Resource	$1,000 8-78	$920 -8.0%	$1,421 +54.5%	$2,457 +72.9%	$3,411 +38.8%	$4,248 +24.5%	$3,792 -10.7%
Thomson FF	$1,000 11-78	$867 -13.3%	$983 +13.4%	$1,416 +44.1%	$1,685 +36.7%*	$1,676 -0.5%	$1,483 -11.5%
Future Fund I	$1,000 7-79		$1,286 +28.6%	$2,325 +80.8%	$3,127 +34.5%	$4,209 +34.6%	$3,732 -11.3%
Gallieo	$1,000 3-79		$822 -17.8%	$1,294 +57.4%	$891 -19.6%*	$914 +19.4%*	$957 +4.7%
Cm. Trend Timing	$963 1-80			$1,263 +31.2%	$1,467 +28.0%*	$1,440 -1.8%	$1,220 -15.3%
Boston I	$957 1-80			$955 -0.2%	$1,065 +19.0%*	$682 -34.6%*	$517 -24.2%
Chancellor I	$942 2-80			$1,046 +11.0%	$1,277 +22.1%	$1,217 +3.1%*	$1,154 -5.2%
Harvest II	$970 2-80			$505 -47.9%	$491 -2.8%	$661 +34.6%	$929 +40.5%
Boston II	$957 8-80			$946 -1.2%	$1,025 +14.7%*	$622 -38.3%*	$485 -22.0%
Peavey I	$876 10-80			$869 -0.8%	$894 +21.9%*	$571 -36.1%	$498 -12.8%
Horizon	$1,000 10-80			$1,039 +3.9%	$1,095 +5.4%	$1,503 +37.3%	$1,307 -13.0%
Cm. Venture	$950 11-80			$1,017 +7.1%	$1,374 +49.9%*	$1,568 +25.0%*	$1,437 -8.4%
Chancellor FFF	$1,000 3-81				$751 -4.9%*	$964 +28.4%	$429 -55.5%
Western	$1,000 11-81				$922 -7.8%	$423 -54.1%	$351 -17.0%

Source: Reprinted from *Futures* Magazine, 219 Parkade, Ceder Falls, Iowa 50613, Darrell Jobman, "Public Pools: Down But Not Out," March 1984, p. 51.

* Includes distributions.

TABLE 6.2. LIFETIME RETURNS[a]

Funds

Year started:	1978	1979	1980	1981	1982	1983
	Harvest I +461.0	Future Fund +273.2	Commodity Venture +82.8	Tactical +81.2	McCormick I +7.6	Commonwealth +14.3
	Resource +279.2	Galileo +25.7	Cm. Trend Timing +42.3	Trendview IV +20.4	Clark Street +2.6	Commodore II +8.8
	Illinois +131.3		Chancellor I +33.0	Admiral +19.4	Hutton Reserve -10.7	Mint +8.6
	Major Trend +94.6		Horizon +30.7	LaSalle +12.4	Future Fund II -11.2	N. American II +6.5
	Thomson McK. FF +84.0		Aries +26.0	Matterhorn +4.5	Cm. Trend Timing II -16.1	Pacific +0.1
	Recovery I +27.3		Hutton Part. II +16.1	Enterprise +1.9	Commodity Strategy -27.7	Dearborn -1.5
			Hutton Cm. Part +13.8	Vista -2.3	Thomson CP II -27.7	Gemini -1.5
			Winchester +2.9	Commodore I -8.0	McCormick II -28.3	N. American I -2.1
			Harvest II -4.2	Thomson CP I -8.6	Thomson FF Part I -29.5	Capital -4.3
			Peavey I -24.3	Saturn -17.9	Sycamore -31.0	Peachtree -9.1
			Boston I -37.0	Dean Witter CP -18.2	Boston IV -39.4	Sunshine -9.9
			Boston II -42.0	Sceptre -18.9	Peavey III -39.9	Cm. Venture II -10.9

Peavey II	Monetary	Palo Alto		
−19.0	−42.9	−17.0		
Financial	Boston III	Horizon World		
−25.5	−62.0	−17.8		
Princeton II		Columbia		
−28.9		−18.4		
Global		Chancellor II		
−33.5		−21.1		
Chancellor FFF II		Thomson CP III		
−37.0		−25.3		
Chancellor FFF I				
−37.1				
Princeton I				
−43.0				
Lake Forest				
−46.0				
Midwest		Chancellor Financial		
−54.0		Futures Fund III		
Western				
−64.9		S.E.K. Commodity		
		Fund		

Funds gone: Antares   McLean II

McLean I
Recovery III

Source: Reprinted from *Futures* Magazine, 219 Parkade, Cedar Falls, Iowa 50613, Darrell Jobman, "Public Pools: Down But Not Out," *Futures*, March 1984, p. 50.

[a] Percentage returns, including distributions, at the end of 1983 compared to starting unit values.

fee on profits above a particular amount. The fees charged are typically rather high: from 20 to 30 percent of capital per annum. For the more successful pools this is in line with their performance. As for the others, it is the price one pays to have others carry the heavy burden of psychological stress associated with futures trading, and to provide professional management. Whether the professional managements' performances vindicate the substantial fees is a matter the trader/investor must judge for himself or herself.

Just as performances and fees vary considerably, so to do the amounts required to participate in a commodity futures pool or fund. Typically, the public funds require a minimum of $5000 or $10,000. Private funds generally require greater commitments, and individual managed account minimums usually begin at $50,000, though some of the large brokerage firms have $25,000 minimums.

CHOOSING THE GAME

Having made the decision to trade commodities, the investor has a number of alternatives from which to choose. Some persons prefer to concentrate on grains, others on meats, and still others on currency or financial futures. Some may adopt an eclectic approach to trading, selecting on the basis of fundamental or technical analysis what appear to be especially promising trades. Besides choosing which commodities to trade, other questions regarding the approach to, and style of trading, need to be answered.

Straight Long or Short

The simplest approach to futures trading is to establish either a long or short position; that is, to buy in anticipation of a price increase, or sell in anticipation of a decline. The appropriate position to establish is a matter the trader will have determined from fundamental and/or technical analysis, or from some hunch about the likely direction of price.

For hedgers the question of whether to be long or short is answered by the cash position held. The hedger with an inventory of wheat in storage is long cash wheat and thus would be short wheat futures; that is, have a short hedge. The copper fabricator who will need to buy copper bars in the coming months is short cash copper, and thus would be long copper futures.

Hedgers are in futures for a different reason than speculators. Hedgers—if they are truly hedging—are seeking to reduce their risk and willing to forgo possible cash position profits to, at the same time, pass on potential cash position losses. We shall not consider hedgers further in this section.

Traders who hope to profit from price movements through straight long or short positions have relatively uncomplicated strategies: "buy low, sell high" or, for short positions, "sell high, buy low." While simple in concept, the profitable execution is far from easy. And, the risk incurred is large in the sense of swings in the trader's equity being relatively great. In technical terms the variance tends to be great relative to the expected return: that is, the coefficient of variation tends to be large. Equivalently, the "risk to reward" ratio is large, to use trade jargon.

Spreads and Straddles

At one time there was a distinction made between the terms "spread" and "straddle." Today they are used synonymously, with spread being encountered more often among traders. Those who trade spreads or straddles are referred to as "spreaders," never as "straddlers," though the term would seem equally appropriate.

In trading spreads, the speculator anticipates making a profit from correctly predicting the *relative* price movements between two futures contracts. The contracts may be for different delivery months of the same commodity, in which case one has an *intracommodity* spread, or for different commodities, whether in the same delivery month or not. In the latter case one has an *intercommodity* spread.

In agricultural commodities there may be differences between contracts in different crop years of the same commodity that are as great, or greater, than the differences between two different commodities in the same crop years. For example, the old and the new crop May and November soybeans may be more different in terms of the fundamentals driving their prices than May corn and May beans, both old crop contracts.

When shortages develop in carryover, old crop inventories, the old crop futures prices can move above those of the new crop contracts. There is no limit on how far the nearby, old crop contract prices can go above the deferred contracts, except that the price rise will be moderated by the price elasticity of demand for the commodity and the availability of substitutes.

In normal circumstances *carrying charge* markets prevail in physical commodities. This means that the difference in price between an October and a March contract for a commodity will reflect what it costs to store the commodity for 5 months. If the price differential is greater than carrying charges traders could earn arbitrage profits by taking delivery of the October contract at its expiration, storing it to March, then making delivery against the expiring March contract. In the contrary case of the price differential being less than carrying charges arbitrageurs would sell the October and buy the March. For this to produce a profit, however, time must remain before the October expires for most arbitrageurs because there is no way to put a short position into storage. Only those who use the commodity in question can be assured of a profit, provided the deliverable grades are acceptable for its purposes. These arbitrageurs will deliver cash inventory against the expiring October contract if necessary. Then they will take delivery of the March at expiration. What they have done by this is to exchange the higher actual inventory carrying charges for the lower implied charges of the futures markets.

Those who use the physical commodity, and thus have an inventory of it, may be able to make arbitrage profits when the implied carrying charges in the futures markets are too low. However, speculators cannot hope to have the same chance to profit. They must instead put on the spread with sufficient time remaining before the nearby contract expires for it to work to their advantage. If their analysis is correct, the relative prices will move apart to reflect full carrying charges. But, since short positions cannot be stored, they cannot carry a position between contract expirations. In principle they could, of course, purchase cash commodity to deliver against the expiring nearby contract, then carry the open long position to expiration, or as long as necessary to make the anticipated profit. In practice, persons outside the trade will be well advised to avoid such complications to their lives.

Interest Rate Spreads. For many commodities a major component of carrying costs is the cost of the money tied up in inventory; that is, interest. Thus, if interest rates are expected to decrease, carrying charges should consequently decrease; if rates rise, so too will carrying charges. In the case of commodities like the precious metals, interest costs loom large in the picture of total carrying costs. If, for example, gold is at $350 an ounce, a contract of 100 ounces is worth $35,000. If at the same time interest is at 10 percent per annum, by having funds tied up in cash gold inventory the trader forgoes $3500 in earnings. If the inventory is financed with borrowed funds, the cost is a cash outflow of $3500, a forceful reminder of the cost of money!

Continuing the previous gold example, if interest rates were to rise to 12 percent the interest cost would rise $700 to $4200. If rates were to fall to 8 percent, the interest cost decreases $700 to $2800. This assumes, of course, that there is no change in the price of gold. Rising interest rates not only increase carrying costs, they also tend to accompany expectations of increased inflation. This favors the price of gold with an increase, which is magnified in the deferred months by the interest effect. If the relationship between a nearby and a distant contract (with a maturity one year beyond it) is given by

$$P_D = P_N(1 + i) \tag{1}$$

then the change in P_D is expressed in differential form as

$$dP_D = dP_N + idP_N + P_Ndi \tag{2}$$

The first term on the right-hand side is the change in the price of the nearby contract. The second term is the interest effect of the change in nearby price, and the last term reflects the effect of a change in interest rate. Together, the second and third terms reflect the interaction of price change in gold and interest rate change.

What makes carrying charge interest rate spreads worthwhile is that the margin requirement is low (around $500 per spread) and that the potential for loss or gain is comparatively well defined, at least at the extremes of interest rate range experienced in the past decade. For a $500 margin deposit the spreader stands to make well over 100 percent on his or her money if right. If not, losses will not mount so quickly that the trader has no chance to act defensively and exit the position.

It must be mentioned that interest rate spreads like those in precious metals do not work the same way in other commodities. In fact, with other commodity futures, a *bull spread* means one is long the nearby contract, short the deferred; a *bear spread* means short the nearby, long the deferred. The reason for these appellations is that in a bull market prices of nearby futures tend to rise faster than those of the more distant contracts. Conversely, in a bear market, nearby prices tend to fall faster. With the precious metals, however, one finds just the opposite tendencies. There are no crop year effects to cause a squeeze in the near months in the case of the metals. And interest rate effects outweigh other carrying charges because the precious metals have great value density. One hundred ounces of gold, worth perhaps $35,000, occupies only a few cubic centimeters. A hundred ounces of gold thus occupy a very small space in a vault, and the storage and insurance do not amount to much. Contrast this with a contract for 5000 bushels of corn, for example, worth perhaps $15,000 and occupying space approximately equivalent to a railroad car. Or, compare to a contract of live cattle; 40,000 pounds of cattle on the hoof not only occupy space but must be fed, watered, and otherwise looked after, including veterinary care if necessary. Obviously the differences in carrying charges are vastly different.

Intracommodity Spreads. Interest rate spreads in the metals are intracommodity spreads. Other intracommodity spreads are based on perceived price anomalies between different contract months of the same commodity. For example, a trader may feel that market sentiment about old crop corn usage and remaining stocks may be overdone, vis-à-vis expectations concerning the prospects for a bumper crop in the coming year. He or she may decide in February to sell a May contract and buy a December if the trader believes that old crop supplies will prove more abundant relative to new crop than the market reflects. Another trader, believing that old crop carryover will be less than expected relative to the new crop, may buy the May and sell the December.

Intracommodity spreads based on a long position in a nearby, old crop contract and a short position in an old crop contract have a well defined cap on the loss that may be incurred. That loss is equal to the change in carrying costs plus commissions and opportunity cost on the margin deposit. The trader, if necessary, can generally take delivery of the nearby contract, store the commodity, then deliver against the deferred.[11]

Intracommodity spreads in which the trader is short the old crop and long the new have the potential for disaster. The reason for this is that a severe rundown in old crop inventory can cause a sharp run-up in price, and just how far the price can go relative to the as yet unharvested new crop is indeterminable in advance. The price spread will be braked by availability of substitutes and slackened demand as the price of the old crop rises. But the spread trader should be aware of the danger of severe losses being incurred in such a spread.

Intercommodity Spreads. An intercommodity spread is based on a long position in one commodity with a simultaneous short position in another. Not all such combinations can be considered as spreads. There must be a reasonable linkage in the prices of the two commodities, and the linkage must be direct for a spread to be a *recognized spread*. On recognized spreads the margin requirement is usually the larger of the two individual margins rather than their sum. And the commission is somewhere between the commission on one and the commission on both commodities if traded separately.

Recognized intercommodity spreads include corn versus wheat, soybeans versus end products (oil and meal);[12] gold versus silver, T-bills versus T-bonds, and lumber versus plywood. The common thread running through such spreads is that each set of long and short positions is in futures that are affected by the same factors of supply and demand. Some spreads, such as T-bonds or GNMAs versus lumber, are not recognized spreads. However, if the trader can make a sensible case as to how and why two such different commodities react similarly to the same factors, many brokers will try to make some accomodation.

It is the common influence on both futures that makes for a spread. The two should normally move together in response to certain major factors, such as weather or interest rates. The normal price relationship provides the trader with a sense of which way prices are likely to move when the normal relationships become distorted. The risk in intercommodity spread trading is that the price relationship might become still more abnormal before it comes back. Spread profits can be made on either movement from normal or back to it; so too can losses.

Risk Considerations

It is often heard that spread trading is less risky than trading straight positions. This may be true in most cases, though there are exceptions. In trading different crop years of pork bellies, for example, the risk can be greater in a spread than in trading just one of years, and this may be reflected in the margin being larger, not smaller, for such a spread. Generally, however, a spread presents less risk than a straight long or short position.

The reason that spreads tend to be less risky is that both contracts tend to move in the same direction, so that convergence or divergence will seldom be abrupt. At least in intracommodity spreads this is the case. In intercommodity spreads there may be occasions where there is a sharp movement in one future and not the other because of a fundamental influence that affects only one of the two commodities. Spread margin requirements reflect this, they are higher for intercommodity spreads.

If a trader confines himself or herself to intracommodity bull spreads the risk will be less than in straight long or short positions. The trader must be careful, however, to ascertain that retendering is permitted in case taking delivery is a consideration. In Chicago Mercantile Exchange lumber, for example, delivery is permitted only at mill site and retendering by traders not permitted. This can allow price anomalies that would otherwise be arbitraged away.

The reason that spreads tend to be lower risk than straight long or short trades is that, by combining long and short positions in highly correlated commodities, one creates a *portfolio* with negatively correlated assets. More will be said about this later. Portfolio theory has an important bearing on money management and risk-return considerations.

Entering and Lifting the Spread

Spreads are usually entered by a spread order that implies both sides will be put on simultaneously, or as nearly so as conditions on the floor permit. There are spread brokers who specialize in these affairs, and they are good at it; nevertheless, traders will find it advisable to use limit orders in spreading, to avoid regrets. Limit orders put the burden on the spread broker to fill within the limit specified. Otherwise, the fill might be at a less favorable spread than the trader anticipated.

Intracommodity spreads present less problem in entering and exiting simultaneously than intercommodity spreads. The fact that in intercommodity spreads both sides are put on in the same trading pit makes them less troublesome than spreads where commodities at different parts of the trading floor, or on different exchanges, are involved. Yet, for most recognized spreads, such as Chicago Wheat/Kansas City Wheat, even the distance involved does not seriously impair broker performance.

In some intercommodity spreads it may be necessary or advisable to "leg in" one side at a time, rather than simultaneously. One should not attempt such a move without the aid of a broker representative who has experience in such matters. It should seldom be necessary to leg in to a spread. If your broker representative recommends it, you should ask for reasons why it is preferable to a spread order in the particular circumstances. By legging into a spread the trader has a larger risk exposure than desirable until the other leg is put in. If there should be trouble in getting the other leg in, perhaps because it is in a distant contract with low volume currently, the in-leg could move to create a larger than anticipated loss.

When lifting a spread or straddle it is generally done both sides at once. However, a spread may be lifted one leg at a time. Why would anyone want to? One good reason is that the trader has come to believe strongly that the market is going to move decisively one way and wants to have a pure play on it. This may coincide with the imminent expiration of the nearby contract if it is an intracommodity spread.

Spreading for the Wrong Reasons

Spreads can be less risky than pure long or short plays. However, they can, and are, sometimes used by traders for other reasons.

A trader who endures an adverse price move, perhaps one that precipitates a margin call, may put on a spread. The spread margin is less than that of the original open long or short position. Thus, the margin call is put off.

Besides forestalling a margin call, converting a losing pure long or short into one side of a spread can buy time for the trader to think. The spread prevents the situation from further rapid deterioration; it may still deteriorate, but more slowly than before.

Unfortunately, converting to a spread does not often improve a losing situation. While it may buy time for the trader to assess the situation more cooly than before, the conclusion is likely to be the same: Get out of the position.

If the trader was bullish he or she probably was long a nearby contract, for it is these that usually have the greatest liquidity and potential for price movement. The fact that the trader was wrong implies that the market may continue to fall. By converting to a spread the trade creates a bull spread: long the nearby, short the deferred (except in the precious metals).

A trader who has a bull spread in a falling market will continue to lose money. The losses will tend to mount more slowly than they did with the original long position. Nevertheless, the losses will grow inexorably. A bull spread in a bear market is a losing situation. No less so is the bear spread in a bull market.

Only by the market turning to vindicate the trader's original prognosis about price direction will a spread improve matters. But just as losses accrue more slowly in the spread, so too will profits. If the situation were to improve it would do so more slowly than if the trader had kept the original position in the first place. And, although the margin on a spread is less, the commission is greater than a pure long or short trade.

Trying to convert a losing trade into a profitable one is not the only flawed rationale for spreading. Traders have tried spreading gold versus silver on the basis of an historical gold/silver price ratio imputed with almost mystical significance by some writers. A trader must not assume that an intercommodity spread will pan out as hoped because the price spread is wider (or narrower) than the historical norm. There may very well exist fundamental reasons to account for the price disparity; it might persist and even go far against the trader's position. In 1984, for example, July corn went to a substantial premium over July wheat, and the premium continued to grow for some time. Normally, wheat is at a large premium to corn, but dry weather during the prior growing season had harmed the corn crop, while winter wheat in the field and the approaching harvest was considered to be faring well.

Notes

[1] We may wish to distinguish a third class of market participant, the arbitrageur. Arbitrage is the process of simultaneously buying in one market and selling in another in order to make a virtually risk-free profit from price anomalies.

[2] If the speculator has to put up margin equal to 10 percent of the value of a futures contract, then a one percent change in the unit price of the commodity will cause a tenfold change in the speculator's wealth.

[3] Fred S. Gehm, *Commodity Market Money Management* (New York: Wiley, 1983), p. 4.

[4] There is considerable variation from broker to broker on commissions. A discount broker may charge only a third of what a "full service" broker charges, for example.

[5] In some countries the question may be answered in law. In West Germany, for example, futures contracts are not enforceable in court because of section 762 BGB (*Burgerliches Gesetzbuch*), which states that *"Durch Spiel oder Wette wird eine Verbindlichkeit nicht begrundet."* (Games and bets do not create liabilities.) Nor do they generally in the United States, but the nature of futures contracts is recognized to be different and socially beneficial.

[6] It is important to avoid discussing the market with one's broker representative. These persons are seldom at a loss for words, even in regard to futures they know little about. Yet their opinions can have an unsettling effect, even on experienced traders. If it is necessary to avoid unsolicited opinions—change brokers.

[7] Darrell Jobman, "Public Pools: Down But Not Out." *Futures* **13,** no. 3 (March 1984): 50–51, 54.

[8] *Ibid.,* p. 51.

[9] Ginger Szala, "Private Funds: Diversity Pays Off." *Futures* **13,** no. 3 (March 1984): 52–54.

[10] *Ibid.,* p. 52.

[11] This is not true in a few commodities, such as lumber, which cannot be taken in delivery and then later retendered for delivery. A trader must learn to always check on the details of delivery, and so on with his or her broker before putting on a spread.

[12] This spread is called the "crush" or "reverse crush" spread, depending on whether the trader is long beans and short end product or the opposite.

7

Money Management—
Playing to Win

Few factors are as important to success in futures trading as proper money management. Even those who have an inspired ability to forecast prices will have reverses occasionally. With proper money management, the reverses can be weathered without catastrophic damage to the trader's equity. Along with money management techniques, self-knowledge about his or her attitude toward risk and return, and ability to cope with adversity are important to the trader.

UTILITY AND RISK AVERSION

Trading results and risks cannot be meaningfully measured solely in dollar terms. The trader's attitude and feelings—his or her *utility*—must play a role.

Each individual feels and reacts differently toward the same situation. Some prefer to keep their funds in the safe harbor of U.S. T-bonds rather than to brave the vicissitudes associated with a potentially far more profitable trade in commodity futures.

Economists developed the basic concepts of utility many years ago to augment the growth of economic theory in what is termed microeconomics.[1] Utility is a measure of personal satisfaction. If something provides a feeling of greater pleasure than something else, it has greater utility.

Recently psychologists have added to the theory of utility by analyzing the choices of test subjects who were posed questions aimed at determining their attitudes toward risk and reward. In particular, it has been discovered that people generally view a cost of a given amount as acceptable, while a loss of the same amount is not; that is, losses have greater negative utility and thus are more "aversive" than costs. Two researchers who have recently contributed in the area suggest that:

> *The framing of an expenditure as an uncompensated loss or as the price of insurance can probably influence the experience of that outcome. In such cases, the evaluation of outcomes in the context of decisions not only anticipates experience but also molds it.*[2]

This has a bearing on the futures trader, who can alternatively view the small losses resulting from protective stop orders either as losses or as costs of trading. Viewing them as losses will be more stressful for most traders than the alternative. Yet the dollars are no different in either case. Therefore, traders would do well to condition themselves to view the ordinary diminishments in equity that are part and parcel of the trading as costs, and avoid referring to them as losses. Otherwise the stress created may adversely affect the trader's performance.

A risk averse person experiences diminishing marginal utility for increasing amounts of wealth. Each extra dollar adds less utility than the last. This person would reject a "fair bet" (one with zero expected value from equal probabilities of gaining or losing the amount of the bet) because the expected utility is negative.

A risk neutral person experiences the same utility from each dollar of wealth. Fair bets would be acceptable to such a person.

Finally, a risk seeker, or risk lover, would receive greater utility from each additional dollar, suggesting greed. The utility of potential large gain in a gamble is so much larger than the utility of the amount bet for such persons that they will take the bet even though the expected *monetary* value is zero or even negative. One should not expect to find many persons with this utility function since they would have a self-destructive tendency to prefer the riskier of two propositions because it offers the greater possible dollar gain.

Most persons will have utility functions like that shown in Figure 7-1. Eventually he or she has a risk averse function for large dollar amounts. For small amounts the function may indicate risk seeking, phasing into risk neutrality, then risk aversion.

In the range of wealth gains and losses regularly experienced, the trader will have a reliable sense of the utilities associated with them. However, for gains or losses outside the range of experience, the trader will be less sure of the associated utilities and this may confuse his or her instincts and make decision making less reliable. For this reason traders should attempt to ascertain their own utility profiles and to estimate the expected utility of each trade before entering it.[3]

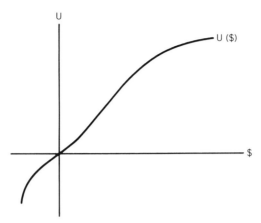

Figure 7.1. Utility of money function for typical person. *Source: Capital Budgeting,* Anthony F. Herbst, copyright 1982, Harper & Row.

CALCULATING PERSONAL UTILITY*

This section presents a method for estimating an individual's utility function. The method could also be used to try to determine a composite utility curve for a group. The treatment here parallels the presentation contained in Teweles, Harlow, and Stone.[4]

The first step is to determine the largest dollar gains your investment decisions have regularly made and the largest dollar losses that have similarly resulted. This may be impossible for many readers. Thus, persons who have not made such decisions will have to imagine what the amounts would be, and try to be perfectly honest about it. This is not a test; there are no right or wrong answers. It is not necessary to do any calculations in reaching your answers, although you may if you prefer.

Let us begin by developing the utility function for a speculator who tells us that he (individually) has regularly made decisions that have resulted in gains of as much as $5000 and losses of as much as $2000. We shall not concern ourselves here with whether these are gains and losses over several months, or with other details of the timing of the amounts. The procedure would not be materially different anyway. Having established the largest regular gains and losses, we write them down as shown in Table 7-1, column (4). The value $5000 is associated with utility of 1.0 and the loss of $2000 with utility 0.0. Other values could have been used for the utilities, such as +1.0 and −1.0, but the scaling is unimportant and by assigning zero utility to the worst outcome the calculations are a little easier.

* This section is adapted from Anthony F. Herbst, *Capital Budgeting* (New York: Harper & Row, 1982).

TABLE 7.1.   COMPUTATION OF A
                SPECULATOR'S UTILITY FOR
                MONETARY GAINS

Probability of			
(1) Best result	(2) Worst result	(3) Computed utility	(4) Dollar cash equivalent
1.0	0.0	1.0	$ 5,000
0.9	0.1	0.9	3,100
0.8	0.2	0.8	2,300
0.7	0.3	0.7	1,500
0.6	0.4	0.6	900
0.5	0.5	0.5	500
0.4	0.6	0.4	− 300
0.3	0.7	0.3	−1,000
0.2	0.8	0.2	−1,300
0.1	0.9	0.1	−1,800
0.0	1.0	0.0	−2,000

Having established utilities of 1.0 for a gain of $5000 with probability 1.0, and 0.0 for loss of $2000 with probability 1.0, we now need to find intermediate values. Suppose now we ask our speculator to tell us if he would accept an investment offering a gain of $5000 with probability 0.9 and loss of $2000 with probability 0.1; in other words, nine chances in 10 of gaining $5000 and one chance in ten of losing $2000. He answers "yes," certainly he would accept such investment. Now we ask if he would pay us $3000 for the opportunity to make such an investment.

Yes, he would. $3200? No, not this much. How about $3100? Maybe. At $3100 he is not sure. For $100 more he will not take the investment, for $100 less he will. Thus in Table 7-1 we write in the second row, rightmost column, the amount $3100.

We repeat the process for gain of $5000 with probability 0.8 and loss of $2000 with probability 0.2. Our speculator will pay up to $2300 but no more for an investment offering these prospects. For each missing value we repeat the process until column (4) is completed. Then we can plot the results obtained, as shown in Figure 7-2, and fit an approximate curve to the points.

In constructing his or her own utility curve for monetary gains and losses, the reader can perform a self-interview or work with someone who will perform the function of interviewer. Further insight into the process is found in Teweles et al.

The curve obtained and plotted in the graph of Figure 7-3 is reasonably satisfactory, except that we do not have enough data points between −$1000

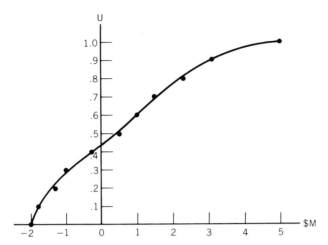

Figure 7.2. Speculator's plotted utility function. *Source: Capital Budgeting,* Anthony F. Herbst, copyright 1982, Harper & Row.

and +$1000 to be confident in the shape of the curve in that range. We can obtain more information by continuing the interview process. Let us begin by constructing Table 7-2 with best result now $1000 and worst result −1000. The associated utilities are, respectively, 0.6 and 0.4.

Values between $1000 gain and $1000 loss are obtained as before. The decision maker is asked if he would accept an investment project offering $1000 gain with 0.9 probability and $1000 loss with 0.1 probability. Yes. Would he pay $1000? No. $950? No. $900? Maybe. Don't know. $850? Yes. We write $900 in column (6) of Table 7-2. The process is repeated until column (6)

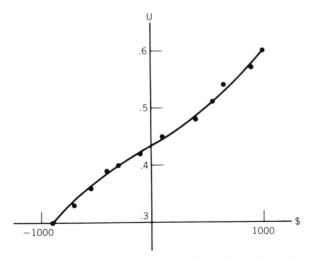

Figure 7.3. Plot of refined utility for a speculator. *Source: Capital Budgeting,* Anthony F. Herbst, copyright 1982, Harper & Row.

TABLE 7.2.   COMPUTATION OF REFINED UTILITY FUNCTION FOR A
SPECULATOR

Best outcome		Worst outcome			
(1)	(2)	(3)	(4)	(5)	(6)
				Computed	Dollar cash
Utility	Probability	Utility	Probability	utility	equivalent
0.6	1.0	0.3	0.0	0.60	$ 1,000
0.6	0.9	0.3	0.1	0.57	900
0.6	0.8	0.3	0.2	0.54	650
0.6	0.7	0.3	0.3	0.51	550
0.6	0.6	0.3	0.4	0.48	400
0.6	0.5	0.3	0.5	0.45	100
0.6	0.4	0.3	0.6	0.42	− 100
0.6	0.3	0.3	0.7	0.39	− 400
0.6	0.2	0.3	0.8	0.36	− 550
0.6	0.1	0.3	0.9	0.33	− 700
0.6	0.0	0.3	1.0	0.30	−1,000

is filled and then the results are plotted. Figure 7-3 contains the graph for the
section of utility curve between −$1,000 and +1,000. The scale is enlarged
from that used in Figure 7-2. After combining the information contained in
Table 7-2 with that of Table 7-1, and plotting the results, we obtain Figure 7-4.
The additional detail for utility between −$1000 and +1000 enables a more
refined approximation. The tentative judgment that our investor is a risk
seeker for monetary gains seems to be vindicated by the additional informa-

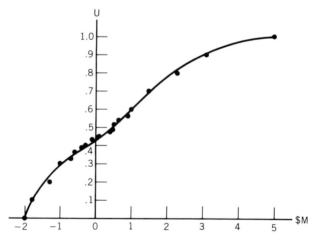

Figure 7.4.   Combined utility estimates. *Source: Capital Budgeting,* Anthony F. Herbst, copyright 1982,
Harper & Row.

tion over the range of about $0 to $1000. Because of the rather wide spread between utility values for dollar amounts in the ranges $-$1000 to $-$2000 and $1000 to $5000, we might want to repeat the procedure for obtaining detail over these ranges, if our speculator's patience has not been exhausted. We shall not do this here, however, since the procedure has been illustrated and the patience of you, the reader, may be running low.

The plotted results obtained from our speculator do not deviate very widely from the fitted curve. In fact, they are very close to it, thus indicating a high degree of consistency in evaluating alternatives over the range of values regularly experienced by the decision maker. We should not have been surprised if the points were much more scattered about the fitted curve. What happens if we now attempt to obtain utility values for dollar gains and losses beyond the range of the decision maker's regular experience? If we attempt to do this, we will most likely find that the decision maker becomes increasingly inconsistent as the monetary values become further and further removed from the domain of his or her experience.

To compute the utility of larger monetary gains, the formula used is

$$U(\text{Gain}) \times Pr(\text{Gain}) + U(\text{Loss}) \times Pr(\text{loss}) = U(\text{Cash Equivalent})$$

which is equivalent to

$$U(G)p + U(L)(1 - p) = U(C)$$

By rearranging the terms, we obtain formulas for computing the utilities of gains and losses outside the range of the decision maker's experience:

$$U(G) = \frac{U(C) - U(L)(1 - p)}{p} \quad \text{and} \quad U(L) = \frac{U(C) - U(G)p}{1 - p}$$

In calculating the utility of gains and losses for extended amounts for commodity traders, it may be advisable to compute them several times. The reason behind repeating the procedure is to find out how consistent the decision maker is in making decisions outside the range of his or her experience. The reader is referred to the excellent discussion by Teweles et al. for a detailed treatment. The main reason for concern about the decision maker's consistency for larger gains and losses than he or she has regularly experienced is this: If judgments do become increasingly inconsistent for larger gains and losses, then the decision maker should either exercise greater caution (something the person will probably do anyway) in evaluating such prospects, or else avoid them entirely if possible. Otherwise it is likely that decisions will be made for which the perceived a priori and a posteriori utilities are different and the decision maker regrets the decision after making it, even before the results are in.

PYRAMIDING

To make large amounts of money, the trader may wish to have multiple contracts. Strategies are adding to the number of contracts carried are called *pyramiding* strategies.

In pyramiding, the trader adds to his or her positions as the price moves favorably by using the growth in equity to provide margin funds. A pyramid can have a broad base with a narrow top or a narrow base with a broad top.

By starting out with several contracts, and adding a progressively lesser number as equity grows, a broad-based pyramid is created. Figure 7-5 illustrates the process. The wide base and narrow top suggest stability and, in fact, this type of pyramid is far more stable than its narrow-base opposite.

Figure 7-6 depicts a pyramid with a narrow base and wide top. This type of pyramid is unstable, as its physical analog suggests.

In the wide base pyramid, as additional contracts are added, there is more equity created toward the bottom of the structure than toward the top. Thus, a reversal in the market is less likely to wipe out the equity unless it is prolonged. With the narrow base pyramid, however, the additional contracts are added with equity generated more with contracts added recently than with those at the bottom. Not only that, but the greater number of contracts rests on this equity cushion that is supported by a small set of contracts. For a given reversal in the price of the futures contract, it is thus more likely that the narrow base pyramid will collapse under the cascading effect of margin calls.

If one wishes to pyramid gains then it should be with the largest number at the bottom, a broad-based pyramid. There are many variations on the basic theme. The sequence 4, 3, 2, 1 is but one of many. It could just as well have been 5, 3, 1; or 4, 2; or 4, 3, 1. The strategy for adding additional contracts also is variable.

Additional contracts may be bought or sold as the commodity price moves favorably by a given amount, say 10 cents per bushel in the case of corn. Or, the trader may add contracts when the increase in equity is some percentage of the required margin (100 percent, 150 percent, etc.). With this latter strategy additional contracts can be added more quickly as the equity growth acceler-

At Time	Action	Pictorial	Total Contracts
$t = n$	Add one	X	10
$t = m$	Add two	XX	9
$t = 1$	Add three	XXX	7
$t = 0$	Buy four	XXXX	4

Figure 7.5. Pyramid with a broad base.

At Time	Action	Pictorial	Total Contracts
$t = n$	Add four	XXXX	10
$t = m$	Add three	XXX	6
$t = 1$	Add two	XX	3
$t = 0$	Buy one	X	1

Figure 7.6. Pyramid with a narrow base.

ates with the addition of contracts. (Warning! The decline in equity upon a price reversal is also greater.)

Judicious pyramiding can lead to great wealth. One can easily take a price chart and show how a successful pyramid could have been constructed. However, it is difficult to do so without benefit of hindsight. As the pyramid grows, even small price changes induce great equity changes, and few trends continue long without volatility increasing. And, for a pyramid to be successfully executed requires that a trend develop after the trader enters the market. Often, there will be no prolonged trend to allow a pyramid to work.

USING STOP ORDERS

The phrase "Damned if you do; damned if you don't" never applied more aptly than to the use of stop orders in futures trading. The skilled placement of stop orders can do much to preserve profits and reduce losses, yet the placement of such orders is one of the most difficult aspects of futures trading to master. Those who have used stop orders invariably can recall occasions when it seemed the market changed course just long enough to stop out their position then reverse course and move in the erstwhile trader's favor. It happens often enough to give credibility to the notion in the minds of some traders: "I'm not paranoid, they're out to get me!" But to trade without using stops is to play the game under a handicap. For this reason, stops are used by many traders despite their uneasiness about them.

Traders frequently use stop orders to enter a position upon the triggering of a technical signal based on chart analysis. At the same time, they often place a stop-loss order to try to limit their losses if the trade does not turn out as expected. Unfortunately, certain chart signals tend to be rather obvious. Other speculators will tend to place their stop orders at the same levels, and floor traders are well aware of this. The floor traders, or "locals" as they are known, will "fish for stops" and, finding them, move the market temporarily—to their profit. Price charts contain ample cases of price spikes that may be explained on the basis of stops being cascaded like a set of dominoes set on end. Given this situation, what can the trader do?

In using stops, there are some guidelines that may help. They are far from perfect but likely to be better than the naive use of stop orders. First, avoid placing stops at obvious chart points. Second, try to use "stop—close only" orders for stop loss protection if your broker will accept them and execute them reliably. Some exchanges will not accept "stop—close only" orders as such, in such cases you must rely on your broker's representative (your "broker") to place the appropriate order at the right time. These orders will often prevent the trader from being stopped out only to see the market reverse and close away from the stop. In cases where the floor traders run the stops, they generally unload positions acquired in the process before the close rather than carry them overnight or over a weekend.

A third possibility is to use "mental" stops, provided one has the time to follow the market and the discipline to act. Unfortunately, most people cannot monitor the market continuously, and most brokers cannot be expected to do it for traders unless the latter's accounts are large enough to warrant the effort. Even those who can follow the market action may find it difficult to act appropriately while under the stress of a market gone against them unless they have worked out a plan of action in advance and strictly follow a policy with regard to enacting the plan.

A fourth alternative is to place formal stops only after a large, sharp price move or "spike" that would have hit a resting stop has occurred. This will work except in cases where the move continues rather than reversing, thus depriving the trader of the advantage afforded by a stop. It also will not work in cases where a second price spike follows the one the trader waited to see before placing his or her stop.

The effective use of stop orders is perhaps the most difficult aspect of futures trading to gain mastery of. However, the importance of stop orders, and the benefits to be had from their effective use, suggest that traders who hope to make money should study and practice their use until mastery is gained.

Limit Moves and Lock-In

Occasionally a futures market moves so strongly that few or even no trades occur within the allowed price range. This sometimes goes on for several days of limit moves. Those who are adversely affected cannot get out until a price is reached at which trading resumes. Stop orders provide little protection against such situations, and losses can be devasting. In many cases, however, they could have been avoided.

Locked-limit moves tend to occur more frequently to the upside for most physical commodities because they can be induced by weather events that threaten supplies. For example, severe freezes in Florida can propel orange juice futures to sharply higher price levels in a series of limit moves that lasts for several days. Similarly, a dry, hot spell in the corn belt can cause grain and soybean prices to go limit up once the drought is acknowledged by crop damage reports. Or, a report that the Soviet Union will be purchasing much greater amounts of grain than expected can induce a sharp upward move in limit steps.

Although there tends to be more limit up moves than limit down, they occur with some regularity as markets top out after a prolonged rise. Traders need to be especially wary of the possibility of a sharp decline upon release of a crop report after a bull market has prevailed for some time. If the report reverses the bullish sentiment with news of less severe crop damage than expected, or larger carryover stocks, and so on, the bull market may collapse sharply, perhaps in a series of limit declines.

To reduce the possibility of being caught in a locked-limit situation traders can do several things. First of all, they should not be short orange juice futures during the freeze season; that should be left to hedgers and gamblers. Second, positions should be reduced or offset after a favorable trend has existed for a long time. That is, if long in an aging bull market or short in an old bear market, positions should be reduced or offset. Third, traders must beware the effects of a major crop report. There was an occasion in 1983 where the grains and soybeans were shocked one way, then the other, within a span of less than two weeks by conflicting USDA crop reports.

CUTTING LOSSES, LETTING PROFITS RUN

One of the most frequent mistakes speculators make is to take small profits and to get out of losing trades only after incurring large losses. There are brokers who encourage this behavior—taking small profits, if not large losses. Brokers live by commissions, and traders who take small profits and small losses generate more commissions than those who let profits or losses run. They rationalize their advice to clients on the basis that a small profit is better than no profit at all. This advice is true, and probably well meant, even if self serving. However, speculators cannot hope to make large profits by taking small ones. Unfortunately, a speculator who ends up with a loss rather than a small profit, by ignoring a broker's advice to sell and secure a small profit, will be vulnerable to similar advice proffered in the future. Having been wrong once when the broker was right, there is a natural reluctance to risk a recurrence: this can lead to trading errors.

The hard and fast rule that all commodity futures speculators should adopt is to let profits run, cut losses short. That is, hold onto winning positions, perhaps with a stop order to exit on a market reversal. And, get out of losing trades quickly, taking small losses rather than letting them grow to large losses. Again, this may be accomplished with stops.

A technique that deserves attention is that of using trailing stops. With this the trader puts a stop loss order under his or her entry price. If this is touched the position is liquidated with a small loss. If the trade is successful, the stop is ratcheted behind the market price. The position is liquidated when the market moves against the position and most of the profit is preserved. In principle, the technique is simple; in practice it is most difficult to apply successfully. Stops placed too close will take the speculator out with small losses in almost every case. Stops placed too far away lead in many cases to larger losses on trades that are bad to begin with than necessary, and on good trades they give up too much profit in taking the trader out. To be successful in using this technique, speculators cannot place stops naively and expect them to work well. They should plan to spend a good deal of time analyzing past market action and volatility as a guide to effective use of stops.

PORTFOLIO THEORY AND DIVERSIFICATION

So far, attention has been focused on individual futures trades. However, few speculators trade only one commodity and, there are good reasons why one should trade several.

The expression "Don't put all your eggs in one basket" was an early precursor of modern portfolio theory.[5] The basic idea of risk reduction through diversification rests on the principle that two or more risky investments in combination are less risky than they are individually. Assume the speculator has two independent trades (i.e., the results are uncorrelated, they don't depend on one another) each with a chance of success of 0.60 (and chance of failure $1.0 - 0.60 = 0.40$). There is only a 0.16 ($= 0.40 \times 0.40$) chance of both failing; the trade-off is that there is only a 0.36 ($= 0.60 \times 0.60$) chance of both succeeding.

If we measure risk by the variance or standard deviation, as is the norm in the literature of finance and economics, then the combination of futures positions is as portrayed in Figure 7-7. The hatched region depicts the set of

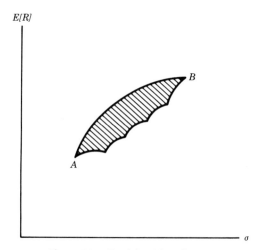

Figure 7.7. Portfolio risk and return.

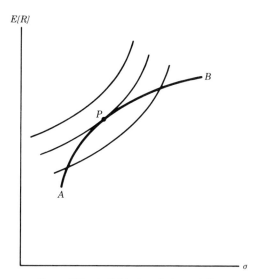

Figure 7.8. Individual trader's portfolio.

feasible (i.e., achievable) combinations of positions.[6] It should be noted that the same return can be achieved with different levels of risk, and for the same level of risk different returns are available.

In Figure 7-7 the set of points along AB is termed the efficient set. This set dominates all other feasible points. A point along AB is preferred to all points below it because, for the same risk, they offer lower returns. A point along AB is also preferred to all points to its right because, for the same return, they incur greater risk. Therefore, the only portfolios of interest are those along AB.

Given that points in the efficient set AB are the only ones of interest, how can we say which of them the individual speculator will choose? The answer lies in the person's utility function, specifically in the set of curves in the $E[R]$, σ space on which the trader is indifferent. These give the risk-return trade-offs for the individual trader. Figure 7-8 shows the interaction of the efficient set with the trader's risk-return indifference set. The chosen portfolio is at point P. Another person, having a different set of risk-return indifference curves, would select a different portfolio.

The development of portfolio theory to the point discussed so far owes much to Markowitz.[7] Introduction of a "risk-free" asset by Sharpe,[8] and the subsequent modifications, lead to a general theory of asset pricing commonly referred to as the capital asset pricing model. We shall not pursue that extension at this juncture because it would tend to divert us from commodity futures, on a long detour. Instead we shall examine the mathematical aspects of diversification.

The essential ingredients of portfolio diversification are expected return $E[R_i]$ on the ith investment, variance or standard deviation on the ith asset, and the covariance between the ith and jth assets.

Expected returns are additive. That is, the return on a portfolio composed of assets i and j in proportion a and b is given by

$$E[R_P] = aE[R_i] + bE[R_j]$$

The variance, which we are using to measure risk, is given by[9]

$$\text{Var}(ai + bj) = a^2 \, \text{Var}(i) + b^2 \, \text{Var}(j) + 2ab \, \text{Cov}(i,j)$$

Assume a speculator who has identified two possible trades, the characteristics of which are given in Table 7-3. The expected net return on a portfolio of one unit of trade A and one of trade B is $175. The variance of return is given by the calculation[10]

$$\text{Var}(A + B) = (0.67)(81) + (0.33)(144) + (2)(0.67)(0.33)(-100)$$

$$= 57.57$$

The relative riskiness of an investment is given by the ratio of risk to expected return. The ratio of variance to expected return is 0.81 for trade A, 1.92 for trade B, and 0.33 for the portfolio of one unit of A and one of B. The risk has been substantially reduced.

In the example just discussed, covariance between A and B is negative (the correlation is -0.93) and this makes the risk reduction stronger than if the trades were positively correlated. Nevertheless, as long as the trades are not perfectly positively correlated, there will be a diminishment in risk.

What if the covariance were to be not -100, but 64? The correlation coefficient would be $+0.59$, and the portfolio variance would be 130.09. The ratio to expected return would be 0.74, which is still less than either trade A or B by itself. This illustrates the principle that as long as the assets selected are not perfectly positively correlated, the portfolio will be relatively less risky than the individual assets.

Although trade B alone offers the higher return, it is also the more risky. Risk and return invariably go hand in hand—the higher the expected return,

TABLE 7.3.   HYPOTHETICAL COMMODITY
                    TRADE DATA

	Trade A	Trade B
Cost	$1000	$500
Expected return	100	75
Variance of return	81	144
Covariance	-100	

the greater the risk. Otherwise, everyone would want to buy the asset, driving up its price and reducing the potential return.

The principle of risk reduction through portfolio diversification plays an important role in money management. Traders who recognize, and incorporate into their trading, the concept that the same return at less risk is better will improve their performance. The principles are simple; nevertheless, speculators will find their successful application far from a trivial challenge.

In applying portfolio diversification, one finds that obtaining the requisite statistical measures can be an elusive goal. In commodity futures, there is some question as to the continuity and stability of statistical parameters from one contract month to another, whether the variance of May wheat is the same as that of September wheat, and whether it is the same for May wheat in one year as it is for another year. Similar problems of parameter stationarity exist in other investments, but they are perhaps more troublesome in futures trading. Nonetheless, the concepts of portfolio diversification, even if not meticulously applied, provide a useful framework for action.

RISK OF RUIN

A futures trader will likely either succeed by growing wealthy or fail by losing the funds committed to speculation. Few will continue for long neither prospering nor losing in a sideways pattern. One thing is certain, if the odds are against the speculator, if he or she has no advantage, then eventually trading capital will be gone. We define *ruin* as the condition of having lost all one's trading capital.

It can give a valuable perspective for us to consider risk of ruin assuming various probability advantages possessed by the trader. If a given speculator assumes he or she has a certain advantage, yet continues to find himself or herself being ruined, then the speculator should try to realistically reassess the assumed advantage. The examples we consider are simple, yet they serve to illustrate the principles involved.

Like many useful risk-related concepts, risk of ruin has its origins in gambling. The probability of eventual loss of all trading capital (i.e., ruin) is given by the equation

$$R = \left[\frac{1 - A}{1 + A}\right]^C$$

where A is the trader's advantage, and C the number of investment units the trader starts with and continues to risk in each trade.[11] Given that P is the probability of a favorable outcome, the trader's advantage is $P - (1 - P)$ or $2P - 1$. Thus, if the odds of a favorable outcome are 55 out of 100, P is 0.55 and A

is 0.10. C is found by dividing the trader's initial capital by the amount risked on each trade.[12]

To illustrate, let us assume a speculator who is considering a futures trade that offers a 0.60 chance of earning 100 percent and a 0.40 chance of losing the entire margin deposit. The speculator has $16,000 trading capital, and the required margin is $4,000. The risk of ruin is given as

$$R = \left[\frac{1 - 0.2}{1 + 0.2}\right]^4 = 0.198$$

or about one chance in five of eventual ruin. In other words, even with the relatively large assumed advantage, there is a genuine threat of eventual loss of all trading capital.

A somewhat different formulation of risk of ruin is necessary to answer the question of what the probability of ruin is before the trader can successfully accumulate W additional units of wealth:

$$R = \frac{[(1 + A)/(1 - A)]^W - 1}{[(1 + A)/(1 - A)]^{C+W} - 1}$$

where A and C are as formerly defined.[13]

Continuing the previous example, what is the probability that the speculator will be ruined before seeing her $16,000 grow to $36,000? It is

$$R = \frac{[(1.2)/(0.8)]^5 - 1}{[(1.2)/(0.8)]^{5+4} - 1} = 0.176$$

or a little more than one chance in six. That this is a lower probability than the risk of *eventual* ruin merely shows that even if the trader has a run of successes in the beginning, if he or she continues to trade *on the same scale,* ruin can still occur. However, after initial success, the trader might decide to scale back the relative amount risked on each trade (increase C).

By increasing the advantage (perhaps by careful study of fundamentals, or technical analysis) the trader's chances for avoiding ruin increase. However, the effect of scaling back the amount risked on each trade can have a similar effect.

If the advantage were to increase to 0.25 the risk of eventual ruin drops to 0.130. But traders can exercise much better control over C than over the odds of success on each trade. And, by reducing the amount risked to half as much as before the risk of ruin drops to 0.039 (C is 8), a remarkable reduction from the former 0.198.

The implications are clear. Speculators should strive for as large an advantage as possible in the odds of success on a trade. They should also risk only a small amount of their trading capital on each trade. It is left as an exercise for the reader to determine the risk of ruin if the trader's advantage is negative, and whether or not a large C value is advantageous in such a case.[14]

Notes

[1] A classic article on utility is that by James Tobin, "Liquidity Preference as Behavior Towards Risk." *The Review of Economic Studies* **67** (February 1958): 65–86.

[2] David Kahneman and Amos Tversky, "Choices, Values, and Frames." 1983 American Psychological Association Award Address, p. 10.

[3] Expected utility is given by the sum of the products of the utilities of the possible outcomes with their probabilities.

[4] Richard J. Teweles, Charles V. Harlow, and Herbert L. Stone, *The Commodity Futures Game* (New York: McGraw-Hill, 1977).

[5] The trite nemesis, "Put all your eggs in one basket and watch the basket very carefully," will be seen to lack any risk reducing benefits.

[6] Because futures contracts are not infinitely, or even finely divisible, the feasible set is not dense. The graphic portrayal is thus not wholly accurate since it suggests a dense feasible set and smooth transition from one portfolio to another.

[7] Harry M. Markowitz, *Portfolio Selection: Efficient Diversification of Investments* (New York: Wiley, 1962).

[8] William F. Sharpe, "A Simplified Model for Portfolio Analysis." *Management Science* **9** (January 1963): 277–293.

[9] More generally, the variance of a linear combination of variables, with weights $a, b, c, \ldots$, is

$$\text{Var}(ax + by + cz + \cdots) = a^2\,\text{Var}(x) + b^2\,\text{Var}(y) + c^2\,\text{Var}(z) + \cdots$$
$$+ 2ab\,\text{Cov}(x,y) + 2ac\,\text{Cov}((x,z) + \cdots + 2bc\,\text{Cov}(y,z) + \cdots$$

[10] Note that the weights are given by $1000/(1000 + 500)$ and $500/(1000 + 500)$.

[11] William Feller, *An Introduction to Probability Theory and Its Applications* (New York: Wiley, 1957).

[12] This formulation assumes a double or nothing situation in which the trader makes or loses 100 percent on each trade.

[13] *Ibid.*

[14] For the nonmathematical a reminder: a probability cannot exceed the value of certainty, which is 1.00.

8

Fundamental and Technical Analysis

Analysis of investments, including commodity futures, can be labeled as fundamental or technical. Although the end results they seek to accomplish may be the same, the means for obtaining them are different, and the underlying philosophical foundations separate.

If markets were perfectly efficient, the practice of either fundamental or technical analysis would be in vain, no one could hope to earn consistently higher returns than could be had by a naive "buy-and-hold" strategy. However, if everyone were to abandon these analytical methods, it is debatable whether or not the markets would continue to be efficient.

The variety of high-priced commodity newsletters published by independent commodity advisors, and those sent to clients by the major brokerage firms, attest to the public's demand for news and analysis. The brokerage firm letters generally concentrate on fundamental analysis. Technical analysis coverage typically ranges from next to none to almost equal to the fundamental. In contrast, the independently published newsletters are overwhelmingly oriented to technical analysis. It would seem that the investing and speculating public prefers to spend its money for technical analysis and information rather than for fundamental.

Some commodity traders use fundamental analysis to try to determine the direction of the market trend and technical analysis for timing their entry to and exit from market positions. In other words, some traders use fundamental analysis to gauge the long-term market factors, and technical analysis to deal with the shorter term influences.

Now, let us examine fundamental and technical analysis. Discussion will be based on the assumption that the commodity markets are less than perfectly efficient.

FUNDAMENTAL ANALYSIS

The foundation for fundamental analysis is supply and demand for the commodity in question. Fundamental analysis involves modeling the supply-demand relationships in a market.

Analysis and modeling of supply and demand is far more difficult than generally realized. To provide useful results, the analyst must not merely deal with static equilibrium conditions for a commodity (itself not an easy task) but must incorporate dynamic influences also. The analyst must identify the relationships with the system he or she is modeling. In a formal model, these relationships become equations in a linked system of equations.

Variables within the model will be either endogenous or exogenous. The former have values determined within the model, whereas the latter are determined by factors external to and possibly independent of the model. An example of an exogenous variable would be average rainfall in a particular corn growing state over some time span.

Since fundamental analysis is concerned with supply-demand modeling, it is useful to examine each of these separately. However, it must be noted that in a dynamic model, supply and demand may have to be treated as interrelated rather than independent. For example, next season's crop production may be a function of this year's demand and the consequent farm production plans and intentions.

Demand

Demand for a commodity may be seasonal or cyclical. For instance, there are seasonal influences on the consumption of beef due to changes in consumer life styles from season to season as evidenced by summertime backyard barbeques.

A commodity's demand is influenced by price and availability of substitutes. Consumers may drink less coffee as the price rises, substituting tea, or soft drinks. If the price of beef gets too high, consumers will substitute pork, poultry, or fish for beef.

Some commodities may be consumed in lesser quantities as consumer incomes rise or their prices fall. These goods are referred to as inferior goods, or Giffen goods. These commodities behave contrarily to the usual price-quantity model in which quantity demanded is a monotone decreasing function of unit price. If consumers really prefer other goods to potatoes, they may not consume more at a lower price but instead use the money no longer needed for potatoes to buy their preferred consumption. If consumers would like to consume more beef, but have been substituting poultry because of its lower price, then as their incomes rise, they may cut back on poultry and expand purchases of beef.

Social and political factors may influence demand for some commodities. For example, consumption of sugar may be constrained by health and weight concerns of consumers. Consumption of commodities like palladium may be affected by the warmth or coolness of the moment between the Soviet Union (the major producer) and other nations.

The cross-elasticity of demand between the commodity of interest and substitutes has a bearing on demand model specification. As an example, demand for corn is not solely determined by the price of corn. It is strongly influenced by the prices of substitutes like grain sorghum or milo, and by those of soybean meal, oats, and so on. Similarly, the price of platinum may be constrained by the substitutability of palladium in some applications, such as petroleum cracking.

Supply

Estimation of supply is no less complicated than for demand. For many agricultural commodities supply may be fixed for all practical purposes from harvest to harvest. This can create a situation of inelastic supply in which quantity supplied cannot increase in response to higher prices until the next planting season.

For many commodities, supply is heavily influenced by weather conditions and crop diseases. For others, it may be affected by the foreign exchange needs of less-developed nations who depend on export earnings. For some commodities, supply may be managed by a dominant producer (as in the case of palladium) or consortium (the Organization of Petroleum Exporting Countries is the outstanding contemporary example).

Cross-elasticities influence supply as well as demand. For example, if the price of cotton is low while that of soybeans is high, significant acreages may be diverted from growing cotton to growing soybeans.

In the case of such futures as U.S. Treasury bills and bonds, supply is a function of the Treasury's financing and refunding requirements. For certain others, like silver, supply is determined in large measure by production of other products (copper, lead, zinc, etc.) where it is a by-product. Copper ore is not mined and processed to produce silver, yet silver is a valuable residual in copper refining.

Price Determination

The objective of fundamental analysis is to determine the commodity price that will prevail for a given set of circumstances. Consider Figure 8-1; the demand curve is representative of an agricultural commodity, which is relatively inelastic because supply is fixed between harvests. The demand curve is not perfectly inelastic because higher prices do elicit additional supply from sources outside normal channels, such as inventories of consumers who become suppliers as they substitute other commodities for their own use.

A shift in demand from *DD* to *D'D'* causes price to increase a relatively

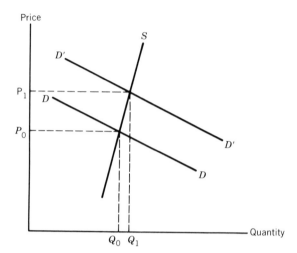

Figure 8.1. Supply-demand interaction.

large amount from P_0 to P_1. Quantity supplied however, increases a comparatively small $Q_0 - Q_1$. Knowledge of the nature of the supply and demand curves and the forces causing a demand shift may thus help the fundamental analyst to predict the relative magnitude of price change.

Figure 8-2 depicts a shift in supply, such as might be the result of a severe drought on corn. The price response in Figure 8-2 is fairly small but, in contrast to the situation shown in Figure 8-1, the change in quantity demanded is large. This is what one would expect for a commodity for which consumers can readily use substitutes.

In Figure 8-3 both supply and demand are relatively inelastic. A shift upward (or to the left) in supply results in a large price increase accompanied

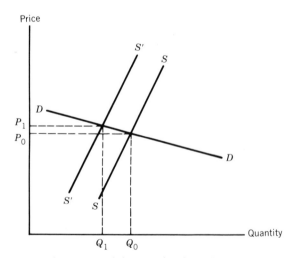

Figure 8.2. Shift in supply, elastic demand.

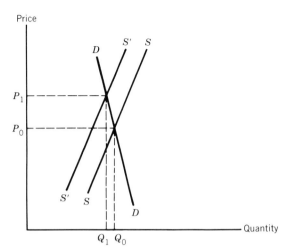

Figure 8.3.   Inelastic supply and demand.

by a relatively small decrease in quantity consumed. Commodities for which good substitutes are not available and for which consumers have strong preferences can be expected to behave as illustrated in Figure 8-3. Commodities like cocoa, coffee, and cotton might be expected to conform to this model in varying degrees.

Market Equilibrium

At any given time, price will move to ration supplies. However, even though a market will adjust to a new equilibrium in a particular time frame, the decisions of producers and consumers will impinge upon the supply-demand balance in subsequent time frames. Under certain conditions, their decisions will lead to a convergence of price to a new equilibrium; under other conditions, price may oscillate explosively.

Consider the supply-demand conditions portrayed in Figure 8-4. If the market were to have a price of P_0 at a given time, suppliers would be willing to provide quantity Q_0, but consumers would only want Q_1 units at that price. Suppliers will only be able to sell Q_1 units. In the next production decision, suppliers will plan to produce Q_1 units, for which they will ask a price of P_1 per unit. However, at a price of P_1, consumers will want Q_2 units. They will decide to buy Q_2 units but, because only Q_1 are available the price will be bid up. Producers will be able to easily sell their production of Q_1 and realize they could have sold more, and at a higher price. In the next round of production, they will produce Q_2 units. The process repeats, with production gradually converging to equilibrium with demand. The process may take some time with agricultural markets or others requiring substantial lead times for production plans to reach fruition. Any disturbance to supply or demand may either shorten or lengthen the time for an equilibrium to be reached.

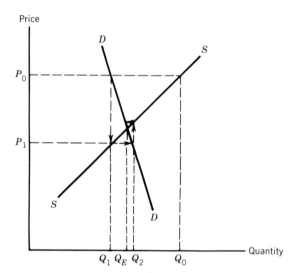

Figure 8.4. Market convergence.

A market may have explosive divergence from equilibrium, until the market eventually collapses. This is portrayed by the "cobweb" model shown in Figure 8-5. Starting at P_0, only Q_1 units will be sold, not the Q_0 units suppliers would like to sell. Producers will have unsold inventory unless they drop the price. For the next production cycle, producers will plan to supply only Q_1 units, and at the lower price, P_1. However, at this price Q_2 units will be demanded, and this will lead producers to plan for stepped up production in the next production cycle. In this system, the divergence from equilibrium be-

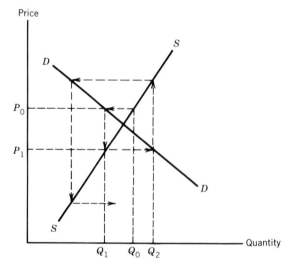

Figure 8.5. Cobweb model.

comes greater and greater until eventually the system must collapse to a level of price and quantity from which the evolution may again begin.

It should be noted that the cobweb model portrayed has a supply function that is relatively less elastic than the demand function. This is precisely the stuff of which many agricultural markets are made: A long production cycle on the supply side coupled with demand that is conditioned by availability of substitutes. In the real world, cobweb models are constrained by the availability of resources for production, so that the explosive divergence is contained.

Practical Considerations

The foregoing discussion of fundamental analysis has attempted to convey what it is about while avoiding specific models for individual commodities. For those who would develop models of their own using fundamental analysis, it will be useful to keep several thoughts in mind.

A supply-demand model, if it is to be useful in commodity trading, must be able to forecast. That is, the model must be able to use available, historical data to yield likely values for future time periods. Thus, identification of leading variables and relationships incorporating them is important to model development.

As a corollary to the necessity of finding leading variables, construction of models based on contemporaneous observations on all variables will be of little if any value to the commodities trader. One must distinguish between models that are useful for explanatory or pedagogical objectives and those that are useful for forecasting. While the forecasting models may be of interest to those with explanatory or pedagogical objectives the converse is not as likely to be true.

The difficulty of identifying and including variables and relationships that are significant, while excluding the myriad that do not contribute to better forecasts, must not be ignored. Nor should the necessity of revalidating and reestimating shifts in relationships be overlooked.

In principle, fundamental analysis has strong rational appeal. In practice, it may more often than not fail to perform as well as reason would lead one to expect.

An Example

To illustrate what is involved in construction a model for fundamental analysis let us consider sugar, which is traded in New York (in two different contracts, domestic, and world or No. 11) and overseas, most notably in London. Table 8-1 contains summary information on factors affecting the supply and demand of sugar. It is clear that a number of influences exist that cannot be easily dealt with quantitatively, such as the social and political-economic or those involving crop diseases and weather. It is also clear that to try to include

TABLE 8.1. FACTORS IN THE SUPPLY/DEMAND MODEL FOR SUGAR

Supply	Demand
Climate factors	End product categories
Northern temperate	Softdrinks and beverages
Southern temperate	Confectionery
Tropic and sub-tropic	Commercial baking
Crop factors	Individual/household use
Cane	Chemical and miscellaneous
Beets	Alternative products
Crop diseases and weather	Substitutes (corn sweetener and
Alternate crops/land uses	synthetics)
Inventory factors	Social
Carryover stocks in supplier hands	Tastes, health and lifestyle factors
Political-economic factors	Inventory factors
Cartel pricing and production agreements	Carryover stocks in hands of users
Government subsidies to producers	Political/economic factors
Political factors affecting production	Government subsidies to consumers
	Political factors affecting demand

all the listed influences would be expensive in terms of time and resources and still yield a model that is far less than perfect.

In practice, one would not attempt to include *all* supply and demand influences in a model. The marginal value of each additional variable declines just as the cost of incorporating it increases; eventually the cost of adding another factor is no longer justified. Thus, a crucial consideration in constructing a model for fundamental analysis is to identify those variables that contribute most in explanatory power and put them into the formal model while excluding the others. This is not to say that the omitted variables are of no importance; they may be used to shade the results of the formal model, for example. Certain variables may have to be excluded from the formal model because they are mathematically awkward to deal with or because insufficient history exists for one to estimate their parameters. Nevertheless, the impact of some influences may be examined in light of their likely impact on the market, assuming the market is in equilibrium at the current price. For example, a hurricane which crosses Cuba and destroys much of the cane cannot be included in a model of sugar prices except stochastically. However, once the hurricane's contact is imminent, or past, one can surmise the effect on equilibrium price.

The West German firm of F.O. Licht & Company is the world's authoritative source of data on sugar. Anyone who wishes to construct a model for the price of sugar would have to utilize that firm's data or else try to duplicate the expensive process of gathering and processing information into usable form. The main types of information that seem to be used in fundamental analysis are such things as planting intentions, crop conditions during the growing season, carryover stocks, and rate of disappearance (i.e., usage). The measure and influence of the more ephemeral factors is up to the model builder to determine.

A good model for fundamental analysis is one that provides statistically reliable price forecasts (at least the *direction* of likely price movement) while using variables parsimoniously. That is, a good model should be as simple as possible while still yielding useful forecasts.

TECHNICAL ANALYSIS

At the core of technical analysis is the premise that the market price at any time is revealed by the pattern of prior price movements. As a result, those who employ technical analysis use price patterns to predict the direction of future price movement. Although price data is at the center of technical analysis, other, related data are also employed by some practitioners. These data include such things as trading volume and open interest besides modified price series.

In its traditional form, technical analysis relys solely on price patterns for what they may portend about the likely future direction of price movement. Two different methods for graphically recording prices are used: the bar chart and the point and figure, or reversal chart.

In recording prices on a bar chart, a vertical line is drawn between the high and the low price in a given time span (day or week typically). Then a short horizontal tick is drawn out from the settlement price to the right. Sometimes the opening price is recorded with a dot to the left of the appropriate price or a short, horizontal tick to the left.

Figure 8-6 illustrates the construction of a bar chart. This is the type of chart published by the Commodity Research Bureau, Inc. and several other

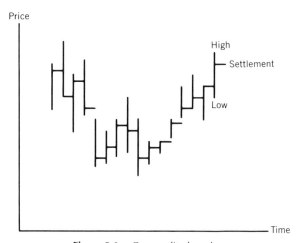

Figure 8.6. Commodity bar chart.

popular services. These charts are straightforward: Each time period's price activity is plotted immediately to the right of the prior period's.

Some chart services plot volume and open interest at the bottom of certain bar charts. The additional information these provide is used by some technical analysts to confirm or augment the price data. Unfortunately, volume information for commodities is available only for the aggregate of all months of a given futures contract. Open interest is available for each contract month.

TRADITIONAL TECHNICAL PATTERNS

Head-and-Shoulders

It is probably safe to say that the head-and-shoulders (H&S) top and bottom patterns are the best known of all technical formations. Figure 8-7 depicts these formations in several variations. The "neckline" is a vital part of H&S patterns.

Figure 8-8 shows an H&S top in March 1980 corn that is itself contained in the head of a much larger H&S formation. (Some might prefer to call the smaller pattern a diamond in this case.) The sharp price decline on June 29, 1979 represents the type of shakeout often seen when traders who have long positions place stop sell orders under a rising trend line. A price dip triggers these sell orders which has a cascading effect: As the price reaches lower levels, new stop orders are touched, and these put further downward pressure on price as they are executed. *In essence, what one has when stop sell orders are hit in a price decline, is an anomaly of supply temporarily increasing in response to lower price levels.*

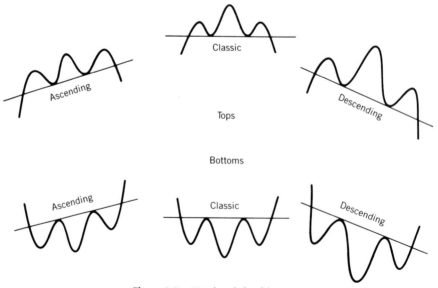

Figure 8.7.   Head and shoulders patterns.

Figure 8.8. H & S top.

Figure 8-9 shows May 1978 wheat evolving from a head-and-shoulders bottom into what appeared in January 1978 as an H&S top. Similarly, Figure 8-10 displays the evolution from an H&S top in December 1979 live hogs into what seemed to be an H&S bottom. Such sequential patterns may be explained by the presence of cycles in commodity prices. A later section in this chapter does this.

Double Tops and Bottoms

Sometimes instead of a head-and-shoulders formation reaching full development, one finds two lobes extending to the same or nearly the same level. Figure 8-11 illustrates what *appeared* to be a double bottom in January 1982 heating oil from September to November 1981. If the price of this contract had risen above 104, a double bottom would have been confirmed.

Unfortunately for those who bought the January 1982 heating oil in *anticipation* of a double bottom rather than on its *confirmation,* the price broke in late November 1981 and fell sharply during December, as Figure 8-12 shows. The April 1982 contract price fell even more markedly, and this contract's

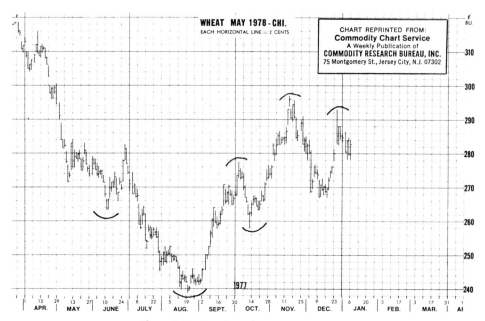

Figure 8.9. H & S tops/bottoms alternating.

Figure 8.10. H & S tops/bottoms alternating.

Figure 8.11. False bottom.

Figure 8.12. False bottom.

price behavior in November may have signaled the subsequent across the board price decline in all contracts.

The double bottom that wasn't in January 1982 heating oil illustrates a basic difficulty with technical analysis: One does not know if he or she has a particular chart pattern until afterward. All too often, what appeared to be a budding H&S or double top (or bottom) evolved into something else. For the trader, this implies that entry into the market should be done by using stop orders at prices that *confirm* the pattern. This, however, is no panacea, since there may be a cluster of such orders that causes erratic market action and poor order fills when such crucial level is attained. One thus has a dilemma: Whether to anticipate confirmation of a technical pattern and risk being wrong or to wait for confirmation and hope to get a good order fill when other technical analysts have the same idea. It is decisions such as these that separate successful technical analysts-traders from the failures, and decisions such as these that favor those with trading experience in the markets and some appreciation of market fundamentals.

Trends and Channels

Successful commodity traders follow trends. Perhaps one can find surer roads to ruin than fighting a trend, but bucking the market trend will remain close to the top of any list of losing strategies. Certainly one can play the "trends within trend"—the short-term trends that go counter to the long-term market trend—*if* one recognizes the direction of the major trend and enters and exits accordingly. But that is a different matter than blindly going counter to the major trend—and staying with a losing trade.

Figures 8-13, 8-14, 8-15, and 8-16 contain typical trend channels in May 1980 sugar (No. 11 or World Contract), May 1978 orange juice, October 1980 feeder cattle, and September 1981 Deutschemark. Such formations are so ubiquitous that one could scarcely pick up a set of commodity charts published in any given week and not find at least one example.

The channel for May 1980 sugar from April 1979 to September 1979 is less rapidly rising than from September 1979 to December 1979. After November, the channel becomes broader and the upper envelope line would be a better fit if it were curved. This is often a signal that a price movement is close to its end and that a change in trend is not far away. Most technical analysts would have sold in late November or early December 1979 on the downspikes that broke bottom channel supports.

May 1978 orange juice (Figure 8-14) contains several trend channels, including one composed of limit increases in the latter part of January 1977. If it were not for the price action in June 1977, a steady uptrend from March through July would have prevailed. In fact, the June price action had the effect, not of invalidating the trend, but temporarily shifting it upward only to be followed by a "correcting" downward shift a few weeks later.

October 1980 feeder cattle (Figure 8-15) displays a very broad uptrending channel beginning April 1980 and following a steep downtrend starting in

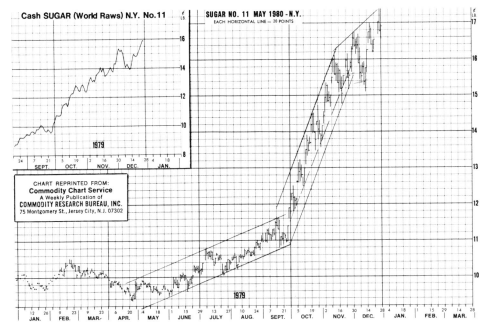

Figure 8.13. Trend channels.

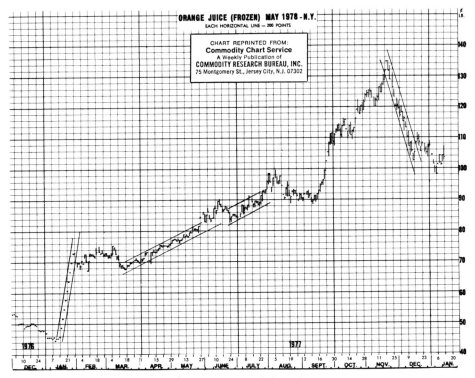

Figure 8.14. Trend channels.

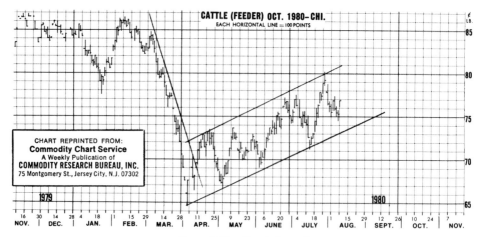

Figure 8.15. Trend channels.

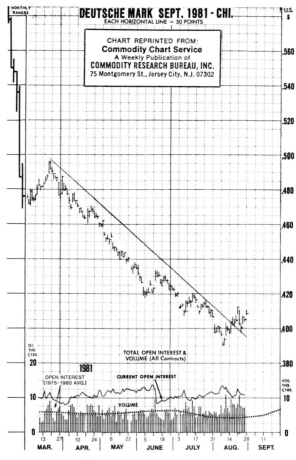

Figure 8.16. Trend channels.

early March. The trends within trend contained in this chart illustrates the trading opportunities that may exist for those who are nimble and quick to identify such short-term countertrend moves.

Seldom does one find a tighter trend for such a long time span as that shown by the September 1981 Deutschemark (Figure 8-16). Only the top of the long channel is drawn on the chart. If one were to draw top and bottom channel lines from March to June 1981 a much tighter channel would result.

Paul H. Cootner,[1] while postulating that prices move in a random walk around their intrinsic value, stated that prices would be contained within "reflecting barriers." He based this on the behavior he felt likely from professional investors, who would buy or sell as price reached these barriers, thus tending to keep price within them. Though Cootner wrote of stocks, it is likely that the same principles apply to commodities. A complete discussion of Cootner's article and related research can be found in H. Russell Fogler, *Analyzing the Stock Market*.[2]

Triangles and Wedges

Figure 8-17, which contains the chart for December 1980 (IMM, Chicago) gold, shows a triangle consolidation in a rising price trend. Similar formations

Figure 8.17. Trend channels plus triangle.

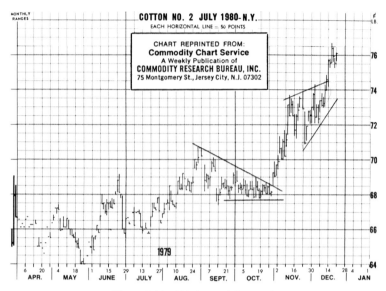

Figure 8.18. Wedge and diamond.

are illustrated in Figure 8-18, which contains July 1980 cotton prices. According to some writers on technical analysis,[3] price tends to continue in the same direction upon leaving the triangle or wedge as it was moving on entry, and such movement is most reliable when the breakout occurs about two-thirds into the triangle.

Although triangles and wedges are common technical patterns, one seldom finds such a pattern with the apex at the left. That is, the price volatility tends to *dampen* as one moves further into the triangle from left to right, rather than to become explosive. If markets followed a truly random walk, one would expect a priori to find as many triangles with their apexes to the left as to the right. An interpretation that may explain the damped oscillatory pattern that is actually found in almost all occurrences of triangles is that the market tends to converge to a new equilibrium. In doing this, price volatility lessens until there is new information considered significant by the market.

Island Reversals

Figures 8-19, 8-20, and 8-21 contain examples of island reversals for December 1980 Swiss franc, September 1980 T-bills, and July 1982 coffee respectively. The "island" for the T-bill contract is noteworthy for having taken almost two months to evolve.

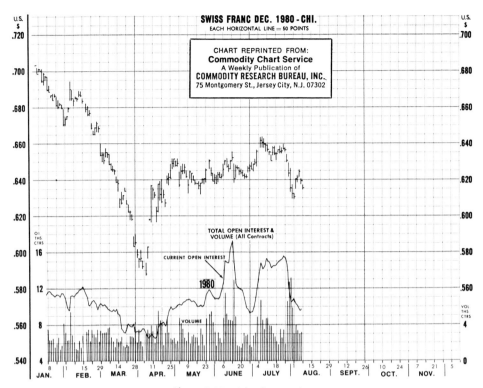

Figure 8.19. Island reversals.

Figure 8.20. Island reversals.

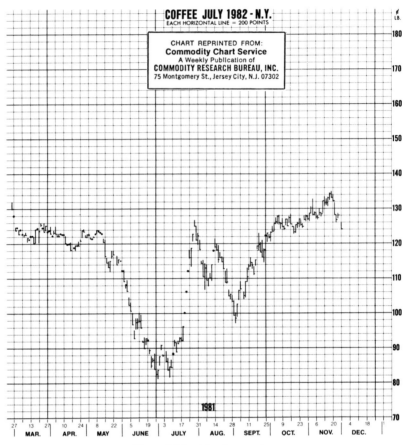

Figure 8.21. Island reversals.

Island reversals result from powerful news that causes a market to abruptly reverse direction, often from a consolidation range wherein prices move in a narrow range. Because these patterns result from significant news developments, the price often continues for quite some time beyond the breakout from the "island."

Other Patterns

Certain other patterns occur with sufficient frequency to warrant identification and labeling, and some traders attach significance to them. A *pennant* is a large price move which, when plotted, serves as the staff, with a triangle or wedge following the large move. A "flag" is similar, but without the triangle shape on the staff. A *key reversal* is a price move to a new high, followed on the same day by a settlement below that of the prior day or a price move to a new low followed by a settlement at a price above the prior day's. These patterns are illustrated in Figure 8-22.

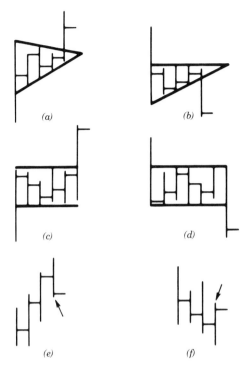

Figure 8.22. Other technical patterns. (a) Up pennant, (b) down pennant, (c) up flag, (d) down flag, (e) key reversal top, and (f) key reversal bottom.

Still more technical analysis patterns have been named. The reader interested in gaining depth in technical analysis is advised to consult some of the excellent works devoted solely to the topic.[4]

Point and Figure Charting

An alternative to the bar chart is the point-and-figure or reversal chart. This method of recording prices requires that the price move some specified distance to be placed on the chart, and thus provides for some filtering of the raw data. With this charting method, there is no time axis; for reference dates may be recorded in the plot area itself.

Figure 8-23 contains a point-and-figure price chart for the Japanese Yen along with the corresponding bar charts for both daily and weekly price ranges.[5] The smoothing effect that the point-and-figure chart has on the data is apparent. So, too, is the smoothing effect of recording the weekly rather than the daily price data.

This point-and-figure chart is based on a three point reversal, with each point set at 0.001. Each vertical distance between lines is worth 0.001, and only reversals in the direction of price of *greater* than 3×0.001, or 0.003 are recorded.

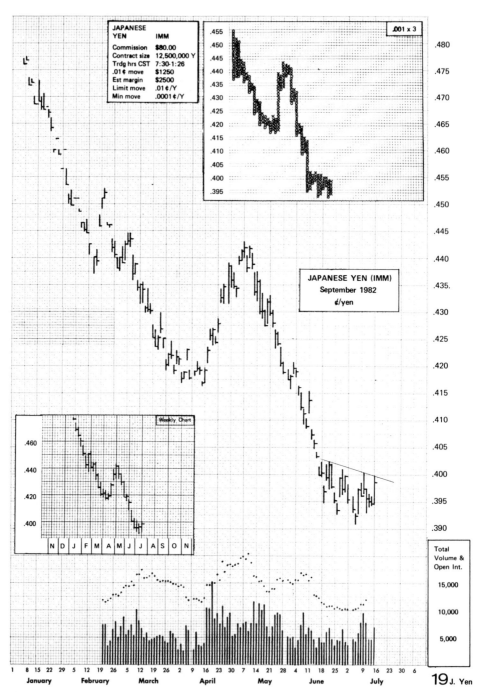

Figure 8.23. Point and Figure chart. Source: Dunn & Hargitt, 22 N. Second Street, Lafayette, Indiana 47902.

How does one decide whether to add X's or O's, or to switch from one to the other? Assume we have a column of X's because the price has been rising for some time. We record one or more X's in the same column only if the day's high is *at least* one box (i.e., 0.001) above the previously plotted price. The high must reach or exceed the scale price for the box in the column to receive an X. We record as many X's as are required.

We continue with our column of X's until we cannot add another X *and* the day's low price is at least three boxes under the box containing the highest X. Then we move one column to the right and fill in the appropriate number of O's. For an O to be recorded, the price must have gotten *at least* as low as the scale price.

The process works in reverse order if we are currently in a column of O's. We add one or more O's to the bottom of the column only if the day's low is at least one box under the lowest O in the column. We switch to X's only if the day's low is not low enough to warrant another O in the column *and* the day's high is *at least* 3 boxes above the scale price of the lowest O.

In addition to the patterns that are held to be useful with bar charts, several additional formations have been defined and are used in point-and-figure charting. For an in-depth discussion, the reader is referred to the excellent treatment by Kaufman.[6] Lerro and Swayne also have an excellent discussion, though the focus is on stocks, not commodities.[7]

There are far fewer firms offering point-and-figure charts than bar charts. One that provides such charts for a comprehensive set of commodity futures is the Chartcraft Commodity Service.[8] Traders can often avail themselves of special offers advertised in *Barron's* or *Futures* magazine to order a sample issue or trial subscription to a variety of chart services at a minimal cost, then choose those that are considered best for an annual subscription.

CYCLES AND TECHNICAL PATTERNS[9]

Both traditional technical analysis and cycle analysis have strong followings. However, the two approaches are generally treated independently and seldom is cycle analysis mentioned in the same breath as a "double top" or "H&S" bottom, except coincidentally, and without regard to cause and effect. Yet, if it were not for cyclical effects, the traditional technical patterns would be much less common than they are.

It can be shown that double tops and H&S tops (and bottoms of both types) can be repetitively generated by the interactions of just two cycles of different periodicity. Trend channels also can be generated by just two cycles. The repetitive generation of uniform patterns in the markets is, of course, unlikely over long spans because of random influences that may cause parameter shifts, and also by cyclical influences external to any simple model containing only a

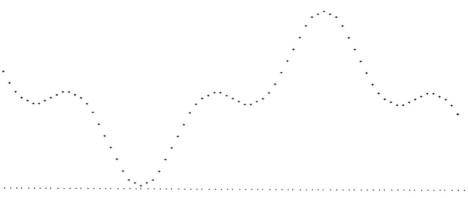

Figure 8.24. Period of longer cycle is three times that of the shorter cycle.

few cycles. Here we shall consider only two cycles at a time. Even so, the results are unambiguous.

Representative patterns are traced over time when the period of the longer of two cycles is an odd multiple of the shorter cycle, and when it is an even multiple. A variety of multiples were examined in preparing this section. However, because of space constraints, only the odd multiples of 3 and 7, and the even multiple of 6 are shown.

When the period of the longer cycle is exactly three times the shorter cycle, a pattern of repeating H&S tops and bottoms results, with a smooth transition from one into the other. This is illustrated in Figure 8-24.

When the longer cycle contains an *even* multiple of the shorter, the pattern that the interaction traces is one of H&S tops (bottoms) alternating with double bottoms (tops). This combination also yields the type of trend channel between tops and bottoms that is often found in actual commodity price movements. This is illustrated for multiple of six cycles in one in Figure 8-25.

Figure 8.25. Period of longer cycle is six times that of the shorter cycle.

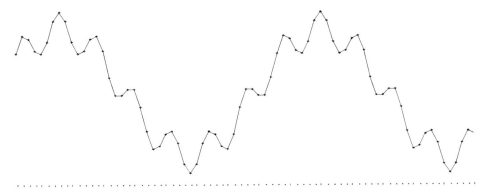

Figure 8.26.   Period of longer cycle is seven times that of the shorter cycle.

If the multiplicity of the longer cycle is a large odd multiple of the shorter, the H&S tops and bottoms alternate. Also, there is a clearly indicated trend channel, with the breaking of the trend coinciding with the transition from head to right shoulder as seen in Figure 8-26.

We have seen only a few representative samples from a great many different combinations of two cycles (a literally infinite number if we allow for noninteger multiples or very long period for the longer of the two cycles). However, examination of these and other combinations allow some generalizations to be drawn.

When the longer cycle is an *even* multiple of the shorter cycle, H&S tops (bottoms) alternate with double bottoms (tops).

When the longer cycle is an *odd* multiple of the shorter cycle, H&S tops alternate with H&S bottoms.

When two cycles are combined, with one having a much longer period than the other, trend channels are created.

It should be apparent that cycle analysis and traditional technical analysis of price charts should not be viewed as competing methods, but rather as complementary tools for putting price action into perspective. The technical analyst who combines the two approaches will have a trading advantage over those who do not. The chart analyst who understands how cycles influence chart patterns should be better able to anticipate the evolution of a pattern from a given point into the future. And, cycle analysts who refer to the charts should be less surprised if prices do not react as the cycles alone would suggest, when important chart points are crossed and chartists react. Market action evoked by violation (or confirmation) of important chart support or resistance levels may cause phase shifts in otherwise consistent cycles. Market participants are not, and should not be considered to be, passive with respect to market action, including that influenced by cycles that may be present.

For those who would like to examine combinations of two cycles further on their own, the following equation will be useful:

$$y = A_1 \sin(\omega_1 t + p_1) + A_2 \sin(\omega_2 t + p_2)$$

where y = the value of the combined cycles at time t

A_i = the amplitude, or relative strengths of the component cycles ($i = 1,2$)

sin = the trigonometric sine function

ω_i = the number of cycle repetitions in 360 degrees (2π radians)

p_i = phase shift parameters (Assume these are zero if both cycles are to start together.)

For cycle one to contain seven replications of cycle two, $\omega_1/\omega_2 = 7$. In the figures used in this example, the ratio of A_1 to A_2 was taken to be in the same proportion. In other words, if cycle one was assumed to be seven times as long as cycle two, it was also assumed to be seven times as strong. Those who would rather not work with trigonometric functions can nevertheless examine the combinations of two or more cycles. They can do this by drawing the individual cycles carefully on a sheet of graph paper, then measuring the combined values and plotting these as a single cycle on the same page.

Work done so far indicates that the traditional technical patterns of triangles, wedges, pennants, and so on, require at least three cycles in combination to be produced. Additional insights may be gained by reading the excellent work by Bernstein on commodity cycles.[10]

CONCLUSION

This chapter has examined basic precepts of fundamental and technical analysis. Fundamental analysis, while appealing to reason, nevertheless suffers from the inherent difficulty associated with building a model useful for forecasting as opposed to ex-post or contemporaneous explanation. Technical analysis assumes that the pattern of price behavior over time reveals all that is important about supply and demand, and further assumes that this gives one an advantage in predicting the likely direction of future price movement.

While fundamental analysis suffers from the problems of model building, technical analysis suffers from problems related to pattern validation. In the heating oil "double bottom" example, what appeared to be such a formation beforehand simply did not pan out. Thus it often is with chart analysis: One does not know with certainty whether one has a particular pattern until after the fact. The trader who would use technical analysis to enter or exit the market may therefore be wise to enter with stops at prices validating the pattern, even though this may frequently result in less-than-desirable order fills, and occasionally responding to false price moves.

It was shown that some traditional technical patterns can be constructed by the interaction of *cycles* in price series. In particular H&S and double tops and bottoms, plus trend channels, can be produced by the interaction of price cycles. Price cycles in commodities may have fundamental causes, such as crop season, weather induced effects or, as in the case of financial futures, cycles stemming from the fiscal and monetary activities of the federal government or actions of the Fed. Thus, there may be linkage from fundamental to technical analysis.

Occasionally one hears the proposition that fundamental analysis should be used to pick the market to trade, and technical analysis should be used for the timing of entry and exit. This notion would seem to deserve more attention from traders.

Ultimately, what determines the merit of a particular mode of analysis is how well it works. A study by Taylor suggests that different futures contracts have different "personalities" and that technical patterns therefore have more or less reliability depending on the particular commodity.[11] He found that some patterns not only occur with high frequency, but are reliable (H&S tops and bottoms in pork bellies, for example, 85 and 87 percent reliable). Whether his findings remain valid a decade later remains to be seen.

Taylor's findings suggest that technical analysis, in principle, works. That may help to explain why thousands of traders are willing to spend hundreds of dollars on each annual subscription from among many weekly charting services, and why many keep charts of their own. What the study does not address are the means by which technical analysis can be implemented. One can, for example, become an expert on the rules of poker or bridge, or riding a bicycle or flying an airplane by reading and study. However, there is no substitute for hands-on experience. And, as in other things, different persons have different talents and aptitudes. Some may be able to adapt to profitably trading futures while others less suited by ability or temperament fail.

Notes

[1] Paul H. Cootner, "Stock Prices: Random versus Systematic Changes." *Industrial Management Review* **3** (Spring 1962): 24–45.

[2] H. Russell Fogler, *Analyzing the Stock Market,* 2nd ed. (Columbus, OH: Grid, 1978).

[3] Ted Warren, *How to Make the Stock Market Make Money for You* (Los Angeles: Sherbourne, 1966). Two chapters specifically on futures markets are included.

[4] One is: Anthony J. Lerro and Charles B. Swayne, Jr., *Selection of Securities: Technical Analysis of Stock Market Prices* (Morristown, NJ: General Learning, 1974).

[5] From the Dunn & Hargitt Commodity Service. Lafayette, IN.

[6] P. J. Kaufman, *Commodity Trading Systems and Methods* (New York: Wiley, 1978): Chapter 11.

[7] *Ibid.*

[8] Chart Craft Commodity Service, Larchmont, N.Y.

[9] Anthony Herbst and Betty Herbst, "Bringing Cycles and Technicals Together." *Futures* **13,** no. 3 (March 1984): 104, 106. Reprinted from *Futures* magazine, 219 Parkade, Cedar Falls, Iowa 50613.

[10] Jacob Bernstein, *The Handbook of Commodity Cycles: A Window on Time* (New York: Wiley, 1982).

[11] Robert J. Taylor, "Technical Personalities of Major Commodities. *Commodities* (August 1972).

References

1. Jacob Bernstein, *The Handbook of Commodity Cycles: A Window on Time* (New York: Wiley, 1982).

2. Paul H. Cootner, "Stock Prices: Random versus Systematic Changes." *Industrial Management Review* **3** (Spring 1962): 24–45.

3. H. Russell Fogler, *Analyzing the Stock Market,* 2nd ed. (Columbus, OH: Grid, 1978).

4. Perry J. Kaufman (Ed.), *Technical Analysis in Commodities* (New York: Wiley, 1980).

5. Perry J. Kaufman (Ed.), *Commodity Trading Systems and Methods* (New York: Wiley, 1978).

6. Anthony J. Lerro and Charles B. Swayne, Jr., *Selection of Securities: Technical Analysis of Stock Market Prices* (Morristown, NJ: General Learning, 1974).

7. Arthur Sklarew, *Techniques of a Professional Commodity Chart Analysts* (New York: Commodity Research Bureau, 1980).

8. Robert J. Taylor, "Technical Personalities of Major Commodities." *Commodities* (August 1972).

9. Ted Warren, *How to Make the Stock Market Make Money for You* (Los Angeles: Sherbourne, 1966).

9

Time Series Analysis and Forecasting

Participants in futures markets engage in forecasting of prices or, at least, the directions of price movement. Some may produce forecasts informally, or with little or no conscious analytical effort. Others may resort to complex mathematical modeling based on supply/demand fundamentals. Still others may rely on analysis of price data alone, or with a few closely related variables, to form opinions as to the likely course of coming price movements. It is to this last group that this chapter will likely be of greatest interest.

It poses an apparent dilemma to the author who would, in the same book, write of market efficiency in one chapter, then in another discuss time series analysis and forecasting. This author has decided to take the dilemma by the horns and do both for the following reasons. First, while most of the evidence supports the efficient markets hypothesis, there nevertheless exists a growing body of published research indicating the existence of imperfections. Second, the establishment of a speculative position in a futures market implies that the speculator has forecast that the market price will move favorably to his or her position. Otherwise what would be the point in being in the market, other than to satisfy some masochistic impulse? Third, technical analysis based on chart configurations remains popular, and chart formations can be explained in terms of interactions of cyclical influences (see Chapter 8). This suggests that an understanding of time series analysis may help the chartist anticipate whether a given chart pattern is likely to evolve as originally thought. Fourth, the hedger may wish to incorporate forecasts into a hedging program, for timing purposes.

Forecasting financial markets and futures markets is a task neither easy to do well nor susceptible to naive, mechanistic approaches. Nevertheless, a forecasting approach that consistently provides better odds than tossing a coin for pointing to the correct direction of price movement merits examination.

The techniques discussed in this chapter have proven, and continue to prove their merits in business forecasting. Classic applications of these methods are found in airline passenger numbers, demand for telephone services, and volume of traffic across urban bridges.

FORECASTING METHODS

Many forecasting methods have been developed over the years. It is not the purpose of this chapter to evaluate or even to enumerate all of them. Nor would it be possible, in the confines of one chapter, to cover a topic on which numerous whole books have been written. Instead, this chapter focuses on those methods found to be especially useful in this author's experience.

The methods discussed in this chapter are based on time series analysis; that is, analysis of historical data from the series one wishes to forecast. The simplest of such methods is that of trend following, a technique of undeniable value in a trending market, though always wrong at the crucial turning points. In this chapter we will focus on spectral analysis and the Box-Jenkins methodology. The purposes of the two approaches and the underlying philosophies are somewhat different, yet they are complementary.

Spectral analysis has typically been used to study long time series for which the cyclical components that may be present do not vary greatly over time. Box-Jenkins modeling has been developed for the shorter time series generally found in economic matters. Spectral analysis does not directly provide a forecasting model; however, it can detect cycles within a time series, even cycles not apparent to the eye. This can be useful in determining the likelihood of a potential chart formation evolving into a confirmed action signal. It can also be useful prior to application of other procedures, such as Box-Jenkins, and for analysis of the residuals after fitting a Box-Jenkins model. Also, with knowledge of prominent cycles within a time series one may combine the cycles into a synthetic time series that extrapolates into the future their combined effects. This works well with cycles that are relatively invariant over time, but unfortunately many economic series vary too much for this to be applicable in most cases. Box-Jenkins methodology can provide a forecasting model directly, without resort to other procedures.

The reader may wish to note that spectral analysis assumes any cycles present in the data persist over time, that cycles do not die out. Box-Jenkins analysis, in contrast, assumes that cycles are induced by "shocks" to the system producing the time series under analysis. Such induced cycles are assumed to die out in the absence of new shocks to the system, and thus the series is assumed to revert to "white noise." A white noise series has no cycles that stand out as more significant or dominant than others.

Both spectral analysis and Box-Jenkins methodology depend on computers for their practical application. The amount of calculation required for practical applications is so great that neither method is practicable without a computer. However, this poses a less formidable obstacle than might at first appear. Programs for implementing these models are available from commercial time-sharing firms on their large computers, and programs for microcomputers are beginning to come onto the market at modest cost. For those near a large university it may be possible to purchase computer time directly (usually if sale of such time would not be in competition with commercial services in the area) or to obtain access by enrolling for a course, either for credit or as an auditor, or noncredit student. For the business firm or affluent individual the fine Biomedical P-series programs (BMDP) developed at the University of California at Los Angeles are available with a microcomputer to run them for an initial outlay less than the cost of most intermediate-size cars, and an annual lease fee of a few hundred dollars. The programs one gets are not just for spectral analysis and Box-Jenkins forecasting, but include many other statistical applications as well. And, as an alternative to applying the forecasting methods directly oneself, it may be more efficient and cost-effective to hire a consultant for a specific project.

The following section may be skipped (or skimmed) by those who have an aversion to math. For those comfortable with math it should provide a suitable foundation for reading the technical books listed at the end of this chapter.

SPECTRAL ANALYSIS

Spectral analysis is a probabilistic Fourier analysis; it takes a time series (signal) which is assumed to be generated by a stochastic process and decomposes the signal into its "natural" frequency components. Because in the frequency domain frequency ($= 1$/period) is the independent variable, the impact of the cycle(s) can be determined at any frequency component within the time series. Thus, the results reflect covariance measured at any desired frequency.

To obtain measures of how much of the total variation in an individual series is accounted for by the various length cycle components (power spectrum), two basic approaches are available. One of these uses the finite Fourier transform of the time series into the frequency domain. The other takes advantage of the relationship between the autocovariance of the time series and the Fourier coefficients to work with the autocovariances.

A stationary time series[1] may be considered to be composed of the sum of periodic series plus its mean in the finite Fourier transform:

$$Y_t = \bar{Y} + \sum_{i=1}^{M} \alpha_i \cos(\omega_i t - \theta_i) \tag{1}$$

where $0 \leq \omega_i \leq 2\pi$, $\omega_i = 2\pi i/M$ is the angular frequency, and $M = 1 + N/2$ if N is even, otherwise $M = 1 + (N + 1)/2$, with N here denoting the number of observations in the series. This is equivalent to an alternate form in which the phase angle (a shift parameter determining when the cycle first reaches maximum amplitude after $t = 0$) is not explicitly stated:

$$Y_t = \bar{Y} + \sum_{i=1}^{M} A_i \cos(\omega_i t) + \sum_{i=1}^{M} B_i \sin(\omega_i t) \tag{2}$$

The A and B coefficients in Equation (2) are found from the relationships

$$A = \frac{2}{M} \sum_{t=1}^{M} Y_t \sin(\omega_i t) \tag{3}$$

and

$$B = \frac{2}{M} \sum_{t=1}^{M} Y_t \cos(\omega_i t) \tag{4}$$

The *intensity* associated with a particular frequency is given by

$$I_i = \frac{M}{2} (A_i^2 + B_i^2) \tag{5}$$

and may be viewed as the squared amplitude associated with that frequency weighted by $M/2$. Plotted as a group, the intensities yield the *periodogram*. The *power spectrum* at a given frequency is

$$p(\omega_i) = \lim_{n \to \infty} E[I_i], \qquad 0 \le \omega_i \le 2\pi. \tag{6}$$

One method of spectral analysis is to smooth the periodogram by using a weighting function. With this method each $p(\omega_i)$ is estimated as a weighted average of neighboring intensities.

An important fact is that the autocorrelation function is directly related to the Fourier spectrum. Because of this, the Fourier transformation of the sample autocorrelation function yields the estimated relative average power at any frequency. And the spectral density can be expressed as a function of *angular frequency:*

$$p(\omega_i) = \frac{1}{\pi} \left[1 + 2 \sum_{K=1}^{M-1} r(K) \cos(\omega_i K) \right], \qquad i = 1, 2, \ldots, M \tag{7}$$

where $r(K)$ denotes the sample autocorrelation function, K the index for the number of lags over which the autocorrelation is calculated, and M the number of observations in the data series.

Equation (7) can be stated in terms of *frequency* by substituting for $\omega_i = 2\pi f_i$ and dividing the power at each frequency by $1/M$:

$$p(f_i) = 2\left[1 + 2\sum_{K=1}^{M-1} r(K)\cos(2\pi f_i K)\right], \qquad i = 1, 2, \ldots, M \qquad (8)$$

and $0 \le f_i \le 1/2$. Unfortunately, Equations (7) and (8) do not provide a consistent estimator of the population spectral density, and must be modified to obtain improved estimation. A trade-off is involved. As Bolch and Huang state it,

> This conflict of being able to achieve less bias only at the expense of greater variance is central to spectral estimation, and all that one can do in practice is to choose several different values for L [L ≤ M − 1 is called the truncation point] and compute the spectral estimates for each of these values. In practice, one starts with a value of L which is small (perhaps 10 percent of M) and then increases L. This procedure is called window closing. The spectral density with a small L will give estimates with a high order of bias (low fidelity).[2]

A second method of spectral analysis is to smooth the estimates provided by Equation (8). As Reinmuth and Geurts point out,

> the sample spectrum obtained by substituting the sample autocovariances . . . produces a highly unstable estimate of the actual power spectrum . . . . To accommodate this problem, the sample spectrum . . . is obtained by smoothing the spectral estimates through the use of damping constants . . . called lag windows.[3]

Many lag windows have been proposed (see Dhrymes[4] for a sample of them), but there is a discernible tendency toward preference for the one proposed by Parzen. For example, Bolch and Huang[5] indicate a preference for the Parzen window, noting that it cannot yield negative spectral density estimates.

If we denote the lag window by $\lambda(K)$, then equation (8) becomes

$$p(f_i) = 2\left[1 + 2\sum_{K=1}^{L-1} \lambda(K)r(K)\cos\left(\frac{\pi_i K}{2L}\right)\right], \qquad i = 1, 2, \ldots, 2L \qquad (9)$$

and, with the Parzen window,

$$\lambda = \begin{cases} 1 - \dfrac{6K^2}{L^2}\left(1 - \dfrac{K}{L}\right), & 0 \le K \le \dfrac{L}{2} \\[2ex] 2\left(1 - \dfrac{K}{L}\right)^3, & \dfrac{L}{2} \le K \le L \end{cases}$$

For an illustration of how Equation (9) may be applied to a numerical example, refer to Bolch and Huang.[6]

In computer implementations of spectral analysis Equation (9) is not often used. The reason is that the computational burden is heavy, increasing rapidly as the series length and number of lags used increase. This makes programs employing Equation (9) expensive to run. To overcome this problem the equivalent form is generally used:[7]

$$p(f_i) = 2\left[1 + 2\sum_{K=1}^{L-1} \lambda(K)r(K)\exp(-i2\pi f(K))\right]. \tag{10}$$

Equation (10) takes advantage of the series expansion relationship between the trigonometric functions and e, the base of natural logarithms.

While Equation (10) per se does not offer any advantage over Equation (9), by using what is known as the *fast Fourier transform* (FFT), the saving in computational time, and thus cost, is remarkable. Newland[8] points out that direct evaluation of Equation (10) would require N^2 multiplications, while the FFT reduces the number of operations to $N \log_2 N$. If $N = 2^{10}$, $N^2 = 2^{20}$, but we have $N \log_2 N = 5 \times 2^{11}$. Thus, the FFT requires slightly less than one percent the number of operations. The longer the series being analyzed, the greater the saving. Newland also mentions that with a data series containing 2^{15} observations (i.e., 32,768) the FFT requires only about 1/2000 the number of calculations. Such long series are common in engineering applications, as in vibrations analysis.

It is a characteristic of spectral analysis programs that the periods corresponding to the higher frequencies are much closer together (i.e., a finer "mesh") than those at low frequency. For example, if one is analyzing weekly data the frequency $f = 0.01$ corresponds to a period of 100 weeks, $f = 0.02$ to 50 weeks, and so on. But, $f = 0.20$ corresponds to a cyclical period of 5 weeks, $f = 0.21$ a period of 4.76 weeks. And $f = 0.45$ corresponds to 2.22 weeks, with $f = 0.46$ corresponding to 2.17 weeks. What this means is that high frequency, short period cycles are likely to be found, while long cycles are likely to "fall through" the wider "mesh" associated with the low frequencies.

Two ways by which the problem of wide mesh at the lower frequency, long-periodicity end of the spectrum may be alleviated are: (1) take smaller frequency increments for small (i.e., low) frequency values, letting the increments gradually increase; and (2) "pad" the data by appending a series of zeroes to the end.[9] For those who wish to delve further into this and other matters pertaining to spectral analysis, references are provided at the end of this chapter.

ILLUSTRATION OF SPECTRAL ANALYSIS

A cursory look at Figure 9-1 suggests that cycles may be present in the price (i.e., index) series for T-bond futures. It was decided to perform a Fourier (i.e. spectral) analysis on data for this series, using the average of each day's high, low, and settlement prices. The analysis was performed (after removing the trend) over the frequency range of 0.0285 cycles per unit time to 0.2222 cycles per unit time. This frequency range corresponds to 35.08 days to 4.5 days in the time domain, so any cycles in this range should have been detected.

Table 9-1 contains the cycle amplitude (strength) and phase corresponding to each frequency. The phase provides a measure of how far from the beginning a cycle first reaches its maximum amplitude. There are indications of several cycles being present in the data. Figure 9-2 contains a plot of the amplitude versus frequency, from which peaks in the amplitude may be more readily distinguished.

It is apparent that there are indications of cycles at frequencies 0.0285, 0.0450, 0.0697, 0.1233, 0.1522, 0.1769, and 0.1975 cycles per day, corresponding to periods of 35.08, 22.22, 14.35, 8.11, 6.57, 5.65, and 5.06 days. The high

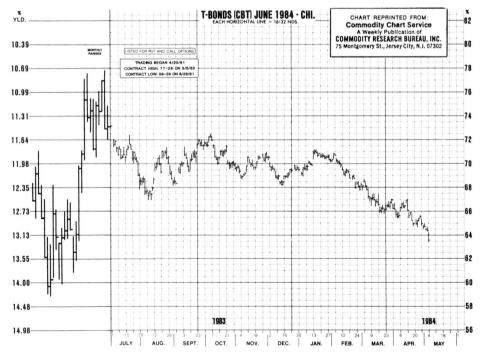

Figure 9.1. June 1984 T-bond futures.

TABLE 9.1.   JUNE 1984 T-BOND FUTURES—FOURIER ANALYSIS

Frequency cycles/unit	Amplitude	Phase degrees	Frequency cycles/unit	Amplitude	Phase degrees
0.0285	19.0485	215	0.1274	4.5543	165
0.0326	10.0635	271	0.1315	3.5256	226
0.0367	4.4423	12	0.1357	2.0933	304
0.0409	7.07	115	0.1398	2.1506	61
0.045	9.3129	172	0.1439	3.8908	137
0.0491	8.6173	220	0.148	5.2659	192
0.0532	5.4715	269	0.1522	5.5687	244
0.0574	1.3003	347	0.1563	4.6888	297
0.0615	3.5039	153	0.1604	3.071	1
0.0656	6.5248	204	0.1645	2.202	99
0.0697	7.6706	250	0.1686	3.2782	187
0.0738	6.8817	296	0.1728	4.3553	247
0.078	4.6736	344	0.1769	4.4984	301
0.0821	1.9007	40	0.181	3.7073	358
0.0862	0.9058	219	0.1851	2.5694	68
0.0903	2.5734	294	0.1892	2.2471	159
0.0944	3.4156	355	0.1934	2.8462	236
0.0986	3.6745	60	0.1975	3.1702	296
0.1027	3.8453	130	0.2016	2.7554	353
0.1068	4.1377	200	0.2057	1.7393	57
0.1109	4.424	268	0.2099	0.966	167
0.1151	4.6348	335	0.214	1.8333	274
0.1192	4.8276	42	0.2181	2.9681	339
0.1233	4.9066	105	0.2222	3.8291	38

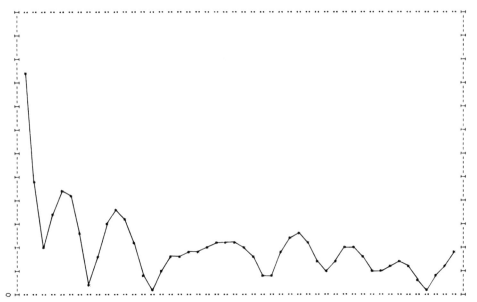

Figure 9.2.   June 1984 T-bond futures, Plot of amplitude (Vertical Axis) vs. Frequency.

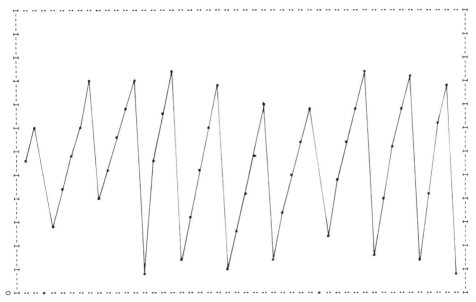

Figure 9.3. June 1984 T-bond futures—Plot of phase (vertical Axis) vs. Frequency.

amplitude for the frequency 0.285 (35.08 days) may be due to incomplete removal of trend prior to the Fourier analysis.

Figure 9-3 contains a plot of phase versus frequency. The graph is typical of those normally encountered, in that gradual phase changes suddenly yield to an abrupt phase change, then go into a set of gradual changes again.

Although there are clear indications of cycles in the T-bond data, the spectral analysis itself does not tell us whether they are statistically significant. It would be useful for us to determine whether or not the indicated cycles are genuine; that is, whether or not they are both consistent and persistent over the period covered by the data. Fortunately there is a test designed specifically for this purpose, the Bartels test, which is described in the appendix to this chapter.

The Bartels tests provides a direct probability measure for whether a cycle's indicated presence could be due to random influences within the data. It is a useful test when properly employed. The reader is cautioned, however, that in analyzing a large number of possible cycles it is likely that one or more cycles will be found that are not genuine even though their test statistics are low. In other words, even with a Bartels' test value of 0.01 for a given cycle, it should be remembered that on average one out of every hundred such cycles is not really present but is an artifact of random influences in the data.

Table 9-2 shows the Bartels test statistics obtained for the T-bond cycles that were indicated to be present. The results are not especially encouraging. A value of 0.5000 means that there is only a 50/50 chance that the indicated

TABLE 9.2.   JUNE 1984 TREASURY
BONDS—TEST OF
SIGNIFICANCE OF
INDIVIDUAL CYCLES

f	Period	Bartels' Test
0.0285	35.08	0.3538
0.0450	22.22	0.5476
0.0697	14.35	0.4996
0.1233	8.11	0.2237
0.1522	6.57	0.4113
0.1769	5.65	0.4289
0.1975	5.06	0.5236

cycle is genuine. The test statistic for a frequency of 0.0285 (35.08 days) cannot be relied on with the limited data used in this analysis. As a rule not much significance should be attributed to any cycle whose period is greater than about one-fifth the time span covered by the data. With 85 daily observations not much confidence can be placed in cycles whose periods are greater than about 17 days, or frequency less than 0.588 cycles per day.

It seems that a cycle of about 8.11 days may be genuine. The probability that evidence of its presence is due to chance is only slightly above one in five. For the other possible cycles we must reserve judgment.

If more observations were used more definitive results might be obtained. However, if attention is restricted to a single futures contract, as a rule only two to three hundred observations can be obtained and, by the time one has them all, the contrast has expired. Under the rule of having at least five times as many data points as the longest cycle observers should not place much confidence in any cycle longer than some 50 to 60 days in any given futures contract. This is a problem in applying spectral analysis to economic data. One needs a great deal of data to identify low frequency (i.e., long period) cycles.

To some extent the problem of sufficient data is diminished if continuity may be assumed across different contract months of a futures contract. With financial futures and perhaps the metals this may be a reasonable assumption. For the agricultural commodities, however, it may be rather tenuous to make this assumption because of factors affecting different crop years in different and perhaps unique ways.

Table 9-3 illustrates what can be found when there are indeed significant cycles in a data series. This table was created by a program which performs a spectral analysis without smoothing the periodogram.[10] The series analyzed was a synthetic series created by combining cycles of known period. Note the strong indications of cycles with periods of about 83 months, 36.7 months, 33.7 months, and 28.36 months. The actual cycles corresponding to these are 85.5, 36.9, 33.9, and 28.36 months within the range covered in the figure.

TABLE 9.3. ILLUSTRATION WITH SERIES OF KNOWN CYCLICAL COMPOSITION[a]

Har-monic	Period	Ampli-tude *10**5	Slope *10**5	Phase
6.0000	104.0000	463.3282	17.8203	4.0796
6.5000	96.0000	591.9955	24.6665	81.0203
7.0000	89.1429	2028.5666	91.0254	4.4143
7.5000	83.2000	2227.9364	107.1123	23.6471
8.0000	78.0000	871.9914	44.7175	41.7368
8.5000	73.4118	365.4103	19.9102	16.5777
9.0000	69.3333	343.9910	19.8456	37.8194
9.5000	65.6842	374.3214	22.7952	10.8130
10.000	62.4000	226.1455	14.4965	33.5484
10.5000	59.4286	311.3358	20.9553	9.1196
11.0000	56.7273	178.4422	12.5825	29.8089
11.5000	54.2609	333.3265	24.5721	7.2880
12.0000	52.0000	167.6513	12.8963	25.6349
12.5000	49.9200	316.4731	25.3584	7.4448
13.0000	48.0000	157.7052	13.1421	22.8468
13.5000	46.2222	397.8434	34.4288	6.3838
14.0000	44.5714	145.5673	13.0637	21.1488
14.5000	43.0345	491.5439	45.6884	6.4839
15.0000	41.6000	139.9803	13.4596	18.5860
15.5000	40.2581	726.4228	72.1766	6.8649
16.0000	39.0000	135.0682	13.8531	15.1601
16.5000	37.8182	2116.2661	223.8358	7.7760
17.0000	36.7059	3190.4542	347.6777	17.2584
17.5000	35.6571	1151.6823	129.1951	27.7772
18.0000	34.6667	2344.6758	270.5395	15.2470
18.5000	33.7297	3308.8634	392.3973	23.8548
19.0000	32.8421	1387.0444	168.9349	30.4801
19.5000	32.0000	730.3967	91.2996	24.7799
20.0000	31.2000	502.2284	64.3883	28.7757
20.5000	30.4390	815.0195	107.1019	26.1846
21.0000	29.7143	308.7885	41.5677	27.3413
21.5000	29.0233	1934.4576	266.6079	25.8525
22.0000	28.3636	2801.2597	395.0494	3.9437
22.5000	27.7333	1626.0228	234.5225	11.3134
23.0000	27.1304	178.9076	26.3774	24.4519
23.5000	26.5532	453.7996	68.3608	11.0718
24.0000	26.0000	139.5307	21.4663	22.0220
24.5000	25.4694	221.3652	34.7657	10.5424
25.0000	24.9600	135.0892	21.6489	22.6135

[a] Based on 624 data points.

As an alternative to the spectral analysis of T-bonds presented earlier in this chapter, and to illustrate that there exist differences in the results that may be expected from different approaches to spectral analysis, we now repeat the analysis based on the procedure used to analyze the synthetic GM series. Figure 9-4 displays a plot of the unsmoothed periodogram versus frequency. Using the same T-bond data we obtain the output contained in Table 9-4. Frequency is plotted rather than period because the plotted points are congested near the origin when period is used, rather than spaced evenly as they are with frequency. The unsmoothed periodogram contains many spikes in the amplitude series. It is unlikely that all spikes correspond to genuine cycles in T-bond futures prices. To clarify matters the periodogram is smoothed, and the series plotted again, in Figure 9-5. Indications of cycles in the smoothed periodogram are less ambiguous and tentative. It would seem that a cycle of about 9.64 days holds promise of being genuine—that is, both consistent and persistent in the data.

Analysis of a cycle of 9.6429 days is shown in Table 9-5.[11] We shall not go into the details of the analytical output here, but will instead simply point out that the Bartels test shows that indications of a cycle of this length could be due to random influences in the data with a probability of only 0.00729—about 73 chances in 10,000. Thus, it would seem that a cycle of some 9.64 days is probably genuine. Additional statistics provided by the analysis support the Bartels test in this regard.

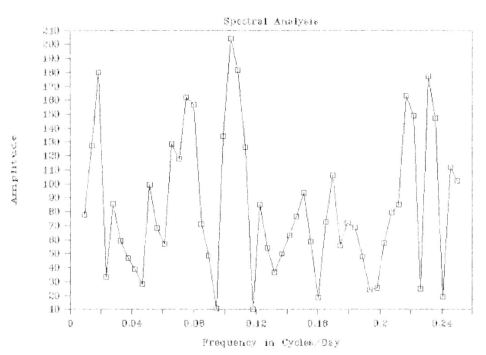

Figure 9.4.   Unsmoothed periodogram of June 1984 T-bond futures prices.

TABLE 9.4. PERIODOGRAM ANALYSIS OF JUNE 1984 T-BOND PRICES[a]

Har-monic	Period	Ampli-tude *10**5	Slope *10**5	Phase
1.0000	108.0000	77.8809	2.8845	15.6889
1.5100	71.5232	127.3822	7.1240	69.8207
2.0200	53.4653	179.8322	13.4541	9.8252
2.5300	42.6877	33.0440	3.0963	17.1548
3.0400	35.5263	85.8087	9.6614	4.3217
3.5500	30.4225	59.1853	7.7818	10.9011
4.0600	26.6010	46.7431	7.0288	6.6011
4.5700	23.6324	39.1308	6.6232	9.0321
5.0800	21.2598	28.0398	5.2756	19.8377
5.5900	19.3202	99.3539	20.5699	3.9040
6.1000	17.7049	68.0805	15.3811	7.8555
6.6100	16.3389	56.7269	13.8876	2.4555
7.1200	15.1685	128.5408	33.8967	7.3192
7.6300	14.1547	117.7799	33.2837	12.7107
8.1400	13.2678	162.0042	48.8413	4.5807
8.6500	12.4855	156.6073	50.1723	8.9655
9.1600	11.7904	71.1181	24.1275	1.0984
9.6700	11.1686	48.3780	17.3265	8.1535
10.1800	10.6090	10.4290	3.9321	8.2671
10.6900	10.1029	134.1040	53.0952	9.5936
11.2000	9.6429	204.2494	84.7257	2.6748
11.7100	9.2229	181.5982	78.7598	5.9874
12.2200	8.8380	126.1054	57.0744	8.7548
12.7300	8.4839	10.0483	4.7376	1.0240
13.2400	8.1571	85.3664	41.8612	1.3208
13.7500	7.8545	53.9989	27.4995	3.1095
14.2600	7.5736	36.4375	19.2444	1.1928
14.7700	7.3121	49.9311	27.3142	1.1913
15.2800	7.0681	63.2365	35.7872	1.9223
15.7900	6.8398	76.4906	44.7328	2.2806
16.3000	6.6258	93.7867	56.6194	3.0265
16.8100	6.4247	58.3792	36.3465	4.1064
17.3200	6.2356	18.6836	11.9852	6.1220
17.8300	6.0572	72.6362	47.9668	1.7999
18.3400	5.8888	106.1726	72.1187	3.2668
18.8500	5.7294	55.8041	38.9595	5.5897
19.3600	5.5785	71.8718	51.5348	2.7499

TABLE 9.4. (Continued)

Har-monic	Period	Ampli-tude *10**5	Slope *10**5	Phase
19.8700	5.4353	68.6451	50.5177	4.8297
20.3800	5.2993	47.9189	36.1699	1.4347
20.8900	5.1699	24.0232	18.5869	3.5840
21.4000	5.0467	25.3625	20.1021	0.8246
21.9100	4.9293	57.4204	46.5956	2.9484
22.4200	4.8171	79.8290	66.2877	4.3861
22.9300	4.7100	85.2506	72.3999	1.8943
23.4400	4.6075	163.0244	141.5293	3.8077
23.9500	4.5094	148.7585	131.9543	0.7309
24.4600	4.4154	24.9632	22.6148	3.2585
24.9700	4.3252	177.1139	163.7976	0.9359
25.4800	4.2386	146.9890	138.7140	2.1693
25.9900	4.1554	19.1682	18.4512	1.0134
26.5000	4.0755	111.5466	109.4809	2.4766
27.0100	3.9985	102.0574	102.0952	0.3470

[a] Logs base e of input data used. First differences of data used: $n = n - 1$

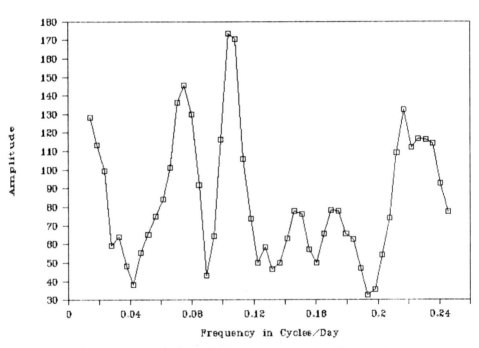

Figure 9.5. Smoothed periodogram of June 1984 T-bond futures prices.

TABLE 9.5. ILLUSTRATION OF TEST FOR SIGNIFICANCE OF
T-BOND CYCLE OF 9.77 DAYS

June 1984 T-Bond Futures
Jan. 1, 1984 thru June 1, 1984
· 9.6429 ITEM ARRAY

THIRDS

NUMBER OF POINTS FROM INPUT FILE= 109   BASE= 0
NUMBER OF LINES 11   POINTS IN ARRAY 110

SECTION	CON A	CON B	AMPLITUDE	PHASE
1	−6.150208E-02	0.1008907	0.1181586	3.768746
2	−0.2999939	0.3416355	0.454655	4.034478
3	−0.1688454	0.6901253	0.7104799	3.296826

IMPROVED PERIOD 9.461061

PREDICTION FOR MIDDLE THIRD 3.517056

F RATIO 3.109571E-02 WITH 9 AND 20 D.F.

HALVES

1	−0.1074844	0.1899731	0.218272	3.718778
2	−0.2615196	0.5401215	0.6001031	3.620608

PROBABLE PERIOD 9.642901

ALL LINES

1	−0.1775002	0.3491352	0.3916653	3.650424

INDIVIDUAL LINES
 0 0 2 5 3 0 1 CHI SQUARE= 13.81818 WITH 6 D.F

BARTELS TEST= 7.294187E-03

F RATIO .1261823 WITH 9 AND 100 D.F

AVERAGE AMPLITUDE = 0.5196466   +−0.2831572

LEAST SQUARES PERIOD= 9.523002   +−0.1519099
LEAST SQUARES PHASE =4.311747   +−0.5424374
USING 10   POINTS

 0 0 2 6 2 0 1 CHI SQUARE= 17.63636 WITH 6 D.F

LINES 1   THROUGH 11

  PHASE RESIDUALS ABOUT L.S. FIT
.1
.
.   111
. 1111   11
. 1
.
.

  AMPLITUDES (MAX.= 1.225788   )
.   1
.
.   1
.   1
.1 11111
.   1
. 1

Despite its shortcomings for economic data, spectral analysis can be useful for obtaining preliminary indications of cyclical influences within a data series. For those who would like to learn more about Fourier analysis of time series and related techniques a list of recommended readings is provided at the end of this chapter.

BOX-JENKINS METHODOLOGY

The methodology developed by Box and Jenkins[3] in recent years is based on the analysis of time series in the time domain. That is, Box-Jenkins analysis does not use frequencies as spectral analysis does, but instead works with days, weeks, months, and so on. These measures generally rest more comfortably with persons outside the physical sciences than does frequency.

There are three separate phases, or steps, to Box-Jenkins methodology: (1) identification, (2) estimation, and (3) validation or diagnostic checking. While mathematically demanding, there is nevertheless a great amount of artistry, of human judgment, in developing Box-Jenkins models. Sometimes different models will yield quite similar results, and choosing the best model will be based on ease of use, the simpler model to be preferred in most cases.

Box-Jenkins models are often referred to as ARMA (autoregressive moving average) or ARIMA (autoregressive integrated moving average) forecasting models. Besides these designations there are the simpler AR (autoregressive) and MA (moving average) models that are special cases of the ARMA or ARIMA classes. We will focus discussion on the ARIMA model since it is the most general.

The basic ARIMA can be written

$$\phi(B)(1 - B)^d Z_t = \theta(B)\varepsilon_t \tag{11}$$

wherein Z_t is the value of the time series at time t, ε_t is a series of random shocks which are independently, normally distributed with zero mean and variance σ^2. $\phi(B)$ is a polynomial of order p in the backshift operator B, which is defined as

$$\phi(B) = 1 - \phi_1 B - \cdot \cdot \cdot - \phi_p B^p \tag{12}$$

$\theta(B)$ is defined similarly to be a polynomial of order q in B:

$$\theta(B) = 1 - \theta_1 B - \cdot \cdot \cdot - \theta_q B^q \tag{13}$$

Finally, $(1 - B)^d$ denotes the differencing operator. Differencing is frequently necessary to achieve stationarity. What this means is that if a time series is not stationary we must take steps to make it stationary. A nonstationary time series is one for which the parameters are functions of time, and thus one for which the mean, variance, and so on, change over time. If a time series is not stationary, its mean, variance, and covariances of the stochastic process we wish to model do not exist, thus invalidating estimation techniques that rely on their existence. Fortunately, for purposes of analysis, most time series can be made stationary by replacing the original data points with their differences. Usually first or second differences ($d = 1$ or 2) are sufficient to obtain stationarity. Overdifferencing must be avoided because it introduces artifacts into the autoregressive structure.

In the case of a series that is stationary for $d = 0$ the model is termed ARMA if it contains both ϕ and θ terms. Otherwise, if $d > 0$ it is termed an integrated model.

A useful shorthand notation is often used for Box-Jenkins models: ARIMA (p, d, q). For various values of these parameters we obtain the following model labels, shown in Table 9-6.

If we assume $d = 0$ and $p = 2$, the left-hand side of Equation (11) becomes

$$(1 - \phi_1 B - \phi_2 B^2)Z_t = Z_t - \phi_1 Z_{t-1} - \phi_2 Z_{t-2} \tag{14}$$

It is clear that there is an infinite number of ARIMA models. The situation is not hopeless, however, because there are two tools to help us narrow the ranges of p, d, and q. The first tool is the autocorrelation function of Z_t, which is the correlation between Z_t and Z_{t-k}. The second tool is the partial autocorrelation function, which is the correlation of Z_t and Z_{t-k} after the removal of the effects of Z_{t-1} through Z_{t-k+1}. The partial autocorrelation thus provides a measure of the strength of the relationship between data points at times t and $t - k$ when the correlations of intervening time periods have been removed.

Each general category of ARIMA (p, d, q) has a unique pair of autocorrelation and partial autocorrelation patterns. Figure 9-6 illustrates the patterns characteristic of simple MA(1) and AR(1) models. Note that either the autocorrelation or partial autocorrelation function "cuts off" or truncates at lag $k = 1$ in the first order models. Second order MA(2) and AR(2) models have similar patterns but truncate after two lags. Thus, for a pure MA(q) or AR(p) model the order of the model is indicated by the lag at which truncation occurs.

That is the good news. Now what about mixed models? Unfortunately the situation tends to be much less straightforward. We may find that there is no truncation in either the autocorrelation or partial autocorrelation series; or, that spikes occur irregularly at various values of k. Such models can present significant challenges, even to experts in applications of Box-Jenkins modeling.

After tentative identification of an appropriate model the next step is estimation of model parameters. Procedures for this are mathematically complex, and are not applied without a computer. The reader interested in such details as the computational procedures is referred to the chapter references.

TABLE 9.6. BOX-JENKINS MODELS IN
TERMS OF THEIR PARAMETERS

	p	d	q
ARIMA models	>0	>0	>0
ARMA models	>0	=0	>0
AR models	>0	>=0	=0
MA models	=0	>=0	>0

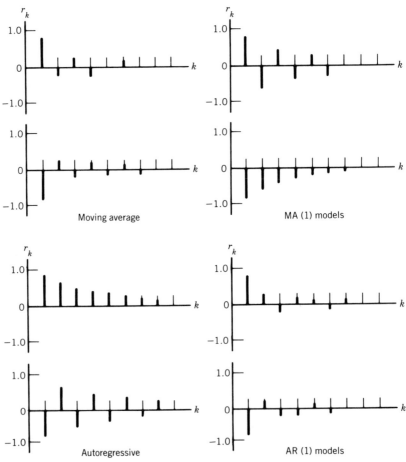

Figure 9.6. Characteristic autocorrelation and partial autocorrelation patterns for first order MA and AR models.

The final step in Box-Jenkins methodology is model testing, or validation. This involves careful examination of the residuals (i.e., forecast errors) obtained in using the model to forecast the points in the time series used to develop the model. If the model is adequate the autoregression and partial autoregression plots should not contain any significant spikes, and should be relatively flat over the range of lags.

The following case study illustrates what is typically involved in identifying, estimating, and checking a Box-Jenkins model.

Case Study: Cash Gold Price. Daily gold prices covering a span of over 1300 days were analyzed. The control card setup for using the Statistical Analysis System (SAS) program package on an IBM 4341 mainframe computer is shown in Figure 9-7. Missing data values, due to holidays, are filled in using values forecast from the observations preceding each missing value. Note that first differences of the data have been taken to achieve stationarity.

Figure 9-8 exhibits the correlations and partial correlations for cash gold. Also shown are the inverse correlations, which are provided by the SAS program, but not generally used for model identification. The autocorrelations and partial autocorrelations suggest that a first order moving average model may be appropriate.

```
 1.     //BJAUSAS JOB B138-AFH,'AFH'
 2.     /*LINES 5
 3.     /*TIME 1
 4.     // EXEC SAS,OPTIONS='LS=70'
 5.     //CASHAU DD DSN=B138.AFH.CASHAU,DISP=SHR
 6.     TITLE DAILY CASH GOLD PRICE;
 7.     DATA GOLD;
 8.     INFILE CASHAU;
 9.     INPUT @6   DAY    YYMMDD8.
10.          @16 PRICE 4.1
11.          @23 INT   4.0
12.          @   VOL      ;
13.     T=_N_;
14.     KEEP DAY T PRICE INT VOL;
15.     LABEL PRICE = CASH GOLD PRICE;
16.     LABEL INT   = OPEN INTEREST -- FUTURES;
17.     LABEL VOL   = DAILY VOLUME -- FUTURES;
18.     FORMAT DAY MMDDYY8.;
19.     ;
20.     PROC ARIMA DATA = GOLD OUT = GOLD;
21.          IDENTIFY VAR = PRICE(1) CENTER NLAG=10;
22.          ESTIMATE Q=1 PLOT;
23.          FORECAST LEAD=1 NOPRINT ID=T;
24.     DATA GOLD;
25.          SET GOLD;
26.          IF PRICE=0 THEN PRICE = FORECAST;
27.          LNPRICE = LOG(PRICE);
28.     PROC ARIMA DATA = GOLD OUT = GOLD;
29.          IDENTIFY VAR = LNPRICE(1) CENTER NLAG=20;
30.          ESTIMATE P=(1)(5) NOCONSTANT ML GRID PRINTALL PLOT;
31.          FORECAST LEAD=1 ID=T PRINTALL;
```

Figure 9.7. Control cards for running a Sample Box-Jenkins analysis.

```
                    DAILY CASH GOLD PRICE
                                18:48 TUESDAY, JUNE 5, 1984
                          ARIMA PROCEDURE
                    NAME OF VARIABLE      =   PRICE
                    PERIODS OF DIFFERENCING=  1.
                    MEAN OF WORKING SERIES=   0
                    STANDARD DEVIATION    =   52.1479
                    NUMBER OF OBSERVATIONS=    1304
                          AUTOCORRELATIONS
LAG COVARIANCE CORRELATION -1 9 8 7 6 5 4 3 2 1 0 1 2 3 4 5 6 7 8 9 1
  0   2719.41    1.00000   I                    |********************|
  1  -1360.8    -0.50040   I          **********|.                   |
  2   71.9889    0.02647   I                    .|*                  |
  3  -23.8429   -0.00877   I                    .|.                  |
  4   0.937199   0.00034   I                    .|.                  |
  5  -12.5282   -0.00461   I                    .|.                  |
  6  -29.4635   -0.01083   I                    .|.                  |
  7   28.2386    0.01038   I                    .|.                  |
  8  -24.6285   -0.00906   I                    .|.                  |
  9   49.6341    0.01825   I                    .|.                  |
 10  -0.572223  -0.00021   I                    .|.                  |
                    '.' MARKS TWO STANDARD ERRORS
                      INVERSE AUTOCORRELATIONS
       LAG CORRELATION -1 9 8 7 6 5 4 3 2 1 0 1 2 3 4 5 6 7 8 9 1
         1   0.78070   I                    .|****************    |
         2   0.60167   I                    .|************        |
         3   0.46823   I                    .|*********           |
         4   0.36253   I                    .|*******             |
         5   0.27570   I                    .|******              |
         6   0.19912   I                    .|****                |
         7   0.12922   I                    .|***                 |
         8   0.07322   I                    .|*                   |
         9   0.02995   I                    .|*                   |
        10   0.00792   I                    .|.                   |
                      PARTIAL AUTOCORRELATIONS
       LAG CORRELATION -1 9 8 7 6 5 4 3 2 1 0 1 2 3 4 5 6 7 8 9 1
         1  -0.50040   I          **********|.                   |
         2  -0.29873   I              ******|.                   |
         3  -0.20661   I                ****|.                   |
         4  -0.14967   I                 ***|.                   |
         5  -0.11789   I                  **|.                   |
         6  -0.11130   I                  **|.                   |
         7  -0.08578   I                  **|.                   |
         8  -0.08017   I                  **|.                   |
         9  -0.04468   I                   *|.                   |
        10  -0.02035   I                    .|.                   |
```

Figure 9.8. Identification phase of Box-Jenkins analysis of cash gold.

Figure 9-9 contains a moving average model for cash gold, centered about the mean of the time series, mu. The *t*-ratio of 44.89 for the MA1,1 term indicates that this term is statistically highly significant. The residuals from fitting this model to the original data series were analyzed, and the autocorrelations and partial autocorrelations of the residuals are shown in Figure 9-10. The model is adequate, though there is a correlation at lag 9 that suggests the possibility that the model might be improved somewhat.

The real significance of this model vis-à-vis the efficient markets hypothesis is that the cash gold market is shown to be less than fully efficient. Whether or not the inefficiency is such that it might be profitably exploited remains to be answered. The purpose of this chapter is to show how Box-Jenkins models may be constructed, not to provide a recipe for making profits. Nevertheless, results such as these provide both hope and justification to those who would seek ways to forecast the direction of market prices, and thus to gain an advantage over those who do not make forecasts (perhaps because they believe that markets are so efficient that it would be futile to try).

```
                        DAILY CASH GOLD PRICE
                                          18:48 TUESDAY, JUNE 5, 1984
                     AUTOCORRELATION CHECK FOR WHITE NOISE
     TO   CHI                              AUTOCORRELATIONS
    LAG  SQUARE DF   PROB
      6  328.48  6  0.000        -0.500  0.026 -0.009  0.000 -0.005 -0.011
                     ARIMA: LEAST SQUARES ESTIMATION
                  PARAMETER    ESTIMATE    STD ERROR   T RATIO  LAG

                  MU          -.00639256    0.251048    -0.03    0
                  MA1,1        0.778685      0.0173461   44.89    1
                  CONSTANT ESTIMATE   =-.00639256
                  VARIANCE  ESTIMATE =    1672.87
                  STD ERROR ESTIMATE =    40.9007
                  NUMBER OF RESIDUALS= 1304
                        CORRELATIONS OF THE ESTIMATES
                                    MU       MA1,1
                     MU          1.000    -0.001
                     MA1,1      -0.001     1.000
                     AUTOCORRELATION CHECK OF RESIDUALS
     TO   CHI                              AUTOCORRELATIONS
    LAG  SQUARE DF   PROB
      6   1.43   4  0.839       -0.014  0.017 -0.005 -0.010 -0.016 -0.014
     12   6.34  10  0.786        0.010  0.013  0.036  0.023  0.012  0.038
     18  23.94  16  0.091        0.014  0.014  0.101 -0.029 -0.027 -0.036
     24  75.12  22  0.000       -0.012 -0.023 -0.024  0.191 -0.019 -0.023
     30  77.35  28  0.000       -0.027 -0.025 -0.002 -0.012  0.011  0.006
     36  85.23  34  0.000       -0.007 -0.007 -0.025 -0.034  0.051 -0.037
     42  92.31  40  0.000       -0.031 -0.057 -0.021  0.005  0.005  0.024
```

Figure 9.9. Fitted B-J model for cash gold price.

```
                          DAILY CASH GOLD PRICE
                                     18:48 TUESDAY, JUNE 5, 1984

                       AUTOCORRELATION PLOT OF RESIDUALS
    LAG COVARIANCE CORRELATION -1 9 8 7 6 5 4 3 2 1 0 1 2 3 4 5 6 7 8 9 1
     0    1672.87   1.00000   |                    |********************|
     1    -23.3907 -0.01398   |                    .|.                  |
     2     29.204   0.01746   |                    .|.                  |
     3     -8.9757 -0.00537   |                    .|.                  |
     4    -16.9529 -0.01013   |                    .|.                  |
     5    -27.2767 -0.01631   |                    .|.                  |
     6    -23.2225 -0.01388   |                    .|.                  |
     7     17.1973  0.01028   |                    .|.                  |
     8     22.4613  0.01343   |                    .|.                  |
     9     60.7038  0.03629   |                    .|*                  |
    10     39.0475  0.02334   |                    .|.                  |
                        '.' MARKS TWO STANDARD ERRORS
                          INVERSE AUTOCORRELATIONS
             LAG CORRELATION -1 9 8 7 6 5 4 3 2 1 0 1 2 3 4 5 6 7 8 9 1
              1    0.01684    |                    .|.                  |
              2   -0.01630    |                    .|.                  |
              3    0.00354    |                    .|.                  |
              4    0.00835    |                    .|.                  |
              5    0.01553    |                    .|.                  |
              6    0.01338    |                    .|.                  |
              7   -0.00970    |                    .|.                  |
              8   -0.01416    |                    .|.                  |
              9   -0.03647    |                    *|.                  |
             10   -0.02343    |                    .|.                  |
                          PARTIAL AUTOCORRELATIONS
             LAG CORRELATION -1 9 8 7 6 5 4 3 2 1 0 1 2 3 4 5 6 7 8 9 1
              1   -0.01398    |                    .|.                  |
              2    0.01727    |                    .|.                  |
              3   -0.00489    |                    .|.                  |
              4   -0.01058    |                    .|.                  |
              5   -0.01642    |                    .|.                  |
              6   -0.01401    |                    .|.                  |
              7    0.01036    |                    .|.                  |
              8    0.01394    |                    .|.                  |
              9    0.03588    |                    .|*                  |
             10    0.02350    |                    .|.                  |
```

Figure 9.10. Analysis of residuals after model fitting.

Notes

[1] A time series without a trend in the mean or variance may be said to be stationary. See B. W. Bolch and C. J. Huang, *Multivariate Statistical Methods for Business and Economics* (Englewood Cliffs, NJ: Prentice-Hall, 1974), p. 273.

[2] *Ibid.* p. 291.

[3] J. E. Reinmuth and M. D. Geurts, "Using Spectral Analysis for Forecast Model Selection." *Decision Sciences* 8 (1977): 138.

[4] P. J. Dhrymes, *Econometrics* (New York: Harper and Row, 1970), p. 442.

[5] Bolch and Huang, *Statistical Methods*, p. 292.

[6] *Ibid.* pp. 293–297.

[7] This results from Euler's formula (see any calculus text) which is $\exp(iz) = \cos z + i \sin z$, where exp denotes the base of natural logarithms, e, raised to the power iz. From this it can be shown that $\exp(-iz) = \cos z - i \sin z$. Adding these equations and dividing by 2 yields $\cos z = (\exp(iz) + \exp(-iz))/2$. For the rationale see Dhrymes, *Econometrics,* pp. 419–422.

[8] D. E. Newland, *An Introduction to Random Vibrations and Spectral Analysis* (London: Longman Group, 1975). Third Impression 1980, p. 150.

[9] "Tapering" is suggested when padding is used, to reduce bias. See Dixon [8], page 687 for a discussion. For another discussion of tapering see Brillinger [4], sections 3.3, 4.3, 5.6, and 5.8. To gain an appreciation of the terminology found in spectral analysis references, compare this to Bloomfield [1], section 5.3.

[10] A program is available from the Foundation for the Study of Cycles, 124 South Highland Avenue, Pittsburgh, PA 15206, that allows the user to specify the range and increments corresponding to frequency. In the author's experience it has performed very well. However, it is based on fitting cycles at each harmonic interval over a specific range, and yields an unsmoothed periodogram. Table 9-3 was produced using a similar program.

[11] A program for this analysis is also available from the Foundation for the Study of Cycles.

References

1. P. Bloomfield, *Fourier Analysis of Time Series: An Introduction* (New York: Wiley, 1976).

2. B. W. Bolch, and C. J. Huang, *Multivariate Statistical Methods for Business and Economics* (Englewood Cliffs, NJ: Prentice-Hall, 1974).

3. G. E. P. Box, and G. M. Jenkins, *Time Series Analysis: Forecasting and Control* (San Francisco: Holden-Day, 1976).

4. D. R. Brillinger, *Time Series: Data Analysis and Theory* (New York: Holt, Rinehart and Winston, 1975).

5. Christopher Chatfield, *The Analysis of Time Series* (London: Chapman and Hall, 1975). (Distributed in the U.S. by Halstead Press, John Wiley and Sons.)

6. James P. Cleary and Hans. Levenbach, *The Professional Forecaster* (Belmont, CA: Lifetime Learning Publications division of Wadsworth, 1982).

7. P. J. Dhrymes, *Econometrics* (New York: Harper and Row, 1970).

8. W. J. Dixon, (Ed). *BMDP Statistical Software: 1981* (Los Angeles: University of California Press, 1981).

9. G. S. Fishman, and P. J. Kiviat, "The Analysis of Simulation-Generated Times Series." *Management Science* **13** (March 1967): 525–557.

10. *Cycle Analysis: A Case Study* Foundation for the Study of Cycles, 1971–1975.

11. C. W. J. Granger, *Forecasting in Business and Economics* (New York: Academic, 1980).

12. John C. Hoff, *A Practical Guide to Box-Jenkins Forecasting* (Belmont, CA: Lifetime Learning Publications division of Wadsworth, 1983).

13. Spyros Makridakis, and Steven C. Wheelwright, (Eds). *The Handbook of Forecasting* (New York: Wiley, 1982).

14. Douglas C. Montgomery, and Lynwood A. Johnson, *Forecasting and Time Series Analysis* (New York: McGraw-Hill, 1976).

15. T. H. Naylor, *Computer Simulation Experiments with Models of Economic Systems* (New York: Wiley, 1971).

16. Charles R. Nelson, *Applied Time Series Analysis* (San Francisco: Holden-Day, 1973).

17. D. E. Newland, *An Introduction to Random Vibrations and Spectral Analysis* (London: Longman Group, 1975).

18. Robert K. Otnes, and Loren Enochson, *Applied Time Series Analysis* (New York: Wiley, 1978).

19. E. Parzen, "Notes on Fourier Analysis and Spectral Windows." Reprinted in E. Parzen, *Time Series Analysis Papers* (San Francisco: Holden-Day, 1967): 190–250.

20. Robert S. Pindyck, and Daniel L. Rubinfeld, *Econometric Models and Economic Forecasts* (New York: McGraw-Hill, 1981).

21. J. E. Reinmuth, and M. D. Geurts, "Using Spectral Analysis for Forecast Model Selection." *Decision Sciences* **8,** (1977): 134–150.

10
Financial Futures

The trading of futures contracts on financial instruments is a relatively new development, having its origins in the latter half of the 1970s. Today there are a variety of actively traded futures contracts, covering a broad range of maturities in the underlying financial instruments. The situation is not a settled one, new contracts are still being developed and existing contracts are subject to a Darwinian "survival of the fittest" evolution which will probably continue to find some contracts fading from the scene while others grow in importance, with contract specifications changing to better match preferences of market participants.

Financial futures contracts have been traded in 30- and 90-day commercial paper, 90-day U.S. T-bills, bank certificates of deposit, Eurodollar deposits, one-year U.S. T-bills, 4- to 6-Year and 10-Year treasury notes, GNMA certificate's of Delivery (CD) and Collateralized Depository Receipts (CDR), and U.S. T-bonds. At this writing there are six contracts with sufficient trading interest to have *The Wall Street Journal* carry full price quotes. Table 10-1 lists these in order of their total open interest (all contract months) at three points in time, and suggests their relative trading importance.

In terms of the total of all futures contracts traded on the CBT in 1980, T-bonds alone accounted for 14.3 percent. On the Chicago Mercantile Exchange's International Monetary Market 90-day T-bills accounted for 15.0 percent of the overall exchange volume. By 1983 the percentages for all interest rate futures contracts on these exchanges (including contracts trading after 1980) were 31.1 and 15.2. When one considers that these contracts have only been traded since the second half of the 1970s, these percentages are especially impressive. What could account for the growth in financials to such large percentages on exchanges that have their origins in wheat and pork bellies?

To be successful, that is, to attract a large volume of trading, a futures contract must appeal to both hedgers and speculators. The underlying commodity, whether it be grain or financial instrument, must have volatile price. The more volatile the price the greater the need for hedging and the greater the prospect for large speculative gains. Financial futures have met both conditions because of the great interest rate fluctuations in recent years.

TABLE 10.1. RELATIVE OPEN INTEREST OF ACTIVE FINANCIAL FUTURES

	Friday, 10 September 1982		Monday, 23 May 1983		Thursday, 8 November 1984	
	Open interest	As % of total	Open interest	As % of total	Open interest	As % of total
U.S. T-bonds (CBT)	160,934	52.0	137,760	50.8	257,277	55.49
U.S. T-bills (IMM)	58,581	18.9	43,046	15.9	49,784	10.74
GNMAs (8%, CBT)	46,211	14.9	44,236	16.3	9,559[a]	2.06
Eurodollars (IMM)	17,392	5.6	22,805	8.4	93,301	20.12
U.S. T-notes (CBT)	13,687	4.4	9,029	3.3	35,143	7.58
Bank CDs (IMM)	12,867	4.2	14,527	5.4	18,565	4.00
	309,672	100.0	291,403	100.0	463,629	100.0

Source: The Wall Street Journal, Monday, September 13, 1982, Tuesday, May 24, 1983, and Friday, November 9, 1984.

[a] Open interest of the GNMA II contract amounted to another 149 contracts, or some 0.03% of the open interest total of the tabulated financial futures above.

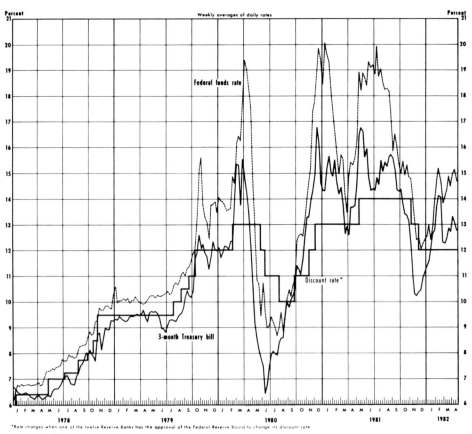

Figure 10.1. Selected interest rates. Source: "The Discount Rate & Market Interest Rate: What's the Connection?," Daniel L. Thornton, Federal Reserve Bank of St. Louis *Review* **64,** no. 6 (June/July 1982): 14.

In Figure 10-1 we have a graphic portrayal of short-term interest rates from 1978 through the first quarter of 1982. The 3-month (90-day) T-bill interest rate ranged from a low of just over 6 percent to a high of almost 17 percent. To gain a clearer appreciation of the volatility in interest rates we might examine the range in the prime rate, the benchmark rate used by banks to set the rates charged on loans to their customers. The prime rate provides an indicator of money market conditions and thus of short-term interest rates. Figure 10-2 illustrates greatly increased rate volatility.

The prime rate is strongly influenced by the discount rate, the rate the FED charges its member banks. Table 10-2 contains a record of the changes in

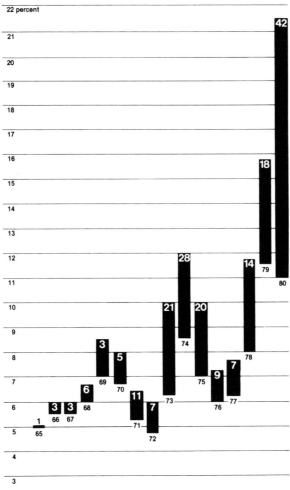

Figure 10.2. Prime Rate 1965–1980. Shows yearly range and number of times rate changed during the course of the year. Source: *Introduction to Financial Futures*, Chicago Board of Trade and First National Bank of Chicago, undated. Copyright Board of Trade of the City of Chicago. Reprinted with permission.

TABLE 10.2. REASONS FOR CHANGES IN THE DISCOUNT RATE

Date	Change	Reason
May 11, 1978	6½ to 7%	Action taken to bring discount rate in closer alignment with short-term interest rates.
July 3, 1978	7 to 7¼%	Essentially the same as above.
August 21, 1978	7¼ to 7¾%	Action taken in view of recent disorderly conditions in foreign exchange markets, as well as the continuation of serious domestic inflation.
September 22, 1978	7¾ to 8%	Action taken to bring discount rate in closer alignment with short-term interest rates, and as a further step to strengthen the dollar.
October 16, 1978	8 to 8½%	Action taken to bring the discount rate in closer alignment with short-term interest rates, and in recognition of the continued high inflation rate and of the current international financial condition.
November 1, 1978	8½ to 9½%	Action taken to strengthen the dollar and to counter continuing domestic inflationary pressures.
July 20, 1979	9½ to 10%	Action taken in view of the recent rapid expansion of the monetary aggregates, to strengthen the dollar on foreign exchange markets and to bring the discount rate into alignment with short-term interest rates.
August 17, 1979	10 to 10½%	Action taken in view of the continuing strong inflationary forces and the relatively rapid expansion in the monetary aggregates.
September 19, 1979	10½ to 11%	Action taken to bring the discount rate into alignment with short-term interest rates, and to discourage excessive borrowing from the discount window.
October 9, 1979	11 to 12%	Action taken to bring discount rate into closer alignment with short-term rates, and to discourage excessive borrowing.
February 15, 1980	12 to 13%	Concern about the increased price of imported oil adding to inflationary pressures underscored the need to raise the discount rate and maintain firm control over the growth of money and credit.
May 30, 1980	13 to 12%	Action taken entirely in recognition of recent substantial declines in short-term market interest rates to levels below the discount rate.

TABLE 10.2. (Continued)

Date	Change	Reason
June 13, 1980	12 to 11%	Essentially the same as above.
July 28, 1980	11 to 10%	Essentially the same as above.
September 26, 1980	10 to 11%	Action taken as part of a continuing policy to discourage excessive growth in the monetary aggregates.
November 17, 1980	11 to 12%	Action taken in view of the current level of short-term interest rates and the recent rapid growth in the monetary aggregates and bank credit.
December 5, 1980	12 to 13%	Action taken in light of the level of market rates and consistent with the existing policy to restrain excessive growth in money and credit.
May 5, 1981	13 to 14%	Action taken in light of the current levels in short-term market interest rates and the need to maintain restraint in the monetary and credit aggregates.
November 2, 1981	14 to 13%	Action taken against the background of recent declines in short-term interest rates and the reduced level of adjustment borrowing at the discount window. It is consistent with a pattern of continued restraint on the growth of money and credit.
December 4, 1981	13 to 12%	Action taken to bring the discount rate into better alignment with short-term interest rates that were prevailing recently in the market.

Source: "The Discount Rate and Market Interest Rates: What's the Connection?" by Daniel L. Thornton, Federal Reserve Bank of St. Louis *Review* **64,** no. 6 (June/July 1982): p. 12.

Note: Federal Reserve Bulletins released the month of or one month after the announced change in the discount rate.

the discount rate, with the reasons for each change, for the span of 1978 through 1981. It is apparent that there is no one reason accounting for all, or even a majority of the changes.

The influences on the money markets and interest rates are complex and difficult to forecast. It is not only domestic economics that affects the money markets, but international economic and political developments that are important influences. Figure 10-3, an annotated price chart for Chicago T-bond

Figure 10.3. Treasury bond futures prices August 22, 1977-August 22, 1980, shows weekly range of prices and settlement price. *Introduction to Financial Futures,* undated. Copyright Board of Trade of the City of Chicago. Reprinted with permission.

futures, associates various events with bond price movement, and supplies labels for others (such as "Black Tuesday" for bonds).

To a great extent the U.S. government influences the money and credit markets. The government has securities maturing for which it must have money for refunding. It also must obtain funds for its expenditures to the extent tax revenues are inadequate, as they clearly have been for decades of mounting deficits. Table 10-3 illustrates a typical U.S. Treasury security offering schedule, this one for the third quarter of calendar 1985. Of some $280.3 billion issued, 44.8 billion represents new cash raised, 16 percent of the total issued.

TABLE 10.3. U.S. TREASURY FINANCING SCHEDULE, 1985-Q3 (DOLLAR AMOUNTS IN BILLIONS)

Auction Date		Settlement Date		Issue	Size	Amount Maturing	New Cash[a]	Cumulative New Cash
June	25	July	1	4-year notes	$ 6.5	$ 3.1	$3.4	3.4
	26		2	7-year notes	6.0	—	6.0	9.4
	27		2	20-year, 1-month bonds	4.5	—	4.5	13.9
July	1		3	3 and 6-month bills	14.0	13.5	0.5	14.4
	8		11	3 and 6-month bills	14.4	13.8	0.6	15.0
	9		11	1-year bills	8.5	8.3	0.2	15.2
	15		18	3 and 6-month bills	14.4	13.9	0.5	15.7
	22		25	3 and 6-month bills	14.4	13.5	0.9	16.6
	24		31	2-year notes	9.3	8.4	0.9	17.5
	29	August	1	3 and 6-month bills	14.4	13.9	0.5	18.0
August	1		8	1-year bills	8.8	8.3	0.5	18.5
	5		8	3 and 6-month bills	14.4	14.0	0.4	18.9
	6		15	3-year notes	8.5 ⎤			
	7		15	10-year notes	6.8 ⎬	12.3	9.5	28.4
	8		15	30-year notes	6.5 ⎦			
	12		15	3 and 6-month bills	14.4	14.0	0.4	28.8
	19		22	3 and 6-month bills	14.4	14.0	0.4	29.2
	21	September	3	2-year notes	9.3	8.4	0.9	30.1
	28		5	5-year, 2-month notes	7.0	—	7.0	37.1
	29		5	1-year bills	8.8	8.3	0.5	37.6
September	2		5	3 and 6-month bills	14.8	14.0	0.8	38.4
	9		12	3 and 6-month bills	14.8	14.0	0.8	39.2
	16		19	3 and 6-month bills	14.8	14.0	0.8	40.0
	18		30	2-year notes	9.3	8.4	0.9	40.9
	23		26	3 and 6-month bills	14.8	14.0	0.8	41.7
	24		30	4-year notes	6.5	3.4	3.1	44.8

Source: Institutional Financial Futures division, Drexel Burnham Lambert.

[a] Ignores foreign add-ons.

INTEREST RATE VOLATILITY

With limited funds for lending and for investment in the economy (and worldwide), the borrowing and refunding activities of the federal government exert a powerful influence on interest rates. And, since the private sector must compete for funds with government, those firms willing to pay the higher interest rates will get the funds they require while other firms are "crowded out" of the debt markets. The trend for several decades has been for inexorably increasing growth in federal government deficits as spending increases at a faster pace than revenues.

Such deficits must be financed, and this means sale of Treasury securities to the public and to the Fed. Sale to the public absorbs money that would otherwise be available for private sector investment, and rates are driven higher in the bidding contest between government and private borrowers for the funds they require. Sale to the Fed can result in "monetizing the debt," the modern equivalent of printing currency to pay for government spending. Sale of treasury securities to the Fed results in the creation of a credit to the treasury account at the Fed, on which it can write checks. Monetization of the debt can be highly inflationary, as critics have pointed out to little apparent avail.

When deficits have to be covered, the government has a dilemma: Finance them with debt sold to the public and drive rates higher while depressing the economy, or finance them by monetizing the debt and fanning the flames of inflation. Neither is an acceptable alternative. Neither is politically popular, though a case can be made that many voters prefer inflation to depression, some benefiting from it (debtors especially, at least when mortgage debt was for fixed interest rates).

Neither alternative for financing deficits is politically popular and neither can be used continually without risking deep economic depression on the one hand or hyperinflation on the other. Yet, the deficit must be financed. The implication seems clear: We will have alternating periods in which each method is used and, as a consequence, continued interest rate volatility.

THE TERM STRUCTURE OF INTEREST RATES

Not all interest rates are equal, even for debt issues of the same quality. In times of settled economic conditions, interest rates on short-term maturity issues are lower than on long maturities. Figure 10-4 illustrates such a "normal" yield curve. In Figure 10-4 the lower interest rates are associated with short maturities, and yields rise along with maturity.

Long-term rates are normally higher than short-term because of the greater risk exposure of investing in long maturity securities. The investor in long maturity bonds stands to see his or her capital value decline if the market rate of interest increases. Not only this, but such an investor incurs an opportunity cost: By having funds tied up in bonds when the rate increases, the investor cannot use the funds to invest at the higher market rate.

The longer the maturity of a bond, other things equal, the greater the change in the bond's price in response to a given change in the market rate of interest. Also, a bond with a smaller coupon (that is, lower face interest rate)

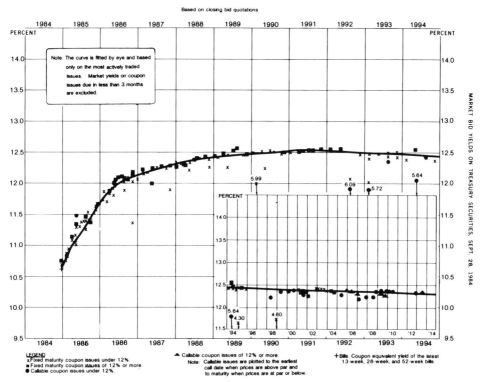

Figure 10.4. Yields of Treasury Securities, September 28, 1984 based on closing bid quotations. Source: *Treasury Bulletin*, September 28, 1984.

will have a larger price change to a given change in interest rate than one with a large coupon. How can we explain the rising yield curve? If we assume that interest rates in general are in their low to moderate range—and they generally are when the yield curve is upward sloping—we can explain its shape on the basis of investor-perceived risk. When rates overall are low, the odds may be viewed to favor an increase rather than a decrease because there is more room for rates to rise than to fall. And, the risk associated with holding a bond increases with the maturity of the bond irrespective of the investor's holding period. If we define risk as variability of returns around the expected or average return—using the variance or standard deviation, as is customary for this purpose—then for a given set of changes in interest rates the risk increases as maturity increases.

If you plan to buy a bond and hold it for one year, a bond that matures one year hence offers you a fixed and known rate of return. But, if you buy a bond maturing in five years, when you sell it a year from now you may not get the price you expected at the date of purchase. Your return is not determined solely by the interest payments you receive, it is also partly a function of the difference in the price you pay and the price you receive when you sell. In the case of the bond maturing on the date you would sell it, you know exactly what you will receive.

Three basic theories are generally considered to cover the likely alternatives accounting for the shape of the yield curve: (1) the pure expectations theory, (2) the liquidity premium theory, and (3) the market segmentation theory. However, the theory that has held up best under the rigors of empirical investigation is a combination of the expectations theory with the liquidity preference theory, or biased expectations theory. This explanation says that future interest rate expectations are important in forming investor preferences, but that risk averse investors prefer short-term bonds and therefore will require a premium over the unbiased long-term rate. Investors must be compensated for parting with the liquidity they would have in a short-term bond portfolio (i.e., one with short duration). This liquidity premium, or extra compensation, is the amount by which actual long-term interest yields exceed the geometric mean of expected short-term rates.

Forward Rates

The forecast, or expected, short-term interest rate over some future time span is a *forward* rate for that time span. Long-term interest rates are an average (geometric) of short-term forward rates.

If the current yield on a one-year T-bill is 9 percent, and the yield on a two-year T-note is 11 percent, then the forward rate (expressed on a yield equivalent basis)[1] on a one-year T-bill to be issued a year hence is 13.04 percent. An investor choosing to purchase two T-bills in sequence, each with a one year life, would earn with certainty 9 percent over the first year and an expected (forward rate of) 13.04 percent over the second year. Assuming the investor believes the forward rate for the second year of 13.04 percent will match the actual rate a year hence, he or she would be indifferent (assuming no transactions costs) between: (1) a two-year T-bond yielding 11 percent, and (2) a T-bill yielding 9 percent over the first year followed by a T-bill a year from now yielding 13.04 percent. To see this more clearly, we will examine the mathematical relationship between the present and forward rates.

The relationship between interest rates is multiplicative, not additive. The reason this is so is that interest earnings may be reinvested—that is, compound interest. An average that did not take compounding into account would be incorrect. The following equation summarizes the example at hand:

$$(1.09)(1.1304) = (1.11)^2 \qquad (1)$$

In general, the term structure of interest rates is given by

$$(1 + i_1)(1 + i_2) \cdots (1 + i_N) = (1 + i_{i,N})^N \qquad (2)$$

where the subscripts correspond to the period over which the rate is expected to prevail and $i_{i,N}$ is the long-term average compound rate over the span from present through period N. Note that the rate $i_{i,N}$ can be found by taking the Nth root of the product of terms on the left-hand side of the expression in Equation (3). It is thus a geometric average rate. With knowledge of interest rates for bonds identical in every respect except their maturities, one can find the individual forward rates algebraically. When the bonds are not identical in every respect but maturity the calculations become much more complex.

Inverted Yield Curve

From time to time short-term interest rates become higher than long-term rates. This generally occurs in times of economic stress, as in 1929, 1973, and 1981, and is followed by economic recession or depression as the economy readjusts. The reason why economic recession follows in the wake of a change from inverted back to normal term structure is not fully understood. It may be due in part to firms postponing new investments until rates decline to what are viewed as a normal level. Then, because of lags between investment spending and its effect on national output and income, the level of economic activity continues to decline for some time after investment has increased.

Figure 10-5 contains an illustration of an "inverted" yield curve. It is important to note that the inverted yield curve of Figure 10-5 lies at a higher level than the normal yield curve of Figure 10-4. In order to have an inverted yield curve, interest rates—both long and short term—must be at levels considered to be high by historical standards. The reason for this is apparent in the explanation of the inverted curve.

Comparison of Figures 10-4 and 10-5 reveals that short-term interest rates have been much more volatile than long-term rates. Short-term rates ranged from about 10.5 to 15.5 percent, a spread of some 5 full percentage points. In contrast, long-term rates ranged from about 10.75 to 12.75—only some 2 full percentate points. It should be noted however, that a move of 2 percentage points in long rates may have a larger effect on the prices of distant maturity bonds than a larger interest rate move in near maturity instruments. Price movement comparisons cannot be made directly by comparing interest rate moves; the relationship of price changes to interest rate moves is not linear. In the case of futures contracts, tables and nomographs are available to determine the price that corresponds to any given interest rate. For cash debt instruments, and small changes in price, duration can help provide useful approximations to price changes. For larger changes, bond tables or computers are necessary.

An inverted yield curve occurs when interest rates move to such high levels that a consensus develops in the markets that rates will soon begin to come down. With this expectation widespread, borrowers will want to borrow short-term rather than raise funds at the higher interest rate costs associated

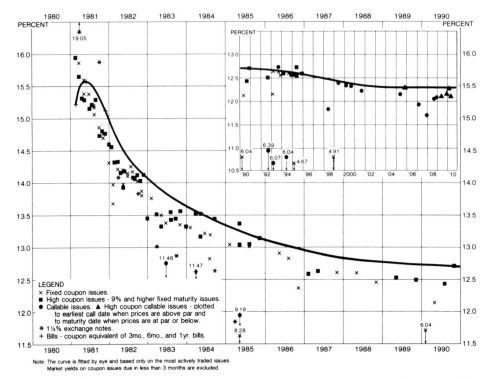

Figure 10.5. Yields of Treasury Securities, November 28, 1980. Source: *Treasury Bulletin,* November 28, 1980.

with long-term borrowing. At the same time, lenders will want to loan long term to avail themselves of capital gains as rates come down.

BOND PRICE AND DURATION

For effective hedging of a cash position using futures contracts, the cash and futures markets must move together. They need not move in a rigid, formula relationship, but must move in a statistically predictable manner up to the maturity or delivery date of the futures contract, at which time the futures price must approach the spot market price. In other words, the basis, or difference between the spot and futures price, may vary up to the expiration of the futures contract. But, the variation must be statistically tractable; that is, basis variation must behave according to a definable stochastic process so that the hedger may assess the risk of a hedge prior to entering into it.

Subject to stochastic variation, the prices of spot financial instruments and the corresponding futures contracts are predictable. This means that financial futures may be used to effectively hedge spot position risks.

A useful summary measure of the effect of an interest rate change on a financial instrument is provided by "duration." Duration can be determined for a particular cash instrument or portfolio of cash instruments. That duration can be compared to the duration of the cash instrument underlying the futures contract being considered for hedging use. If the two durations are equal (or close to equal) the hedge may be expected to be effective.[2]

For a given risk category, the relationship between a bond's price, its face value, nominal rate, and time to maturity is given by

$$P = \sum_{t=1}^{MN} \frac{(i/M)F}{(1 + y/M)^t} + \frac{F}{(1 + y/M)^{MN}} \qquad (3)$$

where P = price, or present value

N = years to maturity

M = interest payment periods in a year

i = nominal, or face annual interest

F = face, or maturity value

y = market rate or yield to maturity on bonds of this risk and other characteristics

Since i, M, and N are constant for a given bond, we may simplify the notation by rewriting Equation (3) as

$$P = \sum_{t=1}^{N'} \frac{I}{z^t} \qquad (4)$$

where $N' = MN$

$z = (1 + y/M)^t$

$I = (i/M)F$ for $1 \leq t \leq N'$, $I = (i/M)F + F$ for $t = N'$

For the vast majority of bonds, all terms are fixed except market price and the return required by the market, or yield to maturity. The direction of causality is for changes in the market rate of interest to induce changes in the market price. It is this price variability that is a major source of risk, both to those who are long bonds and those who are short. Risk of default can be effectively reduced through diversification of bond holdings. Interest rate risk cannot be eliminated by diversification, but it can be offset by hedging.

To be effective, a hedge vehicle must be highly correlated with the thing being hedged. A hedge against adverse bond price movement brought about by interest rate changes should move *proportionately* as much in response to the rate changes. In other words, the *elasticity* of the hedge medium ought to be the same as that of the financial instruments being hedged.

The elasticity of x with respect to y is defined by

$$\eta = \frac{\Delta x/x}{\Delta y/y} \tag{5}$$

where Δ denotes change. The formula in equation (5) is the *arc* elasticity. Elasticity changes over the range of x and y values, the arc elasticity therefore gives an average elasticity measure. Elasticity at a particular point, or pair of x and y, is obtained by taking the limit (as $\Delta y \to 0$) of Equation (3). This yields the elasticity:

$$\eta = \frac{dx/x}{dy/y} \quad \text{or} \quad \frac{dx}{dy} \cdot \frac{y}{x} \tag{6}$$

where dx/dy is the derivative of x with respect to y. The relationship in Equation (6) is referred to as the "y elasticity of x", for example, the "price elasticity of demand."

We are interested in a specific elasticity, the interest elasticity of bond price. For most bonds the relevant variables are the current market price and the required rate of return, or yield to maturity, the interest rate we are concerned with. The interest elasticity of bond price is defined by

$$\eta = \frac{dP/P}{dz/z} = \frac{dP}{dz} \cdot \frac{z}{P} \tag{7}$$

From Equation (4) we obtain dP/dz as

$$\frac{dP}{dz} = \sum_{t=1}^{N'} -tIz^{-t-1} - NFz^{-N'-1} \tag{8}$$

so that

$$\eta = \frac{dP}{dz} \cdot \frac{z}{P} = \frac{z\sum_{t=1}^{N'} -tIz^{-t-1} - N'Fz^{-N'-1}}{\sum_{t=1}^{N'} Iz^{-t} + Fz^{-N'}} \tag{9}$$

If N' is a large number the terms $-N'Fz^{-N'}$ and $Fz^{-N'}$ are small. If we omit them we obtain the following equation:

$$\eta = \frac{\sum_{t=1}^{N'} -tIz^{-t}}{\sum_{t=1}^{N'} Iz^{-t}} = -D \tag{10}$$

Equation (10) is the negative of a measure called *duration*,[3] which is used to gauge the change in bond price for a given change in yield. Note that from Equation (10) we find that duration is the weighted average time that passes— the duration—for the average dollar of present value to be received.

Calculation of duration is relatively straightforward, though tedious. The small computer program displayed in Figure 10-6 is written in the dialect of BASIC commonly encountered on desktop personal computers. To calculate duration the user must supply four values: (1) the number of cash flows, that is, coupon payments, (2) the per-period cash flow, or interest payment, (3) the face value of the bond, and (4) the discount or interest rate. In the program of Figure 10-6 these values are supplied with data statements. It is an easy matter to change appropriate statements so that the values are input from the keyboard.[4]

Now we shall work out in detail the example contained in Figure 10-6 to illustrate how duration is calculated. Calculations are shown in Table 10-4 for a discount (interest) rate of 12 percent.

It is clear from Table 10-4 that the large cash flow and time index at $t=5$ combine to make the duration large: The average dollar of present value is received after 4.14 periods.

```
80  REM *** NUMBER OF CASH FLOWS BEYOND T=0, N
90      DATA 5
100       READ N
110 REM *** UNIFORM PER-PERIOD CASH FLOW, R
120       DATA 100
130       READ R
140 REM *** FACE VALUE TO BE RECEIVED AT T=N, RN
150       DATA 1000
160       READ RN
170 PRINT "WHAT IS THE DISCOUNT (INTEREST) RATE";
180       INPUT K
190 LET F1=1/(1+K)
200 LET C1=1!
210 LET D1=0!
220 LET D2=0!
230 FOR T1=1 TO N
240 LET C1=F1*C1
250 IF T1=N THEN R=R+RN
260 LET TMP1=R*C1
270 LET D1=D1+TMP1
280 LET D2=D2+TMP1*T1
290 NEXT T1
300 LET D=D2/D1
310 PRINT
320 PRINT "DURATION IS   . . . . . . . . . . . . . . .   ";
330 PRINT USING "###.####";D
340 PRINT
350 PRINT "NET PRESENT VALUE (PRICE) OF THE BOND IS";
360 PRINT USING "$$######.##";D1
370 END
```

Figure 10.6. Program to calculate duration for uniform cash flow.

TABLE 10.4. DETAIL OF DURATION CALCULATION[a]

(1)	(2)	(3)	(4)	(5)
			P.V. of	P.V. of
			Cash	Cash
	Cash	12% P.V.	Flow	Flow
t	Flow	Factor	(2) × (3)[a]	× (1)
1	$ 100	0.8929	$ 89.29	$ 89.29
2	100	0.7972	79.72	159.44
3	100	0.7118	71.18	213.54
4	100	0.6355	63.55	254.20
5	1100	0.5674	624.14	3120.70
			$927.88	$3837.17

[a] Sum is the P.V. Therefore, the duration, D = $3,837.17/$927.88 = 4.14.

We are interested in duration because it provides us a convenient means for estimating the change in a bond's price for a given interest rate change. Since duration is the negative of the interest elasticity of bond price given in Equation (7), we may write

$$dP = -D \, dz \, (P/z) \qquad (11)$$

To apply Equation (9), let us assume that the interest rate for bonds of characteristics like that used in Table 10-4 increases by 50 basis points (i.e., half a percentage point) to 12.5 percent. Since we are dealing with changes larger than the infinitesimal dP and dz we replace them in the notation by ΔP and Δz. We find that the half-point change in interest rate produces a price change of approximately

$$\Delta P = (-4.14)(0.005)(\$927.88/1.12) = -\$17.15 \qquad (12)$$

To compare our approximation of a decline in the bond's price of $17.15 with the actual decline we repeat the analysis shown in Table 10-4, with P.V. factors for 12.5 percent. As a bonus we obtain the new duration measure for this higher rate. Table 10-5 contains the calculations.

The estimated bond price is $927.88 − $17.15, or $910.73, the actual bond price is $910.95, 22 cents greater. This is a very good approximation. The error in terms of the actual price decline is only 1.3 percent.

The reason that duration does not provide exact price changes is that duration measures price responsiveness at a single point while we have used it to obtain an estimate over a range between two points. In other words, we have used the point elasticity to estimate the arc elasticity. Nevertheless, as long as

TABLE 10.5. DURATION CALCULATION FOR 12.5 PERCENT[a]

(1)	(2)	(3)	(4)	(5)
			P.V. of Cash	P.V. of Cash
	Cash	12.5% P.V.	Flow	Flow
t	Flow	Factor	(2) × (3)	× (1)
1	$ 100	0.8889	$ 88.89	$ 88.89
2	100	0.7901	79.01	158.02
3	100	0.7023	70.23	210.69
4	100	0.6243	62.43	249.72
5	1100	0.5549	610.39	3051.95
			$910.95	$3759.27

[a] The duration, $D = \$3{,}759.27/\$910.95 = 4.13$.

the change in interest rates is not too great, duration enables us to obtain reasonably close estimates of price change.

HEDGING BOND PRICE RISK

Duration provides a means for estimating the price change in a bond induced by a change in market interest rate. Since duration measures price responsiveness to interest rate changes, an effective hedge requires that the durations of the bond (or bond portfolio) being hedged and that of the instrument underlying the futures contract be approximately equal.[5]

It can be shown that the duration of a bond portfolio is a weighted average of the durations of its individual constituents:

$$D_P = \sum_{i=1}^{n} w_i D_i \tag{13}$$

where w_i is the proportion of the bond portfolio invested in the ith bond. To hedge a portfolio of bonds requires that we have a futures contract for a bond that has duration similar to that of our bond portfolio. Alternatively, for large portfolios, we may be able to use a combination of futures contracts on two financial instruments of different duration, such as T-notes and T-bonds. It will suffice to use two different futures contracts. If we cannot obtain a duration closely matching that of our bond portfolio with two contracts then using three or more will not help to do so. However, it may be more efficient, in the sense of requiring fewer total contracts to reach a given duration, to use more than two different contracts.

If the duration of our bond portfolio is D_P, and the durations of futures contracts on two different financial instruments are D_1 and D_2 such that $D_1 \neq D_2$, then, by proper selection of weights X_1, X_2 we can achieve

$$X_1 D_1 + X_2 D_2 = D_P \qquad (14)$$

However, the smaller hedger may find that the dollar investment represented by $X_1 + X_2$ is greater than his hedging requires. It should be noted that the signs of the X_1, X_2 weights are not constrained to be positive. Negative weights would imply short sales of the corresponding futures contracts.

SUMMARY COMPARISON OF FINANCIAL FUTURES

Currently, the markets and contracts traded in financial futures are continuing to evolve. Consequently, the situation is unsettled and likely to remain so for some time. New contracts are introduced, while existing contracts that have failed to attract sufficient market participation gradually fade away, like the proverbial "old soldiers." Table 10-6 provides a summary of characteristics for financial futures.

In Table 10-1, we have comparisons of the open interest (i.e., number of open contracts, each representing one long position and one short position) of those financial futures with sufficient market participation to be listed in *The Wall Street Journal*.

Clearly the T-bond contract on the CBT is the dominant financial futures contract in terms of relative open interest, accounting for over 50 percent of the total number of financial futures contracts. If the open interest in the smaller T-bond and T-bill contracts on Chicago's MCE were to be included, the dominance would likely be stronger still.

In 1982 and 1983 the GNMA contract had somewhat higher open interest than T-bills, perhaps because it is well-suited to hedging those risks associated with mortgage interest rate changes, risks, such as faced by traditionally thinly capitalized mortgage bankers, many of whom have accepted the advantages of hedging. By November 1984 the GNMAs had fallen to only slightly more than 2 percent of total financial futures open interest.

In mid-1983, T-bills ranked third in open interest just under GNMAs, while these rankings were reversed in 1982. The participation in these markets suggests a rather marked preference for maturity extremes (excepting with GNMAs). The continued small open interest in CDs indicate that hedgers and speculators have not been drawn to this contract. Eurodollar futures have gained greatly, accounting for some 20 percent of open interest in November 1984, second only to T-bonds.

It should be noted that a particular contract does not have to win a popularity contest to be viable. The three most active financial futures seem secure.

TABLE 10.6. SELECTED FINANCIAL FUTURES CONTRACT CHARACTERISTICS

Future	Exchange	Months Traded[a]	Hours Traded (Central Time)	Contract Size	Quoted In	Value of Minimum Fluctuation	Normal Minimum Fluctuation	Value of Limit Move	Limit Move	First Notice Day
T-bonds	CBOT	H,M,U,Z,C,I,P,T	8:00–2:00	$100,000 basis 8%	Per 100 points	1/32 point	$31.25	64/32nds (2 points)	$2,000	Last business day of month preceding delivery month
T-bonds	MACE	H,M,U,Z, current month and 45 consecutive calendar months.	8:00–2:15	$50,000 face value	% of par	1/32 point	15.62	64/32nds (2 points)	1,000	Last business day of month preceding delivery month
GNMA	CBOT	H,M,U,Z out 24 months	8:00–2:00	$100,000 principal balance	Per 100 points	1/32 points per 100 basis points	31.25	64/32nds (2 points)	2,000	Last business day of month preceding delivery month
T-bills annual	IMM	H,M,U,Z	8:15–1:35	$250,000 U.S. T-bills with 1 year maturity	Index = (100% – Yield%)	0.01 per Index	25.00	50 basis points	1,250	On business day following last trade day
T-bills	IMM	F,H,J,M,N,U,V,Z	8:00–2:00	$1 Million U.S. 13-Week T-Bills	Index = (100% – Yield%)	0.01 per Index	25.00	60 basis points	1,500	
T-bills	MACE	H,M,U,Z	8:00–2:10	$500,000 face value	MACE Index	0.01 per Index	12.50	60 basis points	750	
Eurodollar	IMM	H,M,U,Z and spot month	7:30–2:00	$1,000,000	IMM Index	0.01 per Index	25.00	100 basis points	2,500	None
CDs	IMM	H,M,U,Z	7:30–2:00	$1,000,000	Index = (100% – Yield%)	0.01 per Index	25.00	80 basis points	2,000	15th of delivery month
CDs	CBT	H,M,U,Z	7:30–2:00	$1,000,000	Index = (100% – Yield%)	0.01 per Index	25.00	80 basis points	2,000	2nd business day prior to delivery month

[a]
Year 1	F	G	H	J	K	M	N	Q	U	V	X	Z
Month:	Jan	Feb	Mar	Apr	May	Jun	Jul	Aug	Sep	Oct	Nov	Dec
Year 2	A	B	C	D	E	I	L	O	P	R	S	T

And CDs, with over 4 percent of open interest would seem viable if this can be maintained. GMNAs, with just over 2 percent of open interest, may or may not exist as you read this. The markets are ruthless in their judgments of contracts, and only those with continuing appeal will survive.

FINANCIAL FUTURES CONTRACT CHARACTERISTICS

The financial futures are designed to provide trading in interest rates. However, these must be translated into dollars because transactions are settled in currency. Prices move inversely to interest rates. When interest rates move up, the prices of debt obligations fall; when interest rates fall, the prices of debt obligations rise. Unfortunately, a change of x percent in interest rate does not produce a change of x percent in debt instrument price. To overcome this problem, two approaches are followed.

In the case of T-bonds and GNMAs prices are quoted as a percent of par value. In the case of T-bonds and GNMAs, the 100 basis points making up each full percentage point (each basis point = 1/100 of a percent) are divided into 32 parts. That is, each full percentage point = 32/32. Awkward, yes, but practice based on tradition often is. The T-bond contract is based on a bond with 8 percent face, or coupon rate. The cash bond would sell for 100 (i.e., 100 percent of face value) if the market rate of interest on such bonds were 8 percent. When the market rate on cash bonds is above 8 percent, the benchmark bond sells at a discount. A price quotation of 78-03 (78 and 3/32) corresponds to an interest rate yield of 10.672 percent from the underlying bond paying an 8 percent nominal rate. Sliderule type calculators are available from the CBT for quickly finding the approximate yield corresponding to a given bond price.

Trading of T-bonds and GNMAs is based on pricing what amounts to an index of par. A "price" of 78-03 corresponds to a contract value of 78 and 3/32 (78.09375) times the nominal contract value of $100,000. Thus, 78-03 corresponds to a value of $78,093.75. A change of 1/32 of 1 percent of par corresponds to $31.25 (i.e., 0.03125 times $100,000/100). This is the minimum point fluctuation in trading the T-Bond contract on both the CBT and the MCE though the dollar amount associated with a point on the smaller MCE contract is half that of the CBT.

Although dissimilar to one another in other respects, T-bills, CDs, and Eurodollars are similar in the way the pricing of their futures contracts differs from that of T-bonds. Interest on cash T-bills is at discount. This means that the instrument has a fixed maturity value and that the investor receives interest by purchasing the instrument prior to maturity at a lower price—that is, at a discount. Pricing of futures based on these discount instruments is through a simple index. The index is calculated as 100 minus the yield percentage. For example, a yield of 8.5 percent gives an index value of 91.5. It is this index that is traded. On the IMM T-bill contract for example, the minimum fluctuation is 0.01 index point, corresponding to $25.00 on the million dollar nominal contract value (0.01 times $1,000,000 divided by 100.0 divided by 4—the number of 91-day periods per year). Booklets are available, such as that published by the International Monetary Market division of the Chicago Mercantile Exchange, which relate the IMM T-bill Index to the discount rate, the equivalent add-on, or coupon rate, and the discount on $1 million maturity value.

Treasury Bonds

Treasury bonds are sold to finance the federal government's funds requirements. Maturities are long term, extending as far as 30 years. In other countries perpetual bonds have been issued, such as the consols traded in Britain, and a perpetuity issued by the Canadian government.

Treasury bonds are similar to corporation issues except they are considered free of default risk because they are direct obligations of the U.S. government. Investors receive only interest at regular intervals up to maturity or call. Principal is repaid only at maturity or, if retired early, at call.

Treasury bonds, because they are default risk free, provide a measure of the minimum rate of interest on obligations of long maturity. Corporation issues, because there is varying risk of default, trade at higher interest rates, to compensate investors for the greater risk. These other issues follow T-bonds in response to interest rate changes. This makes T-bond futures useful and popular for hedging risks associated with other spot market issues. The relatively great volatility of long-term T-bond prices to interest rate changes makes futures trading in them popular with speculators.

The underlying issue for the CBT T-bond contract is an 8-percent bond, with 20-years to maturity or call. At any given time there may or may not be the actual T-bonds with the exact assumed characteristics. Other bonds that are allowed under the contract specifications may be delivered at premium to or discount from the contract standard.

For a given interest rate the price of the contract standard T-bond can be found easily with the computer program illustrated in Figure 10-7. Calculation of the yield corresponding to a given price for the contract standard T-bond is much more difficult because it requires the solution to a root of a polynomial equation—that is, we must solve for an internal rate of return. Figure 10-8 contains a computer program for finding the rate. Like that in Figure 10-7, it is written in Pascal, a widely used language well suited to such work.

Treasury Bills

Treasury bills are sold at auction weekly by the U.S. Treasury Department through the Federal Reserve Banks. Original maturities are for 91 days, 6 months, or 1 year. Treasury bills are direct obligations of the federal government, and are considered free of default risk. Because of their short maturities T-bills are much less price sensitive to interest rate changes than long term instruments, and are less risky in that sense as well.

```
CONST a=100000.0; n=40; interest=4000.0;

VAR interest_rate, factor,
    decimal_price, price_in_32nds : REAL;

BEGIN

WRITE('What is the T-bond interest rate in percent? ');
READLN(interest_rate);

interest_rate:=interest_rate/200.0;
factor:=EXP(n*LN(1.0+interest_rate));
decimal_price:= (1.0-1.0/factor)/interest_rate*interest+a/factor;
decimal_price:=decimal_price/1000.0;
price_in_32nds:=INT(decimal_price)+(decimal_price-INT(decimal_price))*0.32;
price_in_32nds:=INT(100.0*price_in_32nds+0.005);  (* Round to 2 decimals *)
price_in_32nds:=price_in_32nds/100.0;

WRITE('T-bond decimal price = ',decimal_price:6:3,'   ');
WRITELN('T-bond price in 32nds = ',price_in_32nds:6:2);

(* Copyright (C) 1984 by Anthony F. Herbst.  All rights reserved. *)

END.
```

Figure 10.7.   Program to calculate T-bond price for a given yield.

Treasury bills provide important short-term financing to the federal government. They provide a safe investment medium to those individuals and institutions who are able to loan short term funds. The rates on T-bills of different maturities also may be used as indices on which financial institutions may base their lending rates. For example, a bank's line of credit to an industrial borrower might be stated as the one-year T-bill rate plus 2 percent. The percent add-on, and the measure of rate used—month-end, month average, and so on—vary across institutions.

T-bills are sold at discount rate yield. This means that the purchase of a $1 million, 1-year bill with 360 days to maturity at a 12 percent discount would pay $1,000,000 (1.00 − 0.12) or $880,000. At maturity he would receive $1 million, for a yield of more than 12 percent. In T-bill calculations a 360-day year is assumed. This is in contrast to bond calculations, which assume a 365-day year. This is important to remember for later, when we shall look into rate and pricing formulas.

Treasury bill futures contracts are traded on the International Monetary Market of the Chicago Mercantile Exchange. The active contract at this writing is for 90-day T-bills, also referred to as 3-month or 13-week T-bills. The contract is based on a $1 million, 90-day bill, but 91- or 92-day bills are acceptable for delivery with an appropriate adjustment in price. The formula that gives the price for T-bills of different maturities is $1,000,000 [1 − (days to maturity/360) T-bill yield]

Several additional formulas enable one to easily calculate the values tabulated and published by the exchange. These are the IMM Index, the discount rate, the coupon equivalent, the discount on $1 million, and the price. It must be remembered that the discount rate on T-bills is quoted on a 360-day year, whether for spot market or futures. The coupon-equivalent rate assumes a 365-day year.

$$\text{IMM Index} = 100.00 - \text{discount rate}$$

$$\text{discount} = \left(\frac{\text{days to maturity}}{360}\right) \times \text{discount rate} \times \$1,000,000$$

$$\text{price} = \$1,000,000 - \text{discount}$$

$$\text{coupon equivalent} = \left(\frac{\text{discount}}{\text{price}}\right) \times \left(\frac{365}{\text{days to maturity}}\right)$$

```
Listing for:    tbrate.pas

{$C+,U+}

(* CONVERT FROM 32NDS TO DECIMAL *)
FUNCTION td(x : REAL) : REAL;
        BEGIN
        td:=INT(x)+((x-INT(x))/0.32);
        END;

FUNCTION pow(x,y :REAL) : REAL;
        BEGIN
        pow:=EXP(y*LN(x));
        END;

(* MAIN PROGRAM FOLLOWS *)

   CONST a=100000.0; n=40.0; n1=41.0; interest=4000.0;
   VAR i, x, price, f, df, tbond_price, tbrate : REAL;

   BEGIN
   WRITE('What is the bond price? ');
   READLN(tbond_price);
   f:=1000.0; (* A LARGE NUMBER *)
   price:=td(tbond_price)*1000.0;
   i:=(interest+(price-a)/n)/(price/2); (* FIND APPROX. ANNUAL i *)
   i:=i/2.0; (* CONVERT TO SEMI-ANNUAL RATE *)

   WHILE ABS(f) > 0.000001 DO
      BEGIN   (* NEWTON-RAPHSON SOLUTION METHOD *)
         x:=1.0+i;
         f:=interest*( (1.0-(1.0/pow(x,n))) / i ) + a/pow(x,n) - price;
         df:=interest*( -1.0/(i*i) + 1.0/(i*i*pow(x,n))
            + n/(i*pow(x,n)) ) - a*n/pow(x,n1);
         i:=i-f/df;
      END;

   tbrate:=100.0*2.0*i;
   WRITELN('Rate is ',tbrate:3:4,'%');
   END.
```

Figure 10.8. Program to calculate T-bond yield for a given price.

```
1000 'Program TBILL.BAS: Calculates T-Bill Coupon Equivalent and Cash Discount
1100 '
1200 'Copyright (C) 1984 by Anthony F. Herbst.  All rights reserved.
1300 '
1400 DEFDBL A, D
1500 A=1000000!   'Nominal principal amount
1600 Y360=360!
1700 Y365=365!
1800 INPUT "What is the discount rate in percent";DRATE
1900 DRATE=DRATE/100!
2000 INPUT "What is the bill maturity in days";T
2100 INDEX=100!-100!*DRATE
2200 D=(T*DRATE/Y360)*A
2300 CRATE=(D/(A-D))*Y365/T
2400 PRINT USING " ###.##  ##.##  ##.###  $#####,.##  $######,.##";
              INDEX,100!*DRATE,100!*CRATE,D,A-D
2500 END
```

Figure 10.9. Program for calculating T-bill coupon equivalent and cash discount.

For ease of calculation the computer program in BASIC is provided in Figure 10-9.

Eurodollars

A Eurodollar deposit is defined as any dollar deposit outside the United States, its territories and possessions. Most such dollar balances are carried on the books of major banks and their branches in London, Zurich, and other money centers outside the United States. Tax haven territories also claim a share of Eurodollar deposits. Among these are the Bahamas, Cayman Islands, Panama, Hong Kong, and the Channel Islands.

In the 1950s U.S. banks were prohibited by Regulation Q from paying interest on deposits of less than 30 days, and were limited to paying no more than 1 percent on deposits of 31 to 90 days. Banks outside the United States were not constrained by Regulation Q. They found that dollar deposits could be loaned profitably even when they paid competitive rates to depositors. One writer has attributed the initial Eurodollar loan to the Soviet Union's Norodny Bank in London, which found itself with a fairly large holding of dollars following the Hungarian uprising and the consequent period of increased tension with the United States. In other words, it would seem that history may record that Eurodollars were a Russian invention! By 1966 Eurodollar CDs were being issued by banks in London. These were negotiable instruments that traded at rates below the Eurodeposit rate.

Commercial borrowers in the Eurodollar market can obtain funds from Eurodollar rollover loans. These provide borrower and lender alike a short-term interest rate on funds provided for a relatively long fixed loan period. Typically such arrangements provide a five-year loan on which the interest rate is fixed at intervals of three or six months to the London Interbank offered Rate (LIBOR), plus a negotiated premium over LIBOR.

Because they are outside the United States Eurodollar deposits are not guaranteed by any U.S. agency, such as the Federal Deposit Insurance Corporation (FDIC). However, their size would, in most cases, take them outside the scope of guaranteed deposits even if they were in the United States. The relevant risks related to factors other than interest rate and currency exchange rate volatility are credit risk and sovereign risk.

Credit risk reflects the creditworthiness of the borrower. From the depositor's perspective this is the bank to which the funds are loaned (i.e., "deposited"). From the bank's perspective credit risk is what it faces when lending funds on deposit to commercial borrowers. Credit risk to the depositor of Eurodollars if minimal when deposits are placed with major money center banks; no more such risk than on similar U.S. domestic deposits. However, in the case of deposits placed with offshore branches or subsidiaries of U.S. banks there has been uncertainty regarding the parent corporation's obligation to depositors if the offshore affiliate should fail.

Sovereign risk is that which exists from the fact that the laws and regulations of the country in which the deposits are placed apply. These regulations can be changed by the respective governments at their pleasure. In major world money centers this has not posed a problem. Nevertheless, a change in law or regulation could prove troublesome and costly, and there is ample historical precedent for restrictions on deposits and international capital mobility, albeit not usually in the nations claiming major money centers. Banks attempt to limit their sovereign risk exposure by establishing "sovereign lines" which limit the total they deposit in institutions in any one country.

The Eurodollar futures contract traded on the International Monetary Market of the Chicago Mercantile Exchange is a cash settlement contract. This means that on the last day of trading the Clearing House takes the mean LIBOR for 3-months Eurodollar time deposit funds at the end of trading and at a random time within 90 minutes of the close of trading. The final settlement price is 100 minus the average of those prices, rounded to the nearest basis point (1/100 percent). The dollar value is $1 million times the resulting index.

It will be instructive to examine the methods for calculating interest on Eurodollars. It is assumed that the Eurodollar deposit is for $1 million, and for an original maturity of three months.

A Eurodollar deposit with an original bank add-on interest rate yield of nine percent has a maturity value given by

$$V = (\$1,000,000)(1.0 + 0.09/4) = \$1,022,500$$

The corresponding discount rate is given by

$$(1.0 - x(90/360)(\$1,022,500) = \$1,000,000$$

and x is 8.80%. The functional relationship between the bank add-on interest rate i_A and the corresponding discount i_D rate is given by

$$i_A = (4)[(1.0/(1.0 - i_D/4) - 1]$$

The inverse function is

$$i_D = (4)[1 - (1.0/(1.0 + i_A/4)]$$

By calculating the discount equivalent of the Eurodollar add-on rate, one can make a direct comparison to the T-bill contract, which is quoted on a yield basis. Since CD futures are also quoted on an add-on basis, the above formulas are useful for finding the discount rate equivalent on CDs also.

Eurodollar futures have recently grown significantly in importance. In 1982 they accounted for less than 6 percent of financial futures open interest. In 1984 the percentage had grown to 20 percent. This growth may be atrributed to the unique role that this contract plays in the risk management activities of those firms which operate and invest internationally. Innovative applications, such as combining a gold futures spread trade with a Eurodollar futures contract, provide for a futures portfolio that possesses characteristics similar to other interest rate futures. Eurodollar futures may also be used in combination with foreign currency futures contracts to simulate Eurocurrency hedges in those currencies. Given the growing awareness of the usefulness of Eurodollar futures their niche would seem secure over the near future.

CONCLUSION

As a group, financial futures have met with great success since they were first introduced. Their volume and open interest at this writing suggest financial futures will remain a source of strong trading activity as long as interest rates remain volatile and there prevails a climate of economic uncertainty.

The specific contracts that will be traded in a decade hence will be the products of evolution—a true survival of the fittest in the sense that only those that meet the hedging and speculative demand of the public will be around. New contracts can always be designed, or old ones modified as the need arises.

If economic uncertainty and the concomitant interest rate volatility continue, as they have from the 1970s to this time, it is likely that trading volume will continue to increase. Potential hedgers who, through ignorance, inertia, or regulatory constraints have not yet embarked on hedging programs will have to learn to do so to meet competition from those who have. Speculative interest in these markets too is likely to continue to grow, as the greater leverage and other advantages continue to attract the attention of traders.

Notes

[1] Because different types of quotes are used for T-bills than for T-bonds and notes, this example assumes rates to be stated on a yield equivalent basis.

[2] To determine how effective a hedge would likely be if held over a relatively long period but not maintained until the futures contract expiration is an empirical question. The effectiveness depends on the slope coefficient in regression of the cash instrument price on the futures contract price. This is discussed in the chapter on hedging.

[3] The concept of duration was developed by Macaulay. See Frederick R. Macaulay, *Some Theoretical Problems Suggested by the Movement of Interest Rates, Bond Yields and Stock Prices in the United States Since 1856* (New York: National Bureau of Economic Research, 1938).

[4] For those who have programmable calculators procedures are available or can be developed. For example, owners of Texas Instruments TI-59 can order the program "Time Measures in Investment Analysis," which this author wrote.

[5] Related to the concept of hedging is that of "immunization." Credit for the initial concept of immunization is generally awarded to Redington. See F. M. Redington, "Review of the Principles of Line-Office Valuation." *Journal of the Institute of Actuaries,* **78** (1952): 286–340.

11
Currencies

It has become customary in discussions of currencies and exchange rates to begin with an early history of money and then take the reader up to the present era. This chapter's treatment will break with that custom. Discussion will be focused on those salient features of the current world monetary system that are most pertinent to hedgers and speculators.[1]

On August 15, 1971 President Nixon suspended the United States obligation to exchange gold for foreign holdings of dollars. Despite efforts to put the shattered system of fixed exchange rates back together, such as the Smithsonian Agreement of December 1971, the world was set on a course toward flexible or "floating" rates. Following the brief American closing of foreign exchange markets on March 1, 1973, the era of fixed exchange rates was officially over.

Under the fixed exchange rates of Bretton Woods the U.S. dollar was priced in terms of gold, and other currencies in terms of dollars. Therefore, each currency was priced in terms of each other currency through parities with the dollar. Under floating exchange rates a currency's price in terms of other currencies is based on supply and demand, and on anticipated changes in fundamentals affecting supply and demand. Under floating rates, arbitrage opportunities can develop in which currency A is worth relatively more units of currency B than it is of currency C, given the exchange rate of B for C. Risk free profit can be made by nimble traders who exchange currency C for currency A, then currency A for currency B, then currency B for C to complete the circle.[2]

Countries have strong interests in the exchange values of their currencies vis-à-vis others. High relative values make imports relatively cheap but simultaneously make it difficult for local producers to sell in foreign markets. Low relative values help domestic producers to sell in foreign markets but raise the costs of imported goods. This tends to create a dilemma for national monetary authorities, to the extent they have the freedom to move their currency's value either up or down in relation to others.

Petroleum is priced in U.S. dollars. Thus, countries that could stand to benefit by the increased export sales elicited by reduced exchange value of their currency may find that the increased cost of imported petroleum more than offsets the beneficial effects of the lower currency value. Yet countries that experience increased exchange value of their currencies may find that the relatively lower price of imported petroleum does not compensate for the decline in exports experienced.

The United States in the first half of the 1980s had the highest *real* interest rates in its history.[3] Not only were real U.S. rates high in an historical sense, more importantly, they were much higher than those of other nations. There were several effects of high U.S. rates.

Foreign capital flowed into the United States to earn the higher rates of return available on dollars. This meant that foreign currencies were used to buy dollars, bidding up the price of the U.S. dollar and reducing the relative values of foreign currencies. Initially, the inflow of capital helped to fund the massive and rapidly expanding U.S. federal government's budget deficit.[4]

The high U.S. dollar value made it difficult for domestic manufacturers to sell their products in foreign markets; they were relatively too expensive. Decreased wage and material costs did not develop to offset the higher dollar exchange value.[5] Companies dependent on export markets for their profitability were brought to a state of economic distress.[6]

High real U.S. interest rates also made it more costly for domestic firms to raise capital than their foreign competitors. Higher capital costs tend to favor investment projects offering an early payoff to the detriment of those promising a much larger but deferred payoff. To the extent that these latter investments contribute to an overall synergism within the economy, with technological ripple effects,[7] the effect of high interest rates may be to undermine long-run competitiveness of U.S. industry.

The deleterious effects of high real U.S. interest rates and an immense and growing federal deficit portend continued uncertainty in foreign exchange markets. The industrial nations of Europe need to earn foreign exchange to pay for the petroleum and other imported goods they must buy. The United States cannot let its interest rates delcine sharply or there will be an exodus of capital and a precipitate decline in the dollar's exchange value. The conflicting interests of the United States and other nations in an era of economic recession promote a climate of exchange rate instability.

It is doubtful that anyone fully understands the consequences of the huge U.S. budget deficit, or the trade deficit.[8] But it is probably safe to say that economic uncertainty will be with us for the indeterminate future, and consequently exchange rate uncertainty.

Prior to the increase in real U.S. interest rates, the period of floating exchange rates following 1973 was characterized by different rates of monetary inflation in different nations. Without the discipline imposed by gold backing and fixed exchange rates, governments took the path of least political resistance in their monetary and fiscal affairs. As a consequence, all countries experienced monetary inflation[9] which contributed to cost-push[10] price inflation. But, because the rates of monetary inflation were different, currency exchange values shifted. Rates of monetary inflation remain different, and for that reason currency exchange rates will remain volatile.

EXCHANGE RATE RISK

A U.S. exporter selling to West Germany would like to be paid in dollars because wages, salaries, taxes, dividends, and so on must be paid in dollars. The West German importer would like to pay in Deutschemarks (D-marks), because the value of the dollar in terms of D-marks could increase between the time the sale is made and the time payment is required. Thus, either the exporter or the importer faces a currency risk, depending on whether payment will be in U.S. dollars or D-marks.

Let us assume that the U.S. exporter agrees to accept payment in D-marks. It is now February 15, and the goods sold will be delivered in August, with payment due on August 15. On February 15 the dollar is worth 2.85714 D-marks, equivalently the D-mark is worth $0.35. By the time August 15 rolls around, the dollar will likely be worth either more D-marks or less. If the dollar is worth more, the U.S. exporter will experience a loss. If the dollar is worth less, the exporter will enjoy a gain. Let us further assume the amount of money involved is, on February 15, $10 million or DM28,571,428.57. The invoice will be for this second amount.

If on August 15 the dollar is worth 3.33333 D-marks ($0.30/D-mark) the exporter will receive DM28,571,428.57 which he or she will exchange for $8,571,428.57. Under this scenario, the exporter loses the difference between $10,000,000 and $8,571,428.57, or $1,428,571.43. Such a loss might wipe out the exporter's entire profit margin. This is a risk that the exporter likely will choose to pass on to others, even though by doing so he forgoes the chance to make a windfall gain.

HEDGING THE RISK

Our exporter has two main ways to hedge the currency risk: (1) Sell a forward contract for the DM28,571,428.57, deliverable August 15, or (2) Sell September futures contracts for D-marks[11] in an amount matched to the cash requirement.[12] We will assume that the optimal hedge ratio is 0.95, so that 0.95 futures contracts will be used for each DM125,000 (the standard contract size) in cash to be hedged. In the present case 222 contracts will be sold February 15.

On February 15, 222 September D-mark futures contracts are sold at a price of $0.37/D-mark. Required margin for the exporter, as a *bona fide* hedger, is $250,000. This is borrowed from his or her bank at 12 percent annual interest. If on August 15 the September futures price is commensurate with the spot rate, it may be at $0.305/D-mark. On 222 futures contracts, each for 125,000 D-marks, the exporter makes a profit on the hedge of

	$222 \times 125{,}000$ ($0.370 - $0.305)	
Less:	$250{,}000 \times (6/12) \times 0.12$	Interest on margin loan
Less:	50×222	$50 commission per contract
	$1,777,650.00	Net Gain on futures
Less:	$1,428,571.43	Loss on cash position
	$349,078.57	Net profit on the hedge

Hedges cannot be expected to turn a net profit, but only to reduce losses that would otherwise be incurred. But in such cases as this example, the change in the basis (futures price less spot price) may actually produce a profit. Let us take another look at the hedge, this time in basis terms:

Basis on 2/15: $0.370 - $0.350 =	$0.020	
Basis on 8/15: $0.305 - $0.300 =	$0.005	
Basis change:	$0.015	
Profit on basis change:	= $0.015 \times 222 \times 125{,}000	
	= $416,250.00	
Less:	$ 15,000.00	Margin interest
Less:	11,100.00	Commissions
	= $390,150.00	Net profit on basis change

The difference between the basis change profit of $390,150.00 and the net profit on the hedge of $349,078.57 is $41,071.43. This amount is equal to the loss on the DM821,428.57 difference between the cash position and the 222 futures contracts used in the hedge. At February 15 the dollar value at the spot rate is $287,500.00. On August 15 it is $246,428.57, accounting for the difference of $41,071.43.

With $10,000,000 worth of D-marks to hedge our exporter might have used the interbank *forward* currency market, where the usual transaction is for a million currency units minimum. If our exporter had taken this alternative, DM28,571,428.57 would have been sold on February 15 to a bank, for delivery on August 15 at a specific exchange rate. On August 15, the DM payment would have been turned over to the bank. This is a rather uncomplicated process, provided the hedger has a large enough currency position to hedge. But one must keep in mind that there is an implicit cost in the forward currency market which, while providing profits to the banks, may make the forward market more costly than the futures market. By using the forward market hedgers may exactly match their spot and futures positions and thus eliminate their currency risk exposure, but they pay a price for this protection.

Interbank forward contracts, because they are customized, can be written for any amount and delivery on any future date, though in practice the amount is generally for a minimum of a million currency units. Forward contracts can also be written for a greater variety of currencies than there currently is futures trading. And, the interbank forward market is not limited by the few trading hours that the futures market is open, though this should present no particular problem to most hedgers.[13]

Whether at a given time one should hedge using futures or should use a forward contract cannot be answered in advance. At times, one may be more cost effective than the other. At other times, the cost effectiveness will reverse.[14] The interbank forward and currency futures markets should be viewed as complementary by hedgers. For each hedging situation they will have to decide which offers the better deal at the time.

FUTURES TRADING

Currently there is nominally futures trading in eight foreign currencies on the International Monetary Market (IMM) of the Chicago Mercantile Exchange. But two of the eight currencies (French franc and Netherlands guilder) seldom have any open interest. There has been discussion of trading the Italian lira, but to date no trading has taken place. The actively traded currency futures at this time are the British pound sterling, the Canadian dollar, the West German mark, the Japanese yen, the Mexican peso, and the Swiss franc. Open interest in the peso tends to be far less and margin requirements greater because of its relatively higher volatility than in the other actively traded currency futures.

For all currency futures traded on the IMM, the delivery months are March, June, September, and December. The contract size and price limits vary between currencies. The contract sizes are: British pound, 25,000; Canadian dollar, 100,000; D-mark, Dutch guilder and Swiss franc, 125,000; Japanese yen, 12.5 million; Mexican peso, 1 million; French franc, 250,000. A limit move in any one day is from $750 to $1500 depending on the currency.

Speculators may find interesting and profitable opportunities in currency futures. Spreads between the D-mark and Swiss franc or between the British pound and Japanese yen provide especially promising prospects to those who are adept at forecasting the relative inflation rates and monetary activities of countries or the effect of changing petroleum prices on currency values. Traders should beware, however, that the best laid plans can go awry if the central bank of one country whose currency is in a spread intervenes unexpectedly while the other does not. Spreads between the D-mark and Swiss franc in 1977–1978 were affected by just such a development.

Figures 11.1 through 11.5 contain a recent history of the prices of futures in the British pound, Canadian dollar, Deutsche mark, Japanese yen, and Swiss franc.

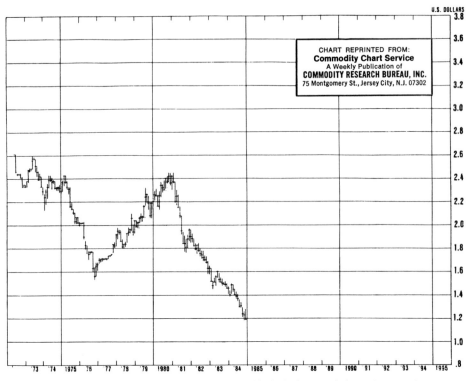

Figure 11.1. British pound, IMM, Chicago (monthly high, low, and close of nearest futures)

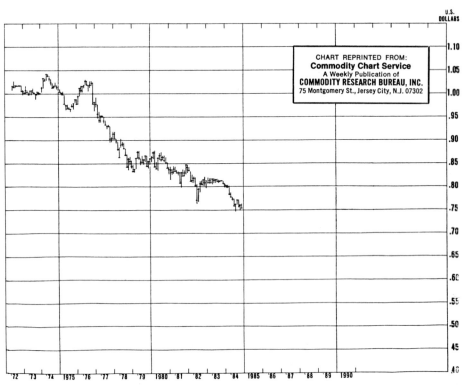

Figure 11.2. Canadian dollar, IMM, Chicago (monthly high, low, and close of nearest futures)

190

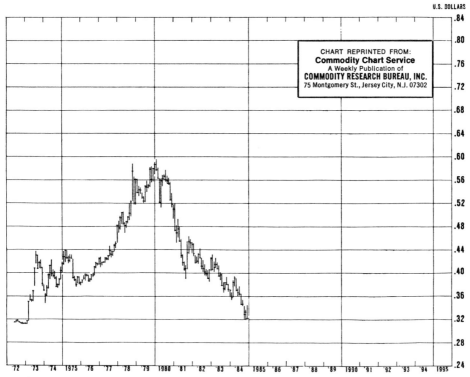

Figure 11.3. Deutsche mark, IMM, Chicago (monthly high, low, and close of nearest futures)

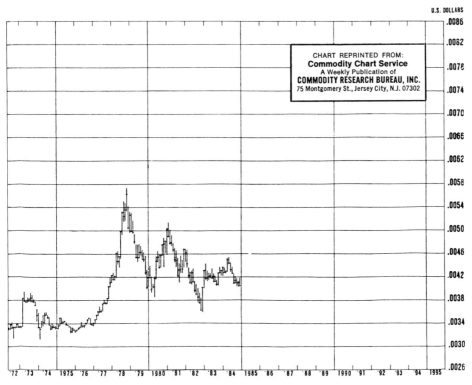

Figure 11.4. Japanese yen, IMM, Chicago (monthly high, low, and close of nearest futures)

191

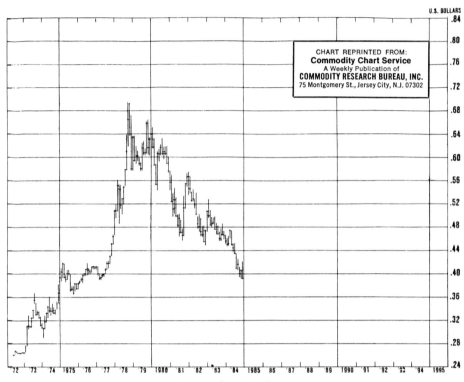

Figure 11.5. Swiss franc.

Notes

[1] For the history and detailed treatment of money and exchange rates see, for example, James E. Higgins and Allan M. Loosigian, "Foreign Exchange Futures," Perry J. Kaufman (Ed.), *Handbook of Futures Markets* (New York: Wiley, 1984): Chapter 47, or David K. Eiteman and Arthur I. Stonehill, *Multinational Business Finance,* 3rd ed. (Reading MA: Addison-Wesley, 1982).

[2] Actually the trades will occur more or less simultaneously. Such arbitrage opportunities can and do develop. However, the actions of arbitrageurs quickly move supply and demand back into equilibrium.

[3] The real interest rate may be defined as the nominal interest rate minus the rate of inflation. Historically, the real rate has averaged between 2 and 3 percent.

[4] Over the longer run the increased debt principal tends to increase the deficit, however, as interest accrues on it.

[5] The institutional realities of labor union contracts and the reluctance of suppliers to reduce prices would in any case tend to prevent costs from declining.

[6] Caterpillar Tractor Corporation, for instance.

[7] Such as the government financed U.S. space program had.

[8] The high dollar value has caused the U.S. imports to greatly exceed exports.

[9] Monetary inflation, or just plain "inflation" refers to increased money supply.

[10] As opposed to demand-pull price inflation, cost-push inflation sees higher prices accompanied by *decreased* output and employment.

[11] The contract month used will normally be that expiring just beyond the cash settlement date of the export transaction.

[12] The exporter will need 228.57143 contracts for a 1/1 hedge, however the optimal match, or *hedge ratio* will normally be less that 1/1.

[13] In the forward market, the performance of the bank's obligation to buy or sell on the due date depends solely on the bank's ability to do so. In the futures market, the exchange guarantees all trades.

[14] Some illumination on this subject is provided in a doctoral dissertation written under this author's academic supervision.

12
Index Futures

In early 1982, futures contracts on stock indices began to trade in the United States. The first index future to trade was the Kansas City Value Line Index contract (KCVLI). This was soon followed by the Chicago Board of Trade (KCBT) Standard and Poor's (S&P 500) 500 Stock Index contract and the New York Futures Exchange New York Stock Exchange Index contract. Because it is not possible to deliver (or take delivery of) an index, these contracts are settled in cash.

Subsequent to trading in stock index futures, contracts have been proposed in such disparate indices as the U.S. Consumer Price Index (CPI) and ocean freight-rate futures (in London). This contract is termed the Baltic International Freight Futures contract.

In principle, virtually any index may be traded as a futures contract. However, the long run success of any such contract is contingent on its usefulness to hedgers, and its acceptance and employment by them.

STOCK INDEX FUTURES

On February 24, 1982 the KCBT began trading in a KCVLI contract. Approval of this contract had been delayed for four years because of an intractable jurisdictional dispute between the SEC, which has authority over the stock markets, and the Commodity Futures Trading Commission (CFTC), which has authority over futures exchanges. New commissioners of both agencies were appointed in 1981, reached an accord, and the KCVLI contract was approved on February 16, 1982.

Shortly after approval of the KCVLI contract the CFTC approved trading of a S&P 500 Stock Index contract by the Chicago Mercantile Exchange. The KCBT sought an injunction to bar trading of other stock index futures for a year, but was not successful. Trading in the S&P 500 contract began on April

21, 1982. The KCBT claimed that the four-year delay in approving the KCVLI contract had compromised its competitive position and that a period of exclusive trading should be granted for it to recover its investment in development. Also KCBT suggested that, should the injunction not be granted, there would be a disincentive to other small exchanges to seek to trade innovative new contracts and thus less competition for the futures industry, concentrated in Chicago.[1]

Rationale for Stock Index Futures

Modern finance theory recognizes two different types of risk in returns from common stocks: "own" or "unsystematic" risk, and "systematic" or "beta" risk. Unsystematic risk in investor returns from any given stock is idiosyncratic, not market related. Unsystematic risk can be eliminated[2] by proper attention to portfolio selection in forming efficient portfolios.[3] Beta, or systematic risk, cannot be eliminated by portfolio selection. Systematic risk is that component of variance in any given security that depends on the market. Therefore, even an efficient portfolio—even the market portfolio, encompassing all securities—contains risk. If the market were to fall, even well diversified portfolios would fall because of their linkage to the market through systematic risk.

Stock index futures contracts provide a means for reducing systematic portfolio risk through hedging. A portfolio manager can thus reduce total risk to an acceptable residual by combining *short stock index futures* positions with the *long cash portfolio* positions they hold in a hedge.

It should be noted, however, that a portfolio hedged with stock index futures, while offering protection against market declines, also puts a ceiling on profits. In other words, by hedging a portfolio with index futures, the portfolio manager avoids downside market risk but simultaneously sacrifices upside capital gains. For this reason portfolio managers may wish to restrict their use of stock index futures to those times in which they feel a steep market decline to be most probable. However, while a fully hedged portfolio is stripped of its capital gains potential, dividends nevertheless would flow as they would without the hedge.

Stock index futures contracts are cash settlement contracts. The settlement "price" at contract expiration is the spot index value at that time. Thus the futures value must converge to the spot index value times the dollar multiplier, which is a constant.

Although the hedging applications of stock index futures provided the compelling rationale for their approval for trading,[4] they may be used by investors as surrogates for holding cash stock portfolios (albeit without dividends, but also with minimal margin requirement) and by speculators. A study by Herbst and Ordway demonstrates how stock index futures may be used with

U.S. T-bills to create an investment portfolio (with two items in it) that offers risk-return advantages over those available from a diversified stock portfolio.[5]

Stock index futures have been controversial since before they began trading, and the controversy has not abated.[6] Some are concerned about the possibility of adverse effects on the nation's equity markets; others appear to be concerned for more personal reasons related to their livelihoods; still others due to an apparent antipathy to speculation of any kind.

Currently stock index futures contracts are taxed by the U.S. federal government in the same manner as other futures contracts. In the last days of the 97th Congress the Technical Corrections Act of 1982 was passed into law. It corrected or clarified some points of tax law, among them the tax treatment of futures contracts having cash settlement. The law provides that regulated futures contracts with cash settlement will receive identical tax treatment to futures contracts requiring delivery of physicals.[7] Investors and traders should be aware that tax laws may be changed, and should not assume that those with conflicting interests will not mount assaults on the current law that may eventually succeed in changing it.

Three stock index futures contracts currently traded have many similarities. The KCVLI, S&P 500, and NYSE contracts are all valued at $500 times their index values, have minimum price changes of $25 (i.e., 0.05 × $500), and identical trading hours of 9:00 A.M. to 3:15 P.M. Central Time (10:00 A.M. to 4:15 P.M. Eastern Time). "Delivery" months are March, June, September, and December. The KCVLI contract's last trading day is the last business day of the delivery month, the S&P 500 is the third Thursday of the delivery month, and the NYSE is the day before the last business day of the delivery month. All three contracts are settled in cash on the business day following the last trading day.

In addition to the three contracts above, traded by competing exchanges, the CBT launched in 1984 its Major Market Index contract (MMI). The CBT's entry into the arena of stock index futures was delayed because of litigation with Dow Jones concerning the proprietary Dow Jones stock indices. The MMI contract is one-fifth the value of the other three stock index futures; the multiplier is $100 instead of $500. It trades from 8:45 A.M. to 3:15 P.M. Central Time. Delivery months are March, June, September, and December. The last trading day is the third Friday of the contract month.

The MMI is based on 20 stocks, 15 of which are also included in the Dow Jones 30 Industrials. To calculate the MMI one adds the prices of the 20 stocks and divides by the divisor value of 4.504832. Stocks included in the MMI are shown in Table 12-1.

The stock index futures contracts are highly correlated with one another. However, they are sufficiently different to provide interesting spread opportunities. The Value Line Index, for example, is a geometric mean while the others are arithmetic means. The stocks included in each are different; some

TABLE 12.1. CHICAGO BOARD OF TRADE MAJOR MARKET
INDEX COMPANIES

American Express	3M
American Tel & Tel (New)	Procter & Gamble
DuPont	Sears, Roebuck
Eastman Kodak	Standard Oil of California
Exxon	U.S. Steel
General Electric	Coca-Cola
General Motors	Dow Chemical
IBM	Johnson & Johnson
International Paper	Mobil
Merck	Philip Morris

are biased toward the so-called blue chip stocks, others are more broadly based. To the extent the stock market is two-tiered, with blue chips moving differently than other stocks, spread profits may be sought by being short one index, long another.

OTHER INDEX CONTRACTS

Consumer Price Index

In 1983, both the MCE and the Cocoa, Coffee, and Sugar Exchange separately proposed to trade price index futures contracts. However, by early 1985 no trading had yet taken place in a price index futures contract.

A CPI contract would provide a means for hedging cost-of-living adjustments to wages, salaries, pension liabilities, and indexed insurance contracts. Research suggests that risks associated with unanticipated changes in the CPI cannot be effectively hedged with a portfolio of other futures contracts.[8]

Freight Rate Index

In the summer of 1984 the Baltic International Freight Futures Exchange announced a series of seminars on freight rate futures for the dry cargo market. The Baltic International Freight Futures contract is based on a historical index that has correlated well with freight rate movements in the international dry cargo market.

The Baltic freight contract is designed to provide hedging protection to shipowners, charterers, agents, and brokers. The unit of trading is the Baltic Freight Index, and contract value is $10 times the index. This is a cash settlement contract, with "delivery" months of January, April, July, and October.

The last trading day is the last business day in the delivery month, with settlement on the following business day. Minimum price movement is 0.5, equivalent to $5.00 per contract.

The Baltic Freight Index is based on a weighted composite of a specified number of dry cargo voyages. The weights are selected according to the importance of each voyage to the market and on historical factors. A panel of Baltic Exchange members each day submits the spot rate that each feels applicable to each voyage. The panel members do not know the rates provided by the others and the information is analyzed by computer to further assure impartial results.

Other Index Futures

The Commodity Research Bureau (CRB) commodity price index, based on 27 commodities (excluding financials, currencies, and stock index futures), will likely be traded as a futures contract, perhaps as early as the end of 1985. The CRB index is analogous to the S&P 500 stock index. The New York Futures Exchange reached agreement with the CRB to trade the index.[9]

A similar index, but one that includes financial futures has been proposed by the CBT.

Notes

[1] Detailed discussion of this and other litigation is provided by Neil S. Weiner, "Stock Index Futures: The Kansas City Board of Trade Value Line Average (VLA) Contract." Perry J. Kaufman (Ed.), *Handbook of Futures Markets* (New York: Wiley, 1984).

[2] In theory, assuming that risk-return parameters are stable.

[3] An efficient portfolio is defined as one with minimum variance for a given target return or, equivalently, one with maximum return for a given level of variance. There are many efficient portfolios.

[4] See for instance Neil S. Weiner, *The Kansas City Board of Trade—Value Line Average (VLA) Stock Index Futures Contract* Kansas City: The Board of Trade of Kansas City, Missouri, Inc., 1980.

[5] Anthony F. Herbst and Nicholas O. Ordway, "Stock Index Futures Contracts and Separability of Returns." *The Journal of Futures Markets* **4,** no. 1 (Spring 1984): 87–102.

[6] "Stock Index Futures Catch on and Spread, Touching Off Debate," *The Wall Street Journal,* April 5, 1983, p. 1.

[7] "Capitol Update." *KC COM-LINE* **3,** no. 1 (January 1983): 2.

[8] Anthony F. Herbst, "Hedging Against Price Index Inflation with Futures Contracts." *The Journal of Futures Markets* **5,** no. 4 (Winter 1985): 489–504.

[9] Ginger Szala, "King of Commodity Indexes Coming to Trading Floor." *Futures* **13,** no. 5 (May 1984): 64–66.

13

Agricultural Commodity Futures

As noted earlier, the first futures contracts ever traded were, undoubtedly, on a tangible, physical commodity. Some have suggested that futures trading in a form identifiable with its modern counterparts began in Japan several centuries ago, with rice the commodity that is said to have been traded. Whatever their early historical antecedents might have been, modern futures trading of grains began in mid-nineteenth century Chicago.

Chicago was, and remains, central to the agricultural trade of the vast grain producing center of the North American continent. It seems natural that a city figuring prominently in the cash, or spot market, for grains would be the locus of the first futures trading for those commodities.

As potential demand for additional agricultural futures contracts became evident to those with a vision of the future, the array of commodities on which futures are traded grew. And, those contracts that either outlived their usefulness or were ill suited to the needs of the respective trade faded from the scene.

Today we find futures trading on a broad spectrum of things besides the traditional agricultural commodities. The list includes not only industrial and precious metals, but financial futures and index futures on things as different as the stock market and ocean freight rates. And, while Chicago remains dominant in the grains, financial futures, and certain other futures contracts, New York has established a dominance in others. Smaller exchanges, serving specialized needs, continue to operate in other cities.

Until recent years, all futures contracts were for tangible, physical commodities. These commodities were fungible: suitable for standardization and grading, and deliverable. Now the distinction between futures on financials and intangibles and those on physical commodities has blurred. At this writing, the New York Mercantile Exchange (NYMEX) has a new potato futures contract that is settled in cash if held to expiration. Prior to this contract's debut, all agricultural futures were settled by delivery if held to expiration. Whether this will set a trend to be followed by other exchanges is unclear at this time.

This section covers those futures contracts that are on an underlying, physical, tangible commodity, whether settled by delivery or cash. Such commodities have mass, occupy space, and are generably storable—some for a short time, others indefinitely. We shall begin with domestic agricultural products.

GRAINS AND OILSEEDS

Futures contracts in recent years have traded on corn, wheat (several varieties), oats, barley, rye, rice (rough and finished), soybeans (and soybean oil and meal), rapeseed, flaxseed, and sunflower seed. Those that have maintained large trading volume over the years are corn, wheat, and soybeans. These are produced in vast quantities, and both producers and large-scale consumers have come to rely on futures markets for hedging. Indeed, it is hard to imagine how grain elevators could operate without futures markets, except with vastly greater capitalization or with some arrangement not consistent with the public interest or government noninvolvement.

CORN

The coarse grain that Americans call corn is the maize the native inhabitants were raising when Europeans first entered the Western Hemisphere. Modern hybrids bear little resemblance to the ancestral variety. The development of highly productive hybrid varieties of corn was a milestone in agricultural history. Were it not for hybridization, yields would be far lower and disease resistance less. Figure 13-1 displays the recent history of corn futures prices.

The proportion of corn production consumed directly by humans in the United States is small, even though more corn is raised than any other grain. But corn is the dominant ingredient in livestock feeding. Corn has also gained attention, since the Organization of Petroleum Exporting Countries raised petroleum prices in the early 1970s, for the ethanol (grain alcohol) that can be produced from it. And, corn is the source of a liquid sweetener that has seen increasing use as a substitute for sugar.

In the United States, corn is planted in late spring and harvested in late summer or early autumn, although some portion of the crop may be harvested much later.[1]

The crop year for corn in the United States begins in October and ends the following September. In the harvest period, prices tend to fall. When on-farm storage facilities are filled and excess is brought to elevators prices are pressed downward. Since wheat and other crops are harvested earlier, space may be at

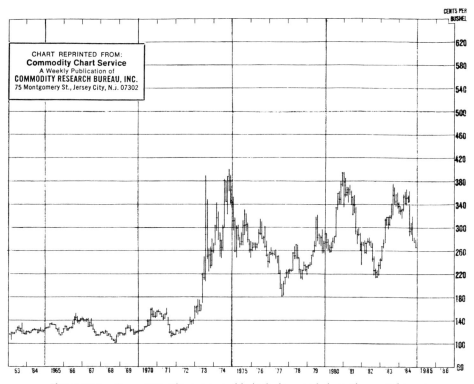

CENTS PER BUSHEL

CHART REPRINTED FROM:
Commodity Chart Service
A Weekly Publication of
COMMODITY RESEARCH BUREAU, INC.
75 Montgomery St., Jersey City, N.J. 07302

Figure 13.1. Corn, CBT, Chicago (monthly high, low, and close of nearest futures)

a premium when corn is brought to market, and the price commanded will consequently be less.

Almost 75 percent of U.S. corn production comes from Iowa, Illinois, Indiana, Minnesota, Nebraska, Ohio, and Missouri—the "corn belt" states. The United States is the world's leading corn producer. In the 1982 to 1983 crop year it accounted for 212.3 million metric tons (i.e., "tonnes"), some 48.3 percent of world production. The second largest producer (China) produced only 28.4 percent as much, though about three times as much as the third largest producer (Brazil).

Seasonally, cash corn prices usually are lowest in the October to December period, then rise to a peak in August to September. Futures prices tend to follow a similar pattern, but one that reflects expectations of lower cash prices during the harvest. (Prices of the nearest futures contract do not dip proportionately as low during harvest as do cash prices.)

Temperature and humidity are strong influences on corn yields. Too much moisture in the spring and plantings may be delayed. Delayed plantings may lower yields and, if the delay is significant, crop maturation may be jeopardized by early frost. If planting is delayed too long, alternate crops may be planted. Too little moisture in the summer and the plants will be stressed and yields lowered. Too little moisture and high temperatures during the critical "tasseling" period and yields may be drastically lowered.

Corn futures prices are affected not only by domestic conditions but also by those in other countries. Export demand for U.S. corn is affected by crop production in importing nations, such as the Soviet Union, and by production in competing exporting nations like Brazil and Argentina. Furthermore, production and carryover stocks of substitute crops can influence corn prices. For example, if wheat prices are low relative to corn, then some wheat will be substituted for corn on feedlots.

Government price support programs can influence corn prices in several ways. Acreage reductions imply reduced crops, though this effect may be diminished to the extent that more fertilizer is used and less productive land is removed from production.

Corn futures are traded in Chicago on the CBT (5000 bushel contract) and on the MCE (1000 bushel contract). Corn is well suited to the beginning futures trader because (1) it tends to be less volatile than many other commodities, (2) the trader is less likely to be whipsawed, and (3) it often follows sustained trends. Traders are well advised to be wary of crop forecast announcement dates because of the potential sharp price movements that often follow them.

SOYBEAN COMPLEX

Soybeans rank third in total U.S. planted acreage, following corn and wheat. Soybeans are legumes, not grains, and are termed oil seed due to the large proportion of oil that may be extracted from them. Figures 13-2 through 13-4 contain the recent price histories of soybeans, soybean meal and oil.

Soybeans have been raised for several millenia. Written reference dates back to the third century B.C. in China, where they were considered one of the "five sacred grains."

Varieties of soybeans number literally in the thousands. The number that is commercially useful in the United States is but a small fraction of the total. However, the vast number of varieties provides a genetic pool useful to plant breeders in developing new varieties with improved qualities. Soybeans have life cycles tuned to the length of the day; that is, tied to the amount of sunlight received each day. This growth characteristic, shared by certain other plants (such as chrysanthemums) is called photoperiodism. Because of this trait soybeans tend to blossom and mature at about the same time even if planted at different times. Even though their total growing seasons may be identical, varieties developed for southerly latitudes will not produce in the North, and vice versa.

In the United States, soybeans are grown in the cornbelt states, the Missis-

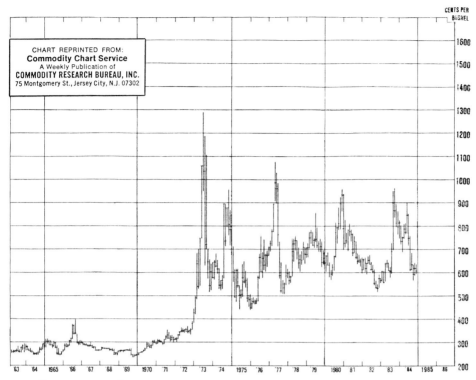

Figure 13.2. Soybeans, CBT, Chicago (monthly high, low, and close of nearest futures).

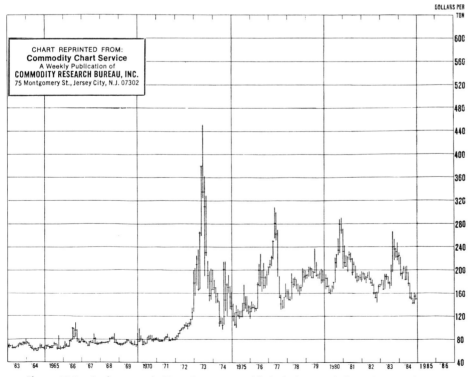

Figure 13.3. Soybean meal, CBT, Chicago (monthly high, low, and close of nearest futures).

205

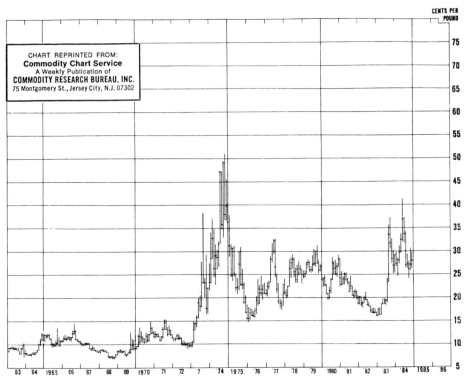

Figure 13.4. Soybean Oil, CBT, Chicago (monthly high, low, and close of nearest futures)

sippi River basin, and the South and Mid-Atlantic states. In the South, soybeans and cotton are alternate crops on much acreage. Over 60 percent of U.S. soybean output comes from the cornbelt states of Illinois, Iowa, Missouri, Indiana, Minnesota, and Ohio.

The United States is the largest soybean producer in the world, accounting for over 60 percent of the world total on average. Brazil, the second largest producer, accounts for about 15 percent. China, in third place, produces about 10 percent, and fourth place Argentina about 4 percent. Although soybeans were introduced into the United States long before, it was not until after World War II that they began to be produced as a major corp. Henry Ford is said to have seen the great potential of soybeans in the first half of the twentieth century. It was not until after his death, however, that his convictions regarding their role would be vindicated.

Soybeans themselves are the means to an end, because it is the oil and the meal they contain for which they are valued. A typical bushel of soybeans weighs 60 pounds. This total yields approximately 11 pounds of oil, 48 pounds of meal, and one pound of waste. Both oil and meal have many uses. Much of the oil is used for cooking or other human consumption. The meal is used principally as a high protein, low fiber ingredient in livestock feed. It contains approximately 44 to 49 percent protein.

Soybean oil, besides its uses in food products, is used for a wide variety of industrial products, including adhesives, inks, plastics, paints, antiknock fuel additives, and disinfectants. Soybean meal, beyond its use in livestock and poultry feeds, has industrial applications in adhesives, coatings, fertilizers, and fillers.

Futures Trading

In the United States, soybeans are traded on the CBT (5000 bushels contract) and the MCE (1000 bushel contract). Soybean meal (100 tons/contract) and oil (60,000 pounds/contract) are traded on the CBT.

Soybean futures contracts, reflecting the worldwide importance of soybeans, are traded in Hong Kong, Brazil, and Japan. Meal is traded in Paris and London; oil is traded in London.

Hedging

Soybean processors who separate the oil from the meal hedge their purchases of soybeans by being long beans and hedge their output by being short oil and meal. This set of positions (long beans plus short oil and meal) is termed a *crushing hedge,* and a processor may be said to "put on the crush." The crush spread protects the profit margin of processors.

When the processing margin on soybeans becomes unprofitable (under 15 to 17 cents/bushel in the mid-1970s) processors may keep operating at a reduced pace while using a *reverse crush spread,* which is the reverse of the normal crush spread. The combined actions of numerous processors would tend to cause price relationships to realign, with bean prices falling and oil and meal prices rising.[2]

Because of contract specifications, crush spreads are only approximate, but close enough. A 5000 bushel soybean contract, at 60 pounds per bushel, contains 300,000 pounds of soybeans. A yield of 11 pounds of oil from each bushel would be a total of 55,000 pounds versus the contract specification of 60,000 pounds. Meal per bushel of 48 pounds translates to 190,000 pounds, or 85 tons, versus a contract size of 100 tons. What this means is that a soybean processor would not have the same number of contracts in beans, oil, and meal if he or she wants a close match between soybeans and end-products. For example, 10 contracts of beans, with nine contracts of oil (540,000 pounds) and 12 contracts of meal (2,400,000 pounds) gives a closer match.

Factors Affecting Soybean Prices

Many fundamental factors affect soybean prices. Weather during the planting, growing, and harvest seasons is obviously an important factor. Availability and prices of competing commodities can cause marked changes in soybean prices. For example, in the early 1970s the sudden disappearance of the anchovy catch off Pacific South America caused a sharp rise in soybean prices. The reason this came about is that fish meal is a high protein ingredient in livestock feed, as is soybean meal.

Although the United States is the dominant soybean producer and exporter, production in other nations can nevertheless influence prices. Brazil, especially, has become an important producer, as has Argentina. While the United States share of world production is still over 60 percent, not long ago it was around 75 percent. As other countries increase their shares, they will become more important influences on price, and weather conditions there will have a greater impact on U.S. futures prices.

In the United States, crop reduction programs applied to wheat, cotton, corn, and other feedgrains have not been applied to soybeans. This has indirectly provided incentive to plant soybeans in place of other crops. In other nations, notably Brazil, government policies have directly encouraged farmers to plant soybeans.

Soybean Speculation

Speculation in soybeans can be extremely profitable or devastatingly costly. It is not uncommon for soybeans to traverse their daily range, as they did in the summer of 1983, from 30 cents above the previous day's settlement to 30 cents beneath it. That translates to a $3000 swing in equity per contract. Few traders can make a profit under such chaotic circumstances.

New futures traders would be wise to consider doing spreads in soybeans, rather than net positions, until they gain experience. Alternatively, they may wish to try to gain experience trading the smaller MCE contracts. Spreads may be more demanding in the sense that, although swings in trader equity tend to be less volatile, the trader may need to acquire more knowledge about soybeans (and end products) than otherwise to succeed. This knowledge may pay off later in better pure long or short plays.

Traders who are bullish on soybeans may wish to go long a nearby contract and short a distant one rather than have an outright long position. If they are correct in their assessments, they will make a profit, albeit smaller than on an outright position. However, the margin required to do a spread is less, and thus the percentage returns on margin deposits may be comparable.

WHEAT

If bread is the staff of life, then wheat is the tree from whence it comes. Wheat is used primarily to produce the flour used in bread, cakes, crackers, cookies, and pasta. It is also used to a lesser extent as a livestock feed ingredient.

There are two basic categorizations of wheat: spring and winter. Spring wheat is planted in the spring and harvested in late summer. Winter wheat is planted in the late summer or early autumn. It lies dormant during the winter, then grows quickly to maturity in the summer months. Winter wheat depends on a reliable occurrence of a protective cover of snow in the colder regions where it is grown. In milder regions snow cover is not required, but moisture must be adequate over the winter months. Figure 13-5 indicates where winter wheat is produced in the United States.

Within the two major wheat categories are many varieties. Each variety tends to be well suited to certain specialized uses. Hard red winter wheat is preferred for flour to be used in bread. Soft red winter wheat works well for cake and cracker flour. Durum wheat is used in pasta production. High protein white spring wheat is blended with lower protein varieties.

Unlike its dominant role in world corn production, the United States in the 1982 to 1983 crop year produced 15.9 percent of the world total, behind number one U.S.S.R. (17.9 percent) and not very far ahead of number three China (14.2 percent).

Although the United States is not the world's largest wheat producer, it *is* the world's largest wheat exporter. The U.S. share of world wheat and flour exports was expected to be just under 41 percent in 1982 to 1983. Canada, the second largest exporter, has roughly half the export volume of the United States.

Wheat prices are affected by weather in the planting and growing seasons just as those of any grain would be. However, because of the wide range of latitudes in the Northern Hemisphere in which wheat is grown, and the differences between spring and winter types, weather effects must be either very extreme or very prolonged to have much effect on overall supply. Then there is the additional supply potential of the Southern Hemisphere, which

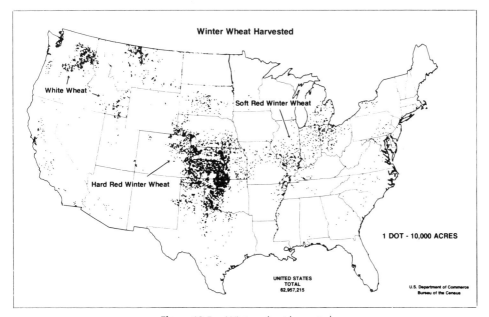

Figure 13.5.   Winter wheat harvested.

further tends to diversify the effects of weather on supply prospects and thus price.

Government price support and acreage reduction programs can affect the production of wheat and therefore the price. Because of the dominant role the United States plays in wheat export trade, any significant reduction is not likely to be immediately offset by other exporting nations. Because wheat can be stored for long periods under suitable conditions, carryover stocks are an important influence on total supply, and thus on price.

Soft red winter wheat is traded on the CBT (5000 bushel contract) and on the MidAmerica Commodity Exchange (1000 bushel contract). Hard red winter wheat is traded on the Kansas City Board of Trade (5000 bushel contract). This is the variety of wheat most often involved in export sales to the Soviet Union. Spring wheat is traded on the Minneapolis Grain Exchange (5000 bushel contracts and 1000 bushel job lots). Feed grade wheat futures are traded on the Winnipeg Commodity Exchange.

Wheat is another good choice for the neophyte commodity trader. In addition to straight long and short positions, there are numerous spread or straddle possibilities based both on different crop years within the same exchange's contracts and on spreads between Chicago, Kansas City, and Minneapolis. Recent price histories of CBT, KCBT and MGE wheat are shown in Figures 13-6 through 13-8.

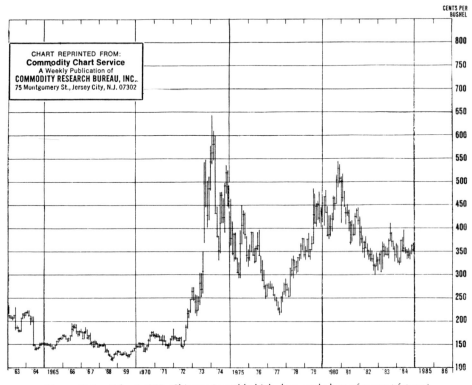

Figure 13.6. Wheat, CBT, Chicago (monthly high, low, and close of nearest futures)

Figure 13.7. Wheat, KCBT, Kansas City (monthly high, low, and close of nearest futures)

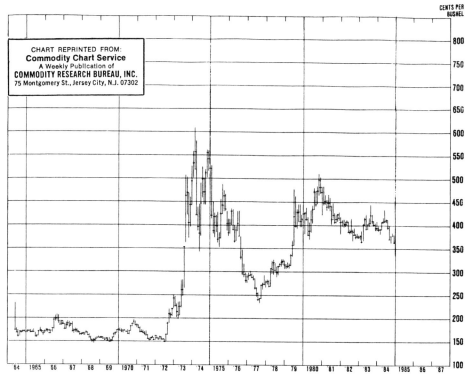

Figure 13.8. Wheat, MGE, Minneapolis (monthly high, low, and close of nearest futures)

OTHER GRAINS AND OILSEEDS

Oats

Oats are far less important in the United States than they were when horses provided the basic transportation. Still, the United States produces a significant amount of oats—about 20 percent of the world total. In oats production the Soviet Union is the clear leader, accounting for about 1/3 of the world total, with the United States in second place, and Canada and West Germany running neck-and-neck for a distant third place.

Oat futures are traded on the CBT and the Winnipeg Commodity Exchange. Oat futures tend to be less volatile than other grains and thus provide a good learning experience for new traders. Some traders are said to have developed strategies for making money by doing their active trading after the first notice day of a contract, a time when most small speculators tend to bail out. Figure 13-9 contains the recent history of CBT oat futures.

Barley

Barley was one of the first grains to be cultivated. Under cultivation in Egypt in the fifth millenia, B.C., barley's history goes back still further in Ethiopa and in Asia. Little barley is consumed directly by humans in the developed nations. In the United States, about half the crop is used for livestock feeding, for which high protein varieties are preferred. The rest is malt-

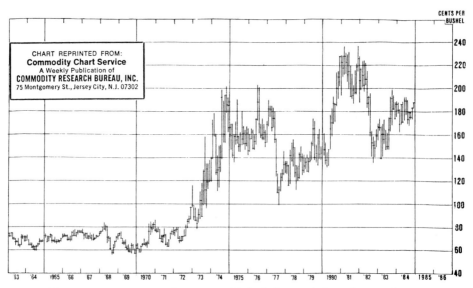

Figure 13.9. Oats, CBT, Chicago (monthly high, low, and close of nearest futures)

ing barley, which often sells for as much as a dollar premium per bushel over the feed varieties. Barley is an adaptable crop and may be grown under a wide range of climatic conditions.

The United States accounts for a small portion of world barley production, about 7 percent in 1982 to 1983. The Soviet Union accounts for about 25 percent, and Canada for about 8.5 percent.

Barley futures currently are traded on the Winnipeg Commodity Exchange.

Rye

Like barley, rye is one of the earliest cultivated grains, and it too can be grown under a wide range of climatic conditions. Rye is the hardiest of the grains, and can be grown further north than the others. It is grown on every continent but Africa.

Rye does not contain gluten, as wheat does. And, since gluten is necessary to produce raised breads, rye is mostly consumed as flour in a blend with wheat. Like other grains, rye can be used in livestock feeds. And, rye is used for some production of Canadian whiskies.

The Soviet Union is the world's largest rye producer, accounting for about 45 percent of the world total. Poland is in second place with about 25 percent of the total. The United States produces only some 2 percent, and Canada 3 percent.

Rye futures are traded on the Winnipeg Commodity Exchange.

Grain Sorghums

Grain sorghums provide an important coarse grain substitute for corn in regions of less moisture and greater heat because they are more resistant to draught. However, total production estimate for the 1983 to 1984 season of 483,056,000 bushels compared to 4204 million bushels of corn indicate that it is only about one-ninth as significant, though important enough to influence the price of corn. At this time there is no trading in grain sorghum.

Oilseeds

In the Northern Hemisphere there are oilseeds of significance other than soybeans: sunflower, cotton, flax, and rapeseed.

Cottonseed, oil, and meal are byproducts of the ginning of cotton. Cotton is raised for its fiber primarily.

Sunflower seed is an important source of edible oil in northern latitudes. The Soviet Union, United States, and China are the three largest world producers, accounting together for about half of world production. The Soviet Union alone produces about a third of world output.

The oil from flaxseed is the well-known linseed oil used for paints, varnishes, printers ink, and kindred purposes. The meal is used to some extent for livestock feeding, the plant fiber is the flax from which linen is woven. However, different varieties have been developed for oil production and fiber production. Canada is the world's largest flaxseed producer, followed by India, the United States, and the Soviet Union.

Rapeseed has become more important with the development of improved varieties of this member of the mustard family that are low in an undesirable oil constituent called erucic acid. Prior to the development of these low-erucic acid varieties, the oil was used primarily for its superior lubricating qualities. Nowadays the oil has become widely used in production of oleomargarine and other products for human consumption.

Canada produces about 25 percent of the world's rapeseed and exports more than half of what it produces. However, the percentage crushed domestically has been rising, and now is about 40 percent of production. China produces much more rapeseed than Canada, and India about the same as Canada. These nations, however, consume their entire domestic productions.

Futures trading in flaxseed and rapeseed is carried out on the Winnipeg Commodity Exchange. A sunflower seed futures contract is listed on the Minneapolis Grain Exchange, but currently it is inactive.

MEATS AND POTATOES

Meat and potatoes are traditional table fare in North America. But, besides going together on the supper table, they share another characteristic that distinguishes them in commodity futures trading: They are more perishable than other commodities traded as futures (i.e. they cannot be stored indefinitely).

Meats

Futures trading in meats is a relatively new development. Only since the 1960s has there been futures trading in meats or livestock. In the United States today, there are active contracts in port bellies, live hogs, feeder cattle, and live cattle. In the past, contracts have been traded in boneless imported beef, frozen turkeys, hams, and broilers.

Unlike those commodities that have traditionally traded as futures, meat and livestock are comparatively perishable. Frozen pork bellies require constant refrigeration, and live cattle and hogs must be fed and watered. Live animals do not remain constant over time; they grow older, perhaps larger, and not necessarily more desirable for their intended uses. Live animals also can become ill and veterinary care is an important cost item.

The success of the contracts in pork bellies, live hogs, feeder cattle, and live cattle stands as testimony to the feasibility of futures contracts on perishable commodities.

Pork Bellies. In September 1961 a futures contract in pork bellies was launched on the Chicago Mercantile Exchange. By 1964 the contract had become active, and after experiencing a bull market in 1965 the volume of trading and open interest have remained high. Pork bellies are a popular contract, whose volatility appeals to many speculators. Figure 13-10 contains a history of pork belly futures prices.

Each hog that is slaughtered yields two pork bellies, each generally weighing 12 to 14 pounds, for a total per animal of about 25 to 26 pounds. Pork bellies are the abdominal walls, with the alternating layers of muscle and fat so evident in the bacon that is produced by slicing them.

Futures contract specification is for 36,000 pounds of 12 to 14 pound pork bellies. Active delivery months are February, March, May, July, and August. Pork bellies put into cold storage prior to December are not eligible for delivery against any futures contract. This prevents a trader from retendering any pork bellies he or she took in one calendar year (before December) in the next year.

Factors Affecting Price. Demand for bacon is relatively price inelastic: Consumers purchase about the same quantities over a rather broad range of prices. For this reason, it is mainly supply that determines the market price. That is, the demand curve is relatively stationary, so that movement of the supply curve causes most price change.

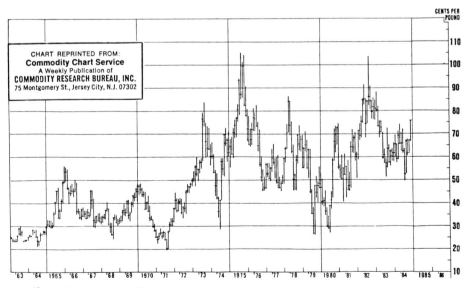

Figure 13.10. Pork bellies, CME, Chicago (monthly high, low, and close of nearest futures)

Pork bellies are produced as a byproduct of hog slaughtering. Hogs are slaughtered primarily because of the other meat products they yield. For this reason, supply does not respond much to changes in price.

The marketing actions of hog producers are strongly influenced by the cost of feed. Because corn is an important constituent of hog feed, the *hog/corn ratio* is a useful index. This ratio is defined as the number of bushels of corn it takes to buy 100 pounds of live hogs. It may be easily calculated by dividing the price of 100 pounds of live hogs by the price of one bushel of corn.

The condition of corn at harvest can influence marketing actions. If the corn is wet, farmers may prefer to feed hogs to greater weights, thus delaying marketing, rather than incur the costs associated with drying the corn for storage. Also, changes in the number of sows in the breeding stock can cause changes of as much as 2 percent in the immediate marketing period. Changes in the amount of pork bellies in storage also can cause changes in price.

Live Hogs. Trading in live hogs began in February 1966 on the Chicago Mercantile Exchange. By 1973 they had grown to equal pork bellies in importance.

The live hog contract is for 30,000 pounds on the Chicago Mercantile Exchange. A 15,000 pound contract is traded on the MCE. A price history is contained in Figure 13-11 for live hog futures.

Live Cattle. Futures trading in live cattle began in November 1964 on the Chicago Mercantile Exchange. This was the first futures contract of its type to trade. Up to its inception, futures contracts had existed only for inanimate, static materials that were relatively immutable in storage. Initially it was questioned whether or not satisfactory grading standards could exist for something as variable in quality and weight as live cattle.

Futures contract specification is for 40,000 pounds of liveweight steers. Contract months are February, April, June, August, October, and December. The MCE trades a 20,000 pound contract, with the same delivery months. Prices are quoted in cents per pound, with a one cent limit move from the previous day's settlement price.

Initially the packing industry strongly opposed futures trading in cattle. Despite the unanimous condemnation by the board of directors of the American Meat Institute, the contract was a success.

Factors Affecting Price. There are many suppliers of live cattle, but comparatively few buyers. Buyers for large grocery chains and large packing houses try to anticipate public demand and make their purchases accordingly. The U.S. public is not accustomed to buying frozen beef, and because it cannot be stored long, beef that is produced is soon sold.

Americans have a traditional taste for beef. To some persons, the words meat and beef are synonomous. Nevertheless, most consumers, even if they prefer beef, will switch to pork, poultry, fish, or other substitute protein when the prices of beef products are too high.

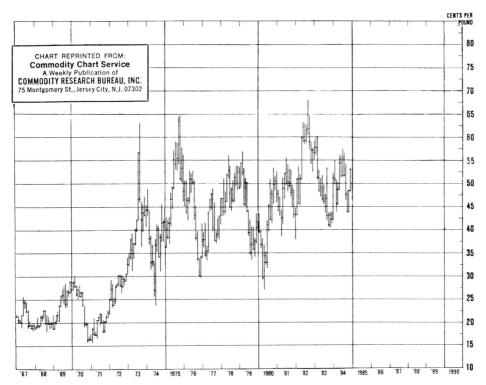

CENTS PER POUND

CHART REPRINTED FROM:
Commodity Chart Service
A Weekly Publication of
COMMODITY RESEARCH BUREAU, INC.
75 Montgomery St., Jersey City, N.J. 07302

Figure 13.11. Hogs (live), CME, Chicago (monthly high, low, and close of nearest futures)

Besides the prices of substitutes, the costs of feed and feeder cattle influence production and marketing decisions. So does the condition of grazing land, though consumers generally have learned to prefer the tenderness of grain fed cattle. Sudden runups in the prices of feed grains, such as in response to drought in the corn belt states, can cause liquidation by cattle feeders. Once in the pipeline, the beef produced by packers and large retailers must be sold. This has often resulted in plentiful supplies at low prices, followed by a period of lesser supply at higher prices.

The production cycle for cattle is lengthy. It takes three years from breeding of the cow to marketing of steak from the calf she produces. Cattle breeders must therefore try to anticipate prices further into the future than most other agricultural producers. When breeders begin holding back cows, heifers, and calves from slaughter, it is indicative of efforts to rebuild herd numbers.

Several cycles have been alleged to exist in cattle numbers and prices. Zimmerman found evidence of a 14-year cycle in cattle production from 1890 to 1951.[3] Bassie found a similar cycle in the number of cattle on farms from 1885 through 1955.[4] Cycles in cattle prices of 2 to 3 years (Hopkins, 1926), 5 to 7 years (Ezekiel, 1938), 7 to 18 years (Hopkins, 1926), 10 to 12 years (Ensminger, 1960), and other periodicities are cited by Wilson.[5] Figure 13-12 contains a history of live cattle futures prices.

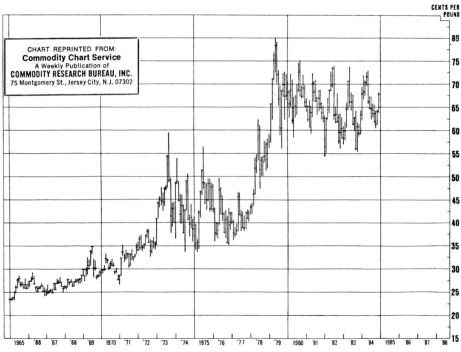

Figure 13.12. Cattle (live), CME, Chicago (monthly high, low, and close of nearest futures)

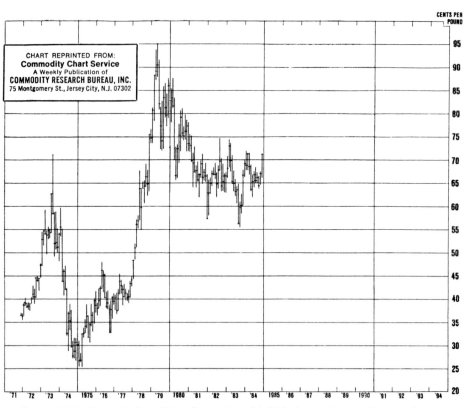

Figure 13.13. Cattle (feeder), CME, Chicago (monthly high, low, and close of nearest futures)

218

Feeder Cattle.   Feeder cattle are bought by feedlot operators for the production of finished cattle. A futures contract in feeder cattle is traded on the Chicago Mercantile Exchange. The contract is for 42,000 pounds in the trading unit and delivery months are March, April, May, August, September, October, and November. Figure 13-13 shows a history of feeder cattle futures prices.

The existence of feeder cattle futures, live cattle futures, and futures on feed grains provide producers with ample opportunities for hedging. For instance, a feedlot operator can, in principle, hedge his or her profit margin by appropriate short positions in live cattle combined with long positions in feeder cattle and grains.

Potatoes

Potatoes are raised in large quantities in many countries. However, because of their perishability (unlike most other commodities traded as futures), and low value to volume and weight, there is little world trade in unprocessed potatoes.

In the United States the western states have become more important in terms of potato production, though Maine and the eastern region remain important. About 70 percent of U.S. production is of russett varieties, most of the balance is round white potatoes.

Potato futures contracts of one specification or another have traded since 1931. Contracts on russets have failed because of various market factors, while contracts on round white potatoes have survived. Few futures contracts that have survived have encountered so much difficulty as have potato futures.

In 1976 there was a default by two western producers who held large short positions and could not deliver their russet potatoes against their open positions. Even if they had grown round white potatoes, they could not have been delivered against the futures contracts, which specified delivery *only* of production from a small region in the northeast. It is interesting that the brokerage firm handling their trading did not take action to avoid the default. Those interested in reviewing the details of the events surrounding the default should refer to issues of *Barron's* in the weeks following the event.

Default in 1976 was not the only scandal to hit the potato futures market. In 1979, 49 of the 57 contracts that were delivered did not meet contract grade specifications. The exchange responded by halting trading in the May contract and expanding the area of delivery to Long Island, upstate New York, and Connecticut. Despite these steps, trading volume has steadily declined.

To revitalize the trading of potato futures, the New York Mercantile Exchange initiated an innovative new contract in 1984. It is the first agricultural futures contract to be settled by *cash*. (With no delivery of physicals there can be no repeat of the 1976 default or the 1979 problem with unacceptable

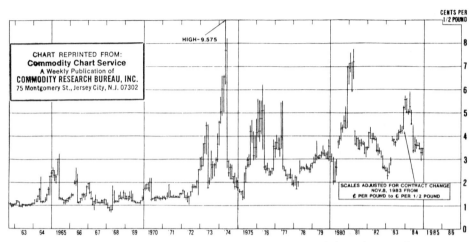

Figure 13.14. Potatoes, NYMEX, N.Y. (monthly high, low, and close of nearest futures)

grades.) The contract size remains at 50,000 pounds which, given the low price per pound, makes it a small contract. It should prove to be popular with new traders for this reason coupled with the fact that potato prices tend to be volatile. Figure 13-14 contains a price history of Maine potato futures.

Notes

[1] When autumn rains soaked fields in Minnesota several years ago, harvest equipment could not be used until the soil had frozen solidly.

[2] For a rationale for reverse crush spreading see Paul H. Cootner, "Speculation and Hedging." *Food Research Institute Studies Supplement* **7**, (1967): 102.

[3] Erich W. Zimmerman, *World Resources and Industries* (New York: Harper & Brothers, 1951).

[4] V. Lewis Bassie, *Economic Forecasting* (New York: McGraw-Hill, 1958).

[5] Louise L. Wilson, *Catalog of Cycles: Part I—Economics* (Pittsburgh: Foundation for the Study of Cycles, 1964): 13–17.

14
Metals

In contrast to agricultural commodities, the metals traded as futures contracts can be stored indefinitely without deterioration. And, some of the metals possess high value to weight and volume ratios. This makes them relatively inexpensive to store. These properties, combined with the fact that production of the rarer "precious metals" is not subject to sharp increases, had made them popular with those seeking protection against inflation.

Currently, futures contracts are traded actively in the United States on the industrial metals aluminum and copper, and on the precious metals gold, silver, platinum, and palladium. Still other metal contracts are traded on the London Metal Exchange, such as lead.

To some extent the line of demarcation between industrial and precious metals is less sharp than in past eras. The use of silver and gold in electronics and other industrial applications, and the use of platinum and palladium for catalysts, and so on, contributes to this.

UNITS OF MEASURE

Industrial metals are normally measured in pounds or kilograms. Precious metals are generally measured in troy ounces or in metric system units of mass. In Middle East gold *souks,* gold is measured by the gram. In the United States and many other English speaking countries it is measured by troy ounce. A troy (or apothecary) ounce is 31.103486 grams whereas an ordinary ounce (avoirdupois) is 28.349523 grams.[1] Therefore, 1 kilogram of gold contains 32.1507 troy ounces, and 100 troy ounces of gold contains 3.1103 kilograms.

GOLD

It is safe to say that no other metal has captured and held the attention of mankind over the ages to the extent gold has. For millennia, gold has served as both a store of value and a standard of value—a *numeraire* by which the relative values of all other things could be measured.

In recent times the official role of gold in national monetary systems has been legislated away. Yet, having removed gold from any official standing in their respective monetary systems, no country has so far shown any intention of disposing of its holdings. Indeed, if gold is unnecessary in modern monetary systems, then the reluctance to part with national hoards presents a paradox.

The main impediment to a gold currency standard would seem to be the opposition of politicians (and their ideological supporters among academic and government economists). They do not wish to be restrained in creation of money by the discipline imposed by a gold standard. But this same reason for opposition provides rationale for favoring a gold standard to those who believe politicians must be restrained in their propensity to expand the money supply. Without a fixed monetary standard, such as gold can provide, the money supply of a nation is subject to the wisdom—or whim—of politicians. Past performance does little to make one confident that this is better than the gold alternative.[2]

Those who argue that remontization of gold would most benefit South Africa and the Soviet Union—countries of which they do not approve—seem to overlook the fact that those countries benefit with or without monetization. Gold producers can sell their output for dollars or other currencies today just as they could exchange gold for dollars under a gold monetary standard with fixed exchange rates.

Figure 14-1 illustrates the relative production of gold by various countries. South Africa is by far the largest producer, accounting for almost half the world total. The Soviet Union is second, with about one-fifth of the world total. Canada is a distant third, with less than one-twentieth of the world total.

But gold production is only part of the story. Gold holdings are also important, and rankings based on them differ from those based on production. Figure 14-2 displays the relative official gold holdings of various noncommunist countries. By this measure, the U.S. government is clearly in first place, with over one-fourth of the world's above-ground gold holdings. West Germany is second with less than half the holdings of the United States, and France is third with holdings near those of West Germany. From there, holdings fall off sharply. South Africa, the largest producer, has an official above-ground stock of gold less than one-twenty-fifth that of the United States!

The primary uses of gold are for the fabrication of jewelry, official coinage (e.g., Krugerrands and Mapleleafs), industrial products, private coinage, and in dentistry. The industrial use of gold has increased with the growth of electronic computers, in which its corrosion resistance and conductivity make it ideal for such purposes as plating contacts.

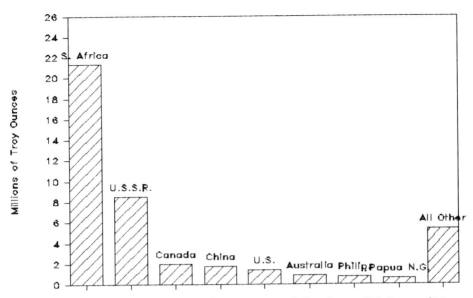

Figure 14.1. World mine production of gold (1982 estimated) Data Source: U.S. Bureau of Mines.

Gold remains the metal of choice for jewelry. In the United States most gold is marketed as 10 to 14 karat (24 karat is 100 percent pure gold), though legally the gold content is permitted to vary from the indicated percentages by a half karat by the U.S. Federal Trade Commission, and fabricators take advantage of this; most U.S. 14 karat gold is actually 13.5 karat, 12 karat is 11.5 karat, and so forth. In Europe and much of the rest of the world, there is a

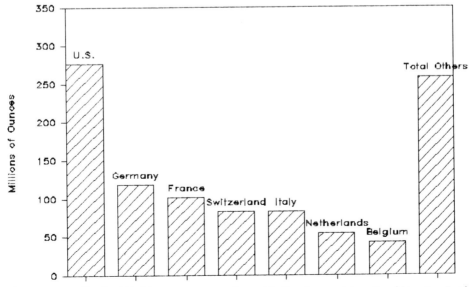

Figure 14.2. Official gold holdings (non-communist world). Data Source: International Monetary Fund.

decided preference for 18 karat gold (75 percent gold content). In the Middle East gold is purchased at least as much for its property as a store of value as for its decorative use. There is consequently little interest in low karat content jewelry or in gold plate. It is common to find gold sold by weight in some Middle East countries rather than by item price as in the United States and Europe. This means that the price of each item in a jewelry store can change from day to day. It also establishes a basis on which owners of gold jewelry can sell it back to the store when currency is wanted.

Factors Influencing Price

In the case of gold, supply tends to be inelastic with respect to price. A doubling of the price could not produce a sustained increase in supply because of the rarity of the metal and the limits of current technology for mining it. In fact, a sharp increase in price might lead to a decrease in supply. This perverse result can arise when producers shut down mining of high grade deposits to turn their efforts to lower grade deposits that had not been profitable to work at lower prices. To the producers, the high grade ore is like money in the bank (some would say better) because, if prices were to fall, it could again be mined profitably, following the closing of work on the low grade ores.

In some applications, such as electronics, demand too is relatively inelastic. Consumption changes little with price changes. It is only in those applications for which the gold content is significant that demand shows much responsiveness. In electronics, in gold coatings for office building window glass, and in gold brazing applications in the aerospace industry, the gold content is too small relative to the overall product value for a price change to have much effect on usage, especially since there are no effective substitutes for some of these applications.

The two factors most closely associated with price movements in gold are political and military conflict and inflation. Political changes can induce citizens to buy gold because of uncertainty about the continued value of their country's currency, or concern that more visible assets might either be taxed more heavily or confiscated. Military conflict can elicit the same responses. Widespread fear that price inflation will get out of control leads those with wealth to seek safe havens. Gold is thought by many to be well suited to the purpose of preserving purchasing power.[3] Its high value to weight and volume make it relatively easy to conceal or transport, and gold holdings are highly liquid—more so than many other physical commodities that might be held as inflation hedges. In times during which gold is preferred to other assets, its price is bid relatively higher as those assets are sold so that gold can be bought with the proceeds.

In the 1980s, a factor tending to complicate analysis of supply and demand fundamentals is the actions of Middle Eastern oil producing countries. When the price of petroleum was high, and revenues exceeded spending commitments, gold was purchased along with other investments that were made. But, when revenues declined from lower prices and decreased production of petroleum pressures mounted to sell off gold and other assets to cover fiscal deficits. The extent to which this has been or will become a significant factor has yet to be determined.

Futures Trading in Gold

From the 1930s to 1975 it was illegal for U.S. citizens to own gold and no futures traded in the United States. Today futures contracts are traded in the United States on the Commodity Exchange, Inc. (COMEX) in New York (100 oz. contracts), the IMM of the Chicago Mercantile Exchange (100 oz. contract), and the MCE, also in Chicago (33.2 oz. contract). Futures contracts are also traded on the Winnipeg Commodity Exchange, the London Gold Futures Market, Hong Kong, Tokyo, and Singapore. Contract size has varied from 1 kilogram to 400 ounces, with most trading today in the 100 ounces (i.e., "centum") contracts. In London gold is normally traded in 400 troy ounce bars. Gold literally trades 24 hours a day worldwide. Futures trading in gold is conducted in the United States just as it is for other physical commodities.

Futures trading in gold presents interesting opportunities for spread traders. Because storage costs are small relative to contract values, most of the price difference between a nearby delivery month and a distant month is due to interest expense—what it would cost to borrow to buy the nearby contract, then store it for delivery later against the expiring distant contract.

Traders should note that spreads in precious metals anticipating price changes are *opposite* to those in other physical commodities. For example, if a trader believed the price of wheat was going to increase, the appropriate spread would be long a nearby contract, short a distant contract. If the price of wheat were to rise, the nearby contract would have a more rapid price increase. In the case of gold, however, the appropriate trade would be short the nearby, long the deferred.[4] If the price of gold were to rise, the interest rate effect would cause the distant contract price to rise relatively more than that of the nearby. Additionally, circumstances that cause the price of gold to rise may also produce an increase in interest rates, thus compounding the effect. Figure 14-3 displays a history of COMEX gold futures prices.

The London Gold Market[5]

Since 1919, at 10:30 A.M. representatives from the five major gold bullion houses (Sharps, Pixley Ltd.; Johnson Matthey Ltd.; Mocatta, Goldsmid Ltd.; Samuel Montagu and Co., Ltd.; and N. M. Rothschild and Sons)[6] meet to determine the price at which they will trade gold that day. This is not trade in futures but trade in spot market physical bullion and forward contracts (the price of forward contract bullion is a function of the spot price and the interest

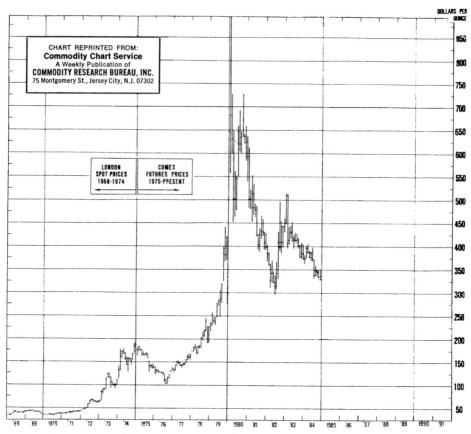

CHART REPRINTED FROM:
Commodity Chart Service
A Weekly Publication of
COMMODITY RESEARCH BUREAU, INC.
75 Montgomery St., Jersey City, N.J. 07302

LONDON
SPOT PRICES
1968-1974

COMEX
FUTURES PRICES
1975-PRESENT

DOLLARS PER OUNCE

Figure 14.3. Gold, COMEX, N.Y. (monthly high, low, and close of nearest futures)

rate plus storage costs). However, it provides a reference to futures markets around the world.

The meetings are held in a room on the ground floor of the Rothschild office building. The room is set up with a table, at which presides a representative of Rothschild's bullion department. At desks facing the table sit representatives of the four other companies. Each desk has a miniature British flag (Union Jack) and a telephone linked directly to that representative's home office.

The session begins with the Rothschild's representative suggesting a U.S. dollar price[7] he feels reflects trading activity earlier in the day. This price is communicated back to their home offices by each dealer in the room. The home offices in turn are linked by telephone and telex to their customers around the world.

Each representative, after conferring with his home office, tells the chairman (i.e., the Rothschild's representative) if he wishes to buy or to sell. Any dealer can call a "time out" by raising the miniature Union Jack on his desk and saying "flag up!"

If no representative offers gold for sale at the suggested price, the chairman raises the price. On the other hand, if there are no buyers, he lowers the price. It is the custom that sellers state the quantity of gold offered at the price for which they are willing to sell. Buyers, in contrast, do not indicate the quantity they are willing to buy.

Finally, when there are both orders to buy and orders to sell, the Rothschild's representative asks for the quantities desired at the currently set price. If the quantity offered at this price is adequate to cover all orders to buy, the price is "fixed" at the current level. Otherwise the price is moved up until enough quantity is offered to cover buy orders. As the price is raised, not only will more be offered for sale, less will be bought, and so the price will be "fixed" quickly.

At 3:00 P.M. the process is repeated for an afternoon fix. Even though the amount of gold actually traded at the morning and afternoon fixings is a small portion of world-wide trading, these sessions are very important. The London fixings provide reference prices at which many private transactions are concluded and a reference point to futures traders throughout the world.

In fall 1984, loan problems of Johnson Matthey Bankers shook the image of impeccable financial integrity enjoyed by the London group, even though the firm accounts for only about 15 percent of London gold market trade. By October 1, 1984 loss of confidence in the group had become a crisis:

> *Several Swiss and American banks threatened to suspend trading with the fix. Worse, they could have "called gold" (refused credit lines and moved to liquidate the bullion balances), leaving the London market up to 100 tons short, [according to] one market source.*[8]

Even though the Bank of England might have been able to find and provide that amount of gold to the group it is likely that much of London's share of the bullion market would have moved to Zurich and New York. According to one authority:

> *For all the prestige and clubby atmosphere the London fix is really just one more price during a continuous stream of prices around the clock and around the world. In the European time zone, for example, Zurich possibly equals London in its volume of gold bullion business.*[9]

Gold futures trading has not fared well in London in its brief history, perhaps because of the longstanding prestige of the physical bullion market in that city and the fact that the Commodity Exchange, Inc. (COMEX) in New York has performed satisfactorily. Of perhaps equal importance is that fact that futures trading profits in the United Kingdom are taxed at up to a rate of 60 percent.[10]

SILVER

In ancient Egypt silver is said to have been more valuable than gold owing to its relative scarcity, due to a lack of domestic deposits. Silver figured prominently in the U.S. monetary system until the 1960s. Its official price relative to that of gold was largely the effect of political considerations. Historically, silver has shared with gold the role of money. However, because of its greater value to weight and volume, gold was generally preferred. And, while a bimetallic standard prevailed in the United States, the price of silver was fixed to that of gold; gold was the standard of value, not silver.

The price ratio of gold to silver has received a good deal of attention as a benchmark for estimating over- or undervaluation of one metal to the other. According to data presented by Jastram[11] for England, the ratio was less than 11.0 in the sixteenth century, rising to a peak of 87.72 in 1944. Following World War II, the British ratio has been as high as 50.05 (1947) and as low as 19.25 (1968). The ratio has been volatile over the years. Popular notions regarding an intrinsic value for the gold/silver ratio today may have their origins in President Franklin Roosevelt's December 21, 1933 decree which set the official price at 1/16 ounce of gold.[12] The notion that the proper ratio is 20/1 likely has its origin in the value ratio of the $20 gold "double eagle" (containing about an ounce of gold) to the silver dollar (containing about an ounce of silver). Investors will be well advised not to put much faith in such ratio today, with both gold and silver prices free of government price support.

Although silver has been less important in international monetary matters than gold, it has been more important industrially. The largest use of silver in recent years has been in photography, which accounts for close to 30 percent of usage. Use in commemorative coins and privately minted medallions accounts for about 20 percent, silverware for just over 10 percent. Jewelry accounts for about three percent. The balance of usage is absorbed in electrical applications, appliances, refrigeration, electronic components, batteries, solder, and other industrial uses. Silver is the best conductor of electricity of the known metals although, unlike gold, it is subject to surface corrosion that renders it less useful for electrical contacts exposed to the air. Silver's superior reflectivity and freedom of color also makes it a superior material for construction of mirrors, in which it is sealed from air contact to prevent tarnish.

Silver consumption in most years since 1971 has exceeded production by significant amounts. Were it not for the large above-ground stocks of silver that were available to fill the deficit, the price would undoubtedly have found and maintained a higher level that it has. If this imbalance continues, it is inevitable that the price of silver will rise to ration demand. For many applications, there is no adequate, cost effective substitute. These applications will of necessity bid whatever price it takes to obtain the silver they require, especially so when the silver represents a minor fraction of the overall cost of their finished output.

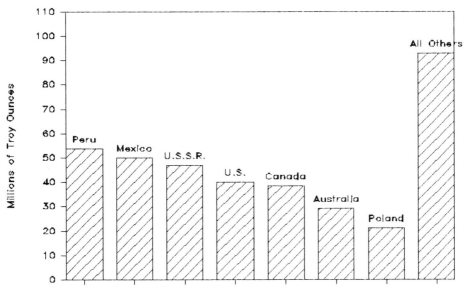

Figure 14.4. World silver production 1982. Data Source: U.S. Bureau of Mines.

Figure 14-4 displays estimated 1982 world silver production by country. Figure 14-5 displays consumption for the same year. It is clear that among the major producing nations, only the United States and Canada are also major consumers, though we cannot be sure of Soviet Union usage because of the secrecy with which they treat their statistics. India is a major consumer of silver, and also holds a large portion of the world's above-ground stocks. In that

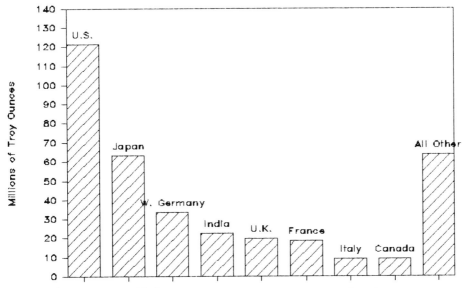

Figure 14.5. World silver consumption 1982. Data Source: Handy and Harman.

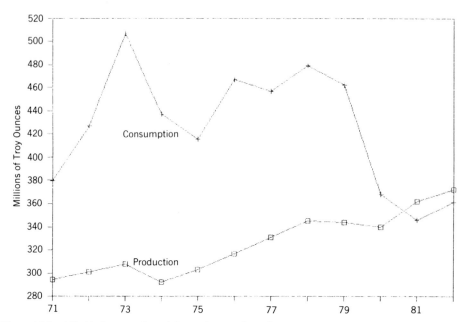

Figure 14.6. World silver supply and demand (1971 through 1982 est.). Data Source: Bureau of Mines; Handy and Harman Production and Consumption.

country, accumulation of silver is both traditional and popular among the populace. In the other major consuming countries, industrial usage is more prevalent, and for many applications silver has no acceptable substitute.

Figure 14-6 contains a plot of silver production versus silver consumption from 1971 through 1982 (estimated). In all but the last few years, characterized by recession in the developed nations, consumption has significantly exceeded mine production. If it were not for large above-ground stocks and recycling, upward pressure on price would have been far greater than it has.

Factors Influencing Price

The primary considerations for forming price expectations are (1) the demand-supply gap characterizing nonrecession years, and (2) technological advances that allow substitution of other materials for silver or recovery of silver that formerly had been lost.

Photography has been the largest area of use for silver. Until recently a large portion of the silver present in film and print paper emulsions was lost in processing, especially by smaller firms. This situation has been changing, however, and the proportion of silver recovered has risen significantly following the sharp price increases in the 1970s. And continued growth in video recording, which uses magnetic tape, but no silver, promises to cut into movie film sales and thus silver consumption.

In August 1981, Sony Corporation of Japan exhibited its "Mavica" electronic still camera, which required no film. The Mavica looks like an ordinary 35mm single-lens reflex camera. But it contains a compact magnetic disk and a special device that records images onto the disk just as a video cassette recorder does on video tape. In early 1982 both Sony and Matsushita introduced new and improved print making machines to overcome the relatively poor quality of the initial version. In addition to the ability to have prints made from the magnetic disk the camera user can view pictures on a television set after they have been taken, and can either store the disks or reuse them. Improvements continue to be announced. In November 1982 Toshiba revealed a camera with a larger format; in July 1983, Nippon Hoso Kyokai and Konishiroku Photo Industry Company revealed prototypes they jointly developed that record *digital* pictures on random access computer memory within a still camera. Not to be outdone, Hitachi disclosed in November 1984 a still camera and color video copier. In 1985 the main impediment to immediate commercialization appeared to be the high price at which the manufacturers believed that retail price would have to be set.[13] It is almost assured, however, that technological improvements will reduce the price to the point where such cameras will eventually provide significant competition to conventional still photography.

As other industrial usage of silver continues to expand, the demand-mine production gap should eventually cause the price of silver to rise to a higher equilibrium level. How long this will take depends on both the size of aboveground silver stocks that can continue to fill the gap and technological advances that will either allow increased recovery, reduced usage, or substitution of other materials.

Futures Trading in Silver

Silver futures are traded on COMEX in New York (5000 oz. contract), on the CBT (1000 oz. contract) and the MCE in Chicago (1000 oz. contract). Futures are also traded on the Winnipeg Commodity Exchange and on the London Metal Exchange. Trading on all but the London Metal Exchange is conducted in the same manner as other North American futures contracts with set delivery months and continuous trading between exchange opening and closing each day. Figure 14-7 contains a price history of COMEX silver futures.

London Metal Exchange Silver Trading[14]

London Metal Exchange (LME) silver is traded with quotes in pounds sterling per troy ounce. Prices are published only for cash, three months forward, and seven months forward on any given day. However, any day up to seven months forward may be traded.

On the LME, dealers sit in a circle called a "ring." Trading starts at 12:05

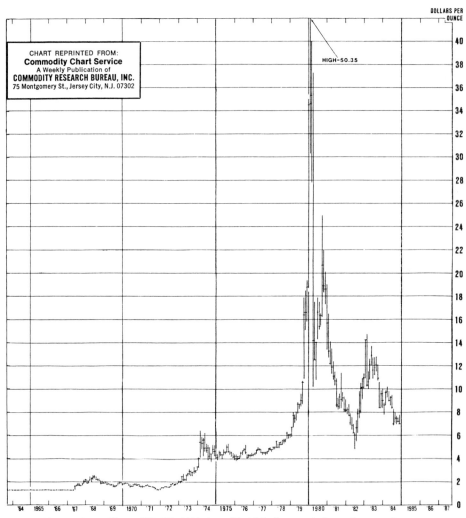

Figure 14.7.   Silver, COMEX, N.Y. (monthly high, low, and close of nearest futures)

P.M. daily. Dealers call out their buy and sell orders for precisely 5 minutes. This process is repeated for five metals: silver, copper, lead, tin, and zinc. Following the calling out of buy and sell orders, there is a 10 minute recess in which the dealers can call their home offices.

After the 10 minute recess, the process is repeated. At the end of this second call a "fixing committee" comprised of three members meets and determines four prices for silver which it announces: (1) cash price, (2) settlement price, (3) three months forward price, and (4) seven months forward price. The committee's prices may be challenged by any exchange member who thinks they do not adequately reflect the activity of the session. If there is no challenge to the committee's prices, they are considered official. The entire proceeding is referred to as the *first session,* or *morning session* (though it proceeds past 12 P.M.).

Later in the day the process is repeated for an afternoon fixing. The afternoon prices are unofficial even though the volume of trading may be greater than the morning session.

At the end of both the morning and afternoon fixings, *kerb* or *exring* transactions occur. For dates other than cash, three and seven months forward, the *prompt date* price may be calculated by extrapolation from the current, or cash date. To perform this extrapolation one first subtracts the cash price from the three month forward price. This yields the total carrying charge for three months. The daily carrying charge is obtained by dividing this difference by the 90 days in three months calendar time. Multiplying the number of days from the current, or cash date to the prompt date and adding to the cash price yields the prompt price.

PLATINUM AND PALLADIUM

Platinum and related metals in what is termed the "platinum group"[15] have many desirable physical and chemical properties. These properties, combined with their rarity, makes them valuable. Although they are often termed precious metals, they may with equal (and perhaps greater accuracy) be called strategic industrial metals.

Platinum (and its near relatives in the platinum group) has great corrosion resistance, exceeding even that of gold. It is malleable and ductile and possesses catalytic properties that make it useful in petroleum cracking, production of sulfuric acid, and other chemical processes. These same properties have brought platinum (and palladium) into use in catalytic converters for automobiles, which in the United States is today the most important use.

The high melting points of platinum and its relatives increase their value in modern applications, although before the modern industrial era this property detracted from their usefulness because of the difficulty it presented (along with their relative hardness).

Platinum has not enjoyed much use as a monetary metal, even though it was used in the coinages of Armenia and Czarist Russia. In the era of its use in coins, platinum was not held in as high a regard as today because there was less application for its valuable chemical and physical characteristics. And it was a relatively common byproduct of other mining and smelting operations in Russia at that time (as it remains today).

Platinum is used in jewelry for its brilliant, corrosion-free finish and wear resistance. For this application, it is most appreciated in Japan, where more than half the amount used goes into jewelry. In the United States and Europe a lesser proportion is used in jewelry. It is useful in settings for diamonds, where its silver color and reflectivity provide for effective display. (Rhodium provides a finish for white gold alloys and silver that resists corrosion and wear, while a thin plated coating is indistinguishable in appearance from the metal under it.)

In some chemical applications, platinum may be the most effective catalyst. It is extensively used in petroleum refining, for example, and in the manufacture of sulfuric acid. Palladium may be substituted for platinum in many catalytic uses, but it requires about three times as much palladium to achieve the same effect. It thus may not be too surprising to see a tendency for the price of palladium to be about one third that of platinum.

Until recent years, platinum's relative scarcity has caused the price to be above that of gold. However, the two metals lately have commanded similar prices. To some extent this may be due to the price depressing effects of economic recession on industrial metals in general.

Figure 14-8 illustrates world production of platinum group metals. The Soviet Union is the largest producer, accounting for over half the world total. South Africa is second, with output accounting for 40 percent of world output. The Soviet Union proportion of palladium to platinum is higher than that of South Africa, and it is the major world source of palladium.[16] About two-thirds of the world's palladium is produced by the Soviet Union, about two-thirds its platinum by South Africa.

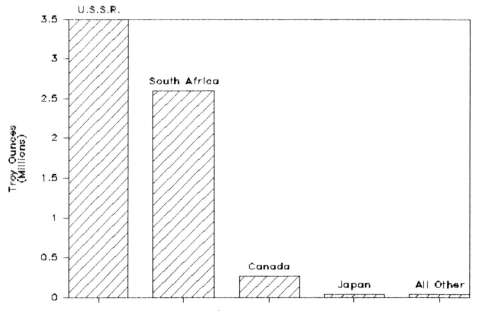

Figure 14.8. World platinum group production, 1982. Data Source: U.S. Bureau of Mines.

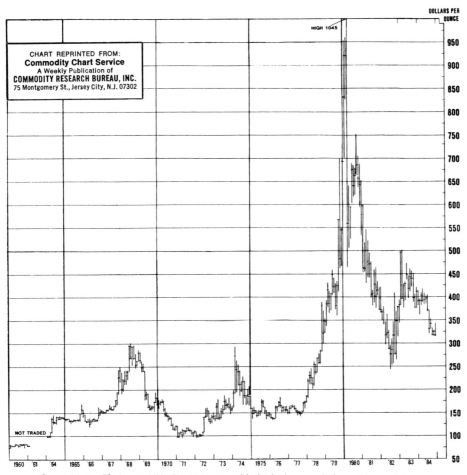

Figure 14.9. Platinum, NYMEX, N.Y. (monthly high, low, and close of nearest futures)

Futures Trading

Figure 14-9 displays the long-term price activity of platinum futures, Figure 14-10 that of palladium futures. Platinum and palladium futures are both traded on NYMEX. The platinum contract is for 50 troy ounces, that for palladium is for 100 ounces.

Futures traders should keep in mind that the marketing actions of the Soviet Union and South Africa can have significant effects on prices. Traders should also check with their brokers regarding the exchange rules pertaining to retendering contracts held into the delivery period to avoid unpleasant surprises.

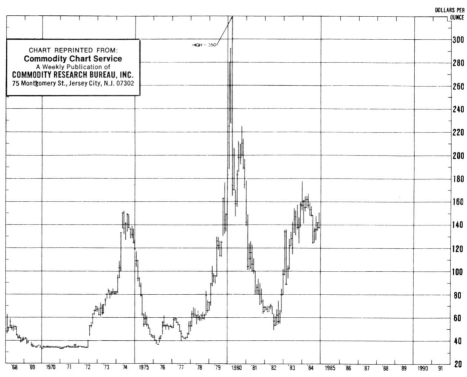

Figure 14.10. Palladium, NYMEX, N.Y. (monthly high, low, and close of nearest futures)

COPPER

Copper is a reddish-colored metal that is both malleable and ductile. It is a superior conductor of both heat and electricity. This makes it useful for cooking vessels and wire. Alloyed with zinc and other metals it forms brass, bronze, and other useful materials. Copper is also relatively corrosion resistant. Copper is probably the first metal to be used by mankind for fabricating tools, in its elemental form and as bronze alloy.

Copper is used extensively in the electrical, automotive, and housing industries. Although it has encountered increased competition from aluminum in recent years, it is still the best material for many uses, combining desirable physical properties with relatively low cost. Copper is also used in the manufacture of ordnance materials, in the form of brass shell casings and gilding metal for small arms projectiles.

Because copper is primarily used as an industrial metal, copper prices tend to move with the health of the economy, rising in good times, falling in recession. This has made copper prices volatile over the years.

Figure 14-11 shows world copper production by country. Chile is the largest producer, with the United States and Soviet Union not far behind. Canada, Zambia, and Zaire follow in fourth through sixth position.

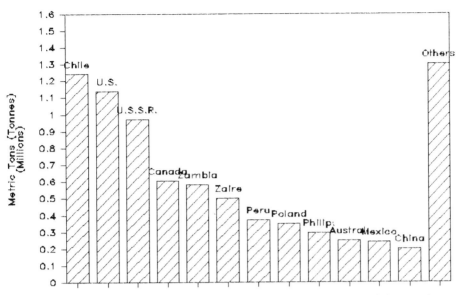

Figure 14.11. World mine production of copper (1982 estimated). Data Source: U.S. Bureau of Mines.

Copper ore is normally removed from open pit mines, where typically only about 8 to 72 pounds of metallic copper are found in a ton of raw ore. Ore is generally crushed and pulverized in a milling operation. Then it goes through a smelting process that removes the metallic copper along with other metals contained in the ore. The copper is then further refined, today generally by electrolytic means, which forms 99.9 percent pure copper on cathode sheets, each weighing about 300 pounds and measuring about 3 1/2 feet square. These cathodes are the most common form encountered in trade today.

In addition to mine output, scrap recovery is an important source of supply. This is in large measure due to the relative corrosion resistance of the metal, as well as the types of use to which the metal is put, such as copper tubing, automobile radiators, electrical motors, generators or alternators, and wire. Much copper is thus easily separated from other scrap for further processing.

Futures Trading

Copper futures are traded on COMEX in New York and the LME. The COMEX contract is for 25,000 pounds of electrolytic cathodes, though other grades, such as fire refined ingots, are deliverable at discount or premium. The minimum price tick is 1/20 cent per pound ($12.50 per contract), and the normal daily price limit is 5 cents per pound ($1250 per contract). Delivery months are January, March, May, July, September, and December.

The LME trades two copper contracts: (1) a high-grade copper cathode and wirebar contract, and (2) a standard copper cathode contract. The first is the more actively traded contract. The LME contracts are for 25 metric tons (i.e.,

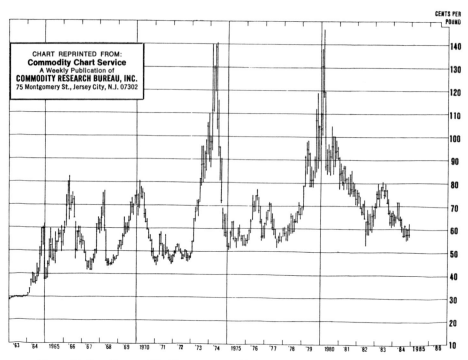

CENTS PER
POUND

CHART REPRINTED FROM:
Commodity Chart Service
A Weekly Publication of
COMMODITY RESEARCH BUREAU, INC.
75 Montgomery St., Jersey City, N.J. 07302

Figure 14.12.   Copper, COMEX, N.Y. (monthly high, low, and close of nearest futures)

tonnes), and spot and three-month forward contracts are traded. The quality of copper traded on the LME is generally somewhat higher than on the COMEX, and thus tends to command a somewhat higher price.

A history of COMEX copper futures prices is contained in Figure 14-12.

ALUMINUM[17]

Aluminum, or, as the British (and some Americans who have trouble with the pronunciation) prefer, "aluminium," is the most plentiful metallic element on earth. However, it does not occur in nature in its free, elemental form, and a great deal of energy must be expended to obtain aluminum from its ore.

In industrial use, aluminum is a very new material. At the end of World War II, output was less than 1 million metric tons (i.e., tonnes). By the early 1980s production exceeded 15 million tonnes.

Aluminum possesses favorable strength to weight ratio, low density, relatively low melting point, corrosion resistance, and is a good conductor of both heat and electricity. Although its ability to conduct electricity is inferior to that of copper, its cost and low density suit it well to long distance overhead power transmission lines. (Problems with connections in homes and offices have posed safety problems that have prevented displacement of copper in those applications.)

Aluminum requires great quantities of energy in its production. One tonne of aluminum metal requires some 117 million Btu of energy. Of this, some 6 million Btu are expended in mining and preparing bauxite ore, 36 million are used to concentrate the bauxite into alumina (Al_2O_3, aluminum oxide), and 75 million to electrolytically remove aluminum metal from the alumina. The energy ratios in these three steps of production are approximately in the relationship of 1 to 6 to 13. The second two steps have led to concentration of production in areas of relatively cheap hydroelectric power: in the U.S. Pacific Northwest, Canada's British Columbia and Quebec, and Norway. The cost of shipping bauxite tends to favor production in areas near sea transportation, which is the lowest cost means of moving bulk material long distances.

Figure 14-13 illustrates the relative importance of various countries in production of bauxite, the primary commercial aluminum ore. Australia is by far the largest producer. Guinea and Jamaica are also large producers, though they individually account for less that half of Australia's production. The Soviet Union and Brazil follow in fourth and fifth places, each with about the same production as the other. Production of bauxite is very important to the economics of some of these countries. Although many countries produce bauxite, the main exporters are Australia, Jamaica, and Surinam. The world recession from 1979 led to a 19 percent decrease in bauxite output in the Western world by 1982 and Jamaican production fell almost 30 percent in that year, with substantial economic repercussions. Aluminum consumption in 1982 was 12.4 percent less than its 1979 peak of 12.6 million tonnes.

Because of energy costs, only about half of bauxite ore is processed into alumina in its country of origin. The other half is processed in the developed

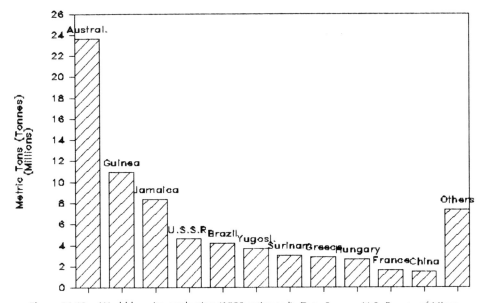

Figure 14.13. World bauxite production (1982 estimated). Data Source: U.S. Bureau of Mines.

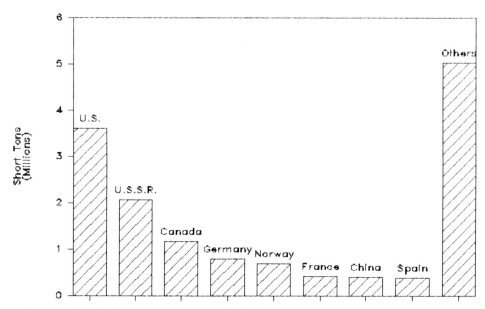

Figure 14.14. World aluminum production (1982 estimated). Data Source: U.S. Bureau of Mines.

countries, particularly the United States, Canada, the Soviet Union, West Germany, and Japan. Prior to the quadrupling of petroleum prices in 1973 to 1974 there was less incentive than afterward to focus production in geographical areas with less expensive hydroelectric power. Figure 14-14 displays the relative aluminum metal production of the major producing countries.

In the United States, 18 percent of aluminum is used in the transportation industry, 21 percent in construction, 11 percent in the electrical industry (including telecommunications), and 30 percent in containers and packaging. The versatility of aluminum is illustrated by the U.S. space shuttle: each vessel requires 9000 pounds of aluminum plates and forgings in its construction, and for each flight uses a new 77,000 pound fuel tank and more than 300,000 of aluminum powder in its fuel.[18]

Factors Influencing Price

The factor most influencing the price of aluminum is the cost of energy. Energy costs influence aluminum supply and demand in two ways. First, increased energy costs tend to increase the costs of mining, transporting, and concentrating bauxite ore into alumina, and the subsequent extraction of metallic aluminum. Second, increased energy costs in the form of petroleum products prompt searches for ways of increasing fuel economy in transportation. This translates into (among other things) searches for ways to reduce vehicle weight. The low density of aluminum combined with its strength (in proper alloys) make it a feasible substitute for heavier materials.[19]

The International Bauxite Association, with its 11 members, has recommended bauxite prices based on the value of U.S. primary aluminum ingot. At the end of 1982 this was at 2 to 3 percent of the ingot price. The recommended alumina price, reflecting the energy costs to process bauxite into alumina, was 14 to 18 percent at the same time. The costs of energy in its various forms, the physical properties of aluminum, and the relative costs of substitutes will likely remain more forceful price influences than the association.

Recycling of aluminum has become an increasingly important factor in supply. However, recycled aluminum is limited in its application to cast products because of the alloying additives and impurities contained in randomly collected scrap.

Futures Trading

Aluminum futures contracts began to trade "on the *London Metal Exchange* (LME) in October, 1978, to a barrage of protest by producers who viewed it as a direct threat to their own pricing system. Three years later the chorus of disapproval [was] singing the market's praises. Producers have even come to depend on it as a useful, independent barometer of aluminum demand."[20]

Several years after the LME contract, aluminum futures began to trade on COMEX in New York. The COMEX aluminum contract is for 40,000 pounds ($\pm 2\%$) of virgin primary aluminum, with certain other grades deliverable at a discount. Delivery months are January, March, May, July, September, and December. Minimum price fluctuation is 5/100 cent per pound ($20.00 per contract) and the normal price limit 5 cents per pound ($2000 per contract) from the prior day's settlement price. Delivery is at seller's option at a number of locations throughout the United States.

The LME aluminum contract is for 25 tonnes ($\pm 2\%$) of 99.5 percent purity primary aluminum, with no more iron content than 0.40 percent and no more silicon content than 0.3 percent. Pricing is in pounds sterling per tonne, with a minimum price change of 50 pence. Trading is for spot and three months forward. Trades may be consummated for any working day within that span.

Notes

[1] A troy pound contains 12 ounces or 373.242 grams. An avoirdupois pound contains 16 ounces or 453.592 grams.

[2] The freedom to buy gold, and gold futures contracts, is the freedom to sell short the promises and assurances of political leaders to control inflation. (Those who believe the assurances can similarly sell gold short.)

[3] The record is not clear in this regard. The inflation hedging effectiveness of gold depends on the timing of one's purchases.

[4] For detailed development of this subject see H. Alan Lipscomb, "Golden Leverage." *On Gold* (DeKalb, IL: Waterleaf Press, 1982): 273–356.

[5] This discussion is indebted to Arnold Brisk, "What You Should Know About the Gold Markets." *1984 Commodity Year Book* (New York: Commodity Research Bureau, 1984): 6–19, and Peter Truell and George Anders, "Quaint Customs and World-Wide Impact Mark Daily Fixings of London Gold Price," *The Wall Street Journal,* March 2, 1983, p. 38.

[6] The two most active houses are Johnson Matthey Ltd. and Samuel Montagu and Co., Ltd.

[7] Most of the world's gold trade is priced in U.S. dollars.

[8] Elias Crim, "London's Key Role in World Gold Market." *Futures* **14,** no. 2 (February 1982): 66–67.

[9] Lowell Mintz, quoted in Elias Crim, *ibid.,* p. 67. Lowell Mintz is a former COMEX chairman.

[10] Crim, "London's Key Role," p. 67.

[11] Roy W. Jastram, *Silver: The Restless Metal* (New York: Wiley, 1981).

[12] To producers it was set at 1/32 ounce because for every 2 ounces they sent to the mint, only one ounce in the form of silver dollars was received in payment.

[13] "Electronic Still Camera." *Focus Japan* **11,** no. 12 (December 1984): 5.

[14] This discussion is indebted to Arnold Brisk, "How to Forecast the Silver Market." *1977 Commodity Yearbook* (New York: Commodity Research Bureau, 1977): 6–20.

[15] The platinum group includes palladium, rhodium, iridium, osmium, and ruthenium.

[16] The Soviets are noted for their success in getting the best prices possible for their sales of commodities. They have been said to withold supplies to help firm up prices, and to sell into price strength. See for example Wendy L. Wall and Kathleen A. Hughes, "Soviet Union Emerges as a Big, Clever Player in Commodities Game," *The Wall Street Journal,* January 29, 1985, p. 1.

[17] This discussion is indebted to an anonymous author who wrote the article *Aluminum: A Brief Analysis* (New York: Shearson/American Express, 1983): 7.

[18] *Ibid.* p. 7.

[19] One of the few drawbacks to aluminum is that it is not easily welded or soldered without special equipment.

[20] Anonymous, "London Metal Exchange's Barometer of Aluminum Demand is Falling." *World Business Weekly* (June 1, 1981): 44.

15

Tropical Products

Cocoa, coffee, and orange juice are clearly tropical products because of their climate requirements. Although sugar is not restricted to the tropics and subtropics, it is convenient to classify it with tropical products. Similarly, although cotton is not restricted to tropical climates, it does require a long, warm growing season and it is reasonable to classify it with tropical products.

COCOA

Cocoa was widely valued in pre-Columbian Central America, where it was used as a beverage by the ruling classes. The Spanish conquistadors took the product to Europe, where it quickly became accepted.

Until Van Houten, a Dutch processor, discovered in the early nineteenth century what we know today as chocolate, demand grew slowly for cocoa beans. He blended the cocoa butter extracted from some beans with sugar and other finely ground cocoa beans (cocoa liquor) to make chocolate. Later, Daniel Peter in Switzerland used milk in place of some of the cocoa butter. In milk chocolate production, the powder resulting from drying the blend of milk, sugar, and cocoa liquor is mixed with cocoa butter and the mixture subjected to "conching." In this stage of manufacture, machines (called conches) with heavy granite rollers blend the mixture by rubbing it across a granite surface.

Cocoa is produced from trees, which contain the cocoa beans in pods the size of small melons. Once harvested, the cocoa beans are fermented for several days. This process is what imparts the characteristic flavor to the beans. Proper control of the fermentation is crucial to the quality of the result. After fermentation, the beans are dried and packaged for shipment. They deteriorate rapidly in heat and humidity and so are not stored in the tropics where they are grown.

Processors clean, roast, and blend the dried fermented beans. Blending is required because of the wide range of flavor and aroma found in the various commercial growths. Following roasting, the shells are removed from the beans, leaving the "nibs." These contain approximately 50 percent cocoa butter. The nibs are crushed to produce "liquor," which, when cooled, is unsweetened baking, or cooking chocolate. The liquor may be pressed to remove as much cocoa butter as the processor wishes. The residual cake is pulverized to make cocoa powder, which varies in quality depending on its remaining cocoa butter content.

The demand for chocolate has been such that the cocoa butter in the beans has been greatly sought. The cocoa powder has been relegated to byproduct status and more produced than the market could readily absorb.

For cocoa, the crop year is from October through September of the following year. This span is divided into the "main-crop," harvested from October to March, and the "midcrop," harvested in May and June. The midcrop is larger for Brazil, but for other countries, the main crop is the dominant production.

The long time required to increase production causes the supply of cocoa to be inelastic in the short run. It takes five years from planting to the first harvest of pods. Then yields tend to increase, reaching a peak in about the fifteenth year. From that time production remains constant for perhaps 15 years. Then, yields decline for some 10 to 20 years.

According to research by Shirk, cocoa appeared to possess a cycle of 3.48 years over the period of January 1923 to August 1959. However, this cycle appears to have faded out after 1960 to 1962. Evidence of a 5 1/2 year cycle has also been alleged.[1] Given that it takes about five years to bring plantings into production, a cycle of this periodicity should not in itself be surprising. However, persistence of such a cycle over the years would suggest an inability of the market to smooth it out, and this itself may present a challenge for dogmatic market efficiency proponents to explain.

At this time there appears to be little seasonality in cocoa prices.[2] However, in the early 1970s there appears to have been some evidence of a seasonal pattern, at least in years in which there were no large carryover stocks.[3]

Figure 15-1 illustrates world production of cocoa. Currently, the Ivory Coast is the world's largest cocoa producer, with Brazil a near second. The combined production of all other Western Hemisphere countries ranks third. Ghana and Nigeria follow in importance. After Brazil they are individually the most significant producers. Cameroon is also significant as an individual producer.

Cocoa futures are traded on the London Terminal Market, in New York on the Cocoa, Coffee, and Sugar Exchange, and on smaller exchanges in Amsterdam, Hamburg, and Paris. Since 1979 the New York contract has been for the same measure as that in London, 10 metric tons (i.e., tonnes). This has facilitated arbitrage between the two markets, although the London contract is quoted in pounds sterling, and the New York in dollars. Delivery months on both exchanges are March, May, July, September, and December.

Figure 15-2 shows a history of New York cocoa futures prices.

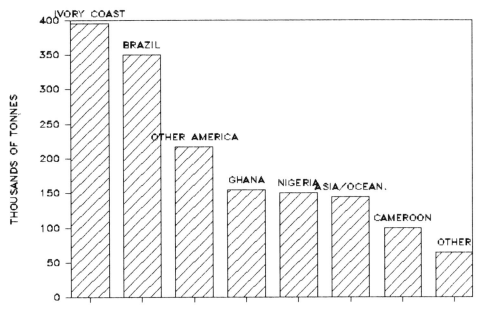

Figure 15.1. World cocoa production 1983–1984. Data Source: Foreign Agricultural Service, U.S.D.A.

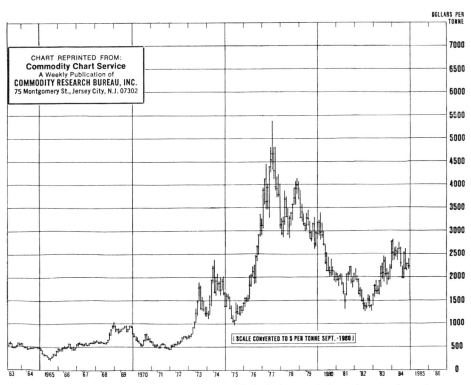

Figure 15.2. Cocoa, NYCSC, N.Y. (monthly high, low, and close of nearest futures)

COFFEE

Coffee is the most important nonalcoholic beverage in world trade. The plant from which coffee beans are harvested is native to the Middle East (*Caffea arabica*). In fact, the well known variety mocha, at one time synonymous with the word coffee, is named for the Red Sea port in South Yemen from which much Arabian Peninsula coffee was exported in the nineteenth century. Today the Middle East coffee production is not a significant force in world export trade, though one may still buy mocha (and Far Eastern java, too!) in specialty shops.

By far the largest coffee exporter in the world is Brazil. Colombia is a distant second, with roughly half the export production. Then come Indonesia and the Ivory Coast, with about one-third Colombia's production. These are followed by Uganda, Mexico, El Salvador, and Guatemala. Figure 15-3 illustrates the relative export productions of coffee growing nations. Clearly, Latin America is the largest producing region, and it was only since the end of World War II that Africa became an important exporting region.

There are two varietal groups of coffee: the mild, flavorful, and aromatic *arabicas,* and the less flavorful *robustas*. The arabica variety is predominant in Latin America, where it grows in mild and constant temperature regions with an altitude above 2000 feet. Unlike other major producers, super producer Brazil grows much of its coffee in a region vulnerable to frosts. Because of Brazil's dominance in world coffee trade, uncertainties about the Brazilian crop brought about by this factor can have a dramatic impact on coffee prices.

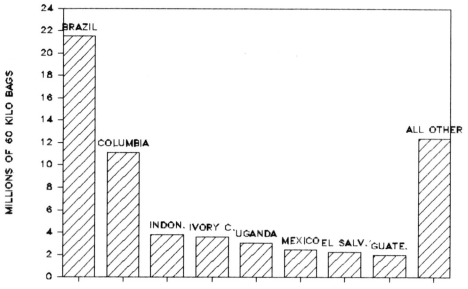

Figure 15.3. Exportable world coffee production 1983–1984 green coffee. Data Source: Foreign Agricultural Service, U.S.D.A.

About three-quarters of African coffee production is from *caffea robusta,* which can be grown in the hotter, lower elevations (500 to 2000 feet) and is disease resistant. Arabicas are restricted to mountainous countries such as Ethiopia and Kenya. Robustas may constitute as much as half the content of "instant" coffees, termed "soluble coffees" in the trade. Robustas are less flavorful than arabicas and thus considered to be of lower quality.

Like cocoa, coffee is produced on small trees. Commercial production requires at least 2 to 3 years beyond planting for robusta varieties, more typically 5 years for arabica. Subsequently, the tree is in its prime for perhaps 15 to 18 years. Then, after about 30 years, the tree declines to such an extent it is not worth keeping. Coffee trees are generally kept trimmed to heights of 8 to 15 feet to facilitate picking of the berries that contain the beans, and to obtain better yields.

Like many other tropical plants, coffee trees may have flowers, ripe, and unripened fruit on its branches at the same time. In Brazil the berries are harvested once a year. In other countries only the ripe berries are picked, and there are two to four annual pickings. Because some berries are not at their peak ripeness when picked, Brazilian coffee tends to be of a lower quality overall than that produced only from berries at their prime.

After picking, the green (i.e., unroasted) coffee beans must be separated from the berry pulp surrounding them. There are two means for achieving this: the natural process and the wet process. The natural process is based on sun drying the coffee berries. This requires a sufficiently long period of warm, dry weather. Wet weather prevents proper drying and adversely affects quality. The wet process begins with mechanical removal of the pulp from the coffee beans, followed by washing and fermentation. As in the fermentation of cocoa beans, this process is crucial to determining the flavor and quality of the coffee produced. After sufficient fermentation the process is stopped by washing, which also further cleans the green coffee beans. Then the beans are dried and cleaned once more. The highest quality "washed arabicas" are produced by this method.

The green coffee beans are exported to consuming countries by a small number of firms. These are shipped to the warehouses of customers in the important port cities of New York, San Francisco, New Orleans, Le Havre, and Antwerp. Coffee beans are blended according to secret formulas designed to assure consistent and distinctive qualities. They are then roasted and packaged for sale to their customers, usually after grinding.

Factors Affecting Price

Demand for coffee is relatively inelastic; consumption does not change much over a wide range of price. Supply is more responsive to price change over the long run, but it can take about five years before new plantings produce commercial quantities of berries.

Supply is much more readily curtailed abruptly than it can be increased. Freezes in Brazil's main coffee growing region generally occur in what corresponds to early summer in the Northern Hemisphere. A bad freeze can harm production for several years, or as long as it takes replacements for frost-killed trees to begin production. Most traders would be well advised to avoid short positions during the freeze season.

Futures Trading

Coffee futures contracts are traded in New York and London. The New York "C" contract is traded on the Coffee, Cocoa, and Sugar Exchange. It is for a trading unit of 37,500 pounds, of washed arabica coffee of certain specified national origins. The now suspended "B" contract was for Brazilian coffee. The "C" contract allows delivery from some 19 different countries, but *not* from Brazil. However, since Brazilian coffee prices are correlated with those from other origins, the "C" contract is still useful for hedging Brazilian coffee. The delivery months are March, May, July, September, and December. Price quotes are in U.S. cents per pound, with a minimum price movement of 1/100 cent per pound. Figure 15-4 contains a history of New York coffee futures prices.

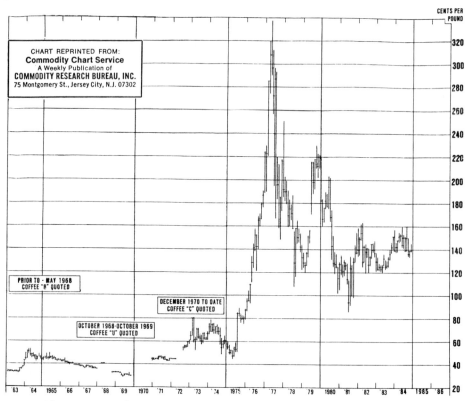

Figure 15.4. Coffee, NYCSC, N.Y. (monthly high, low, and close of nearest futures)

The London futures contract is for robusta coffee. The contract unit is for 5 long tons (2240 pounds per long ton) and price quotations are in British pounds sterling per ton, with a minimum price movement of 0.5 pound sterling per ton.

COTTON

Cotton fiber is produced by plants of the genus *Gossypium*.. Upland cotton is *Gossypium hirsutum*. Long staple cotton derives from the species *Gossypium barbadense*. Cotton is related to okra, and other members of the hibiscus family, as is evident from the appearance of the flowering plant.

The history of cotton is long and complex, going back some 5000 years. Although resisted by the English woolen industry in the 1600s, cotton textiles grew in popularity. The cotton gin, invented by an American, Eli Whitney,[4] made possible the production of cotton on a large scale. Prior to the gin, fiber, and seed had to be separated by slow, laborious means.

Cotton requires six months of warm weather, with a minimum summer average temperature of 80 degree Fahrenheit. More than 75 countries produce cotton, but the United States, Soviet Union, and China together account for half of the world's production.

Cotton is classified by grade, staple, and micronaire. Grade itself is determined by color, content of foreign matter (such as leaves and dirt), and preparation. Staple refers to the length of the cotton fiber: 13/16 to 1 3/32 inch is termed medium and medium-long staple; 1 1/8 to 1 5/16 is termed long staple. Cotton under 13/16 is termed short staple, that over 1 3/8 extra-long staple. Micronaire is a measure of fiber quality related to its maturity when harvested.

In the United States cotton is produced in the Southeast, the Midsouth, and Southwest, and the West. The Midsouth, or Central section covers the High Plains region of Texas, which is subject to drought, to late spring and early fall freezes, and to hail. Irrigation mitigates the dry weather of the region, but the other factors remain. Cotton produced in this region sells at a discount to other U.S. cotton because of its short staple, averaging about 1 inch in length. However, because of its size, this region is an important cotton producer, and when it has damaging weather the price of cotton responds accordingly.

Figure 15-5 shows cotton production for the major producing nations.

Factors Affecting Price

Demand for cotton is affected not only by its own price, but by those of substitutes, such as polyester synthetics and other natural fibers. However, no synthetic fiber has been found that can be produced economically to duplicate

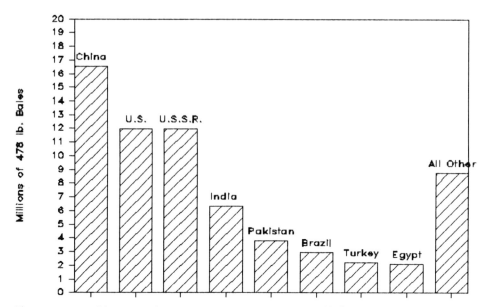

Figure 15.5. World cotton production 1982–1983 (U.S. in 500 pound bales), Data Source: International Cotton Advisory Committee.

the comfort provided by cotton. Many consumers resist all-synthetic fabrics in favor of blends which retain the comfort of cotton while adding the increased wear properties, color fastness, and wrinkle resistance of polyester. Some consumers steadfastly prefer pure cotton for its comfort despite the shortcomings.

Supply of cotton is determined by acreage planted and weather. Planting intentions are affected by a number of factors. Among these are the expected price of cotton, the expected prices of alternative crops that can be grown on the same land, and government programs. In the United States, soybeans can be an attractive alternative to cotton. Since 1929 the U.S. federal government has been an important factor in the cotton market.

During the Great Depression, the Agricultural Adjustment Act of 1933 was intended to support the prices of farm commodities, including cotton. Prices were supported at varying percentages of parity until 1945 when the loan rate rose to 100 percent. After World War II the percentage was reduced so that by 1959 it was at 75 percent. In 1956 the soil bank was started, and farmers were paid for setting aside acreage (i.e., for *not* growing cotton on some of their land). These price support programs kept prices at levels that attracted foreign competition, and production in other countries increased greatly. Toward the end of the 1930s, the United States produced half the world's cotton. Today its share is about one-fifth of the world total, about the same as the Soviet Union.

In the 1970s government policy switched from price supports to more of a free market orientation. The Agriculture Act of 1970 set the U.S. cotton loan rate at 90 percent of the preceding two years' world price. Then, in 1973, the

Agriculture and Consumer Protection Act of that year established payments to producers when prices fell below target levels. In 1980, the Agricultural Act of that year established a system for incrementing the target price by 5 cents a year for 5 years. This, and similar programs for other farm products posed a potential threat to the federal budget that led to the payments-in-kind (PIK) program of 1982.

Under the PIK program, cotton growers were required to reduce acreage by 20 percent to quality for benefits. Those agreeing to a further 30 percent reduction were paid by return of 80 percent of their normal annual yield from stocks of cotton owned by the government under its loan programs. The effect of the PIK program for cotton was to reduce planted acreage to its lowest level since the years following the U.S. Civil War.

Futures Trading

Cotton has been traded in recent years in New York and New Orleans. Currently, trading is on the New York Cotton Exchange for a trading unit of 50,000 pounds (500 bales). Delivery months are March, May, July, October, and December. Minimum price tick is 1/100 cent per pound, or $5 per contract. The normal daily price limit is 2 cents a pound, or $1000 per contract.

Figure 15-6 contains a history of NYCE cotton futures.

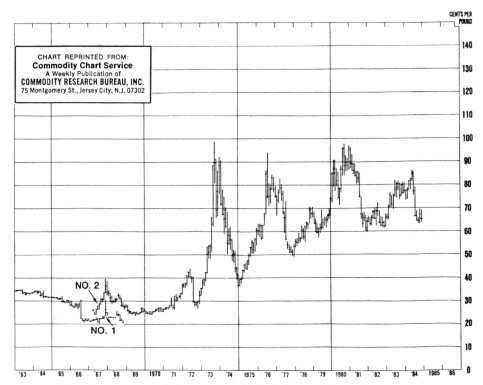

Figure 15.6. Cotton, NYCE, N.Y. (monthly high, low, and close of nearest futures)

ORANGE JUICE

"I traded commodity futures once, some years ago," admitted the president of a large Boston firm. "My broker put me into orange juice futures. He sold a couple of contracts in December, just before a freeze," Thus began the true story of one erstwhile commodities trader. He hasn't traded any commodity contract since that time.

Orange juice futures are traded on the Citrus Associates of the New York Cotton Exchange. The trading unit is for 15,000 pounds of frozen orange juice concentrate, U.S. Grade A. Delivery months are January, March, May, July, September, and November. The minimum price fluctuation is 5/100 cent per pound, or $7.50 per contract. The daily price limit is 5 cents per pound, or $750 per contract. Unlike most commodity futures, this is a limit range. For example, if the price were to trade 1 cent under the previous day's settlement early in the day, then rally strongly, the price could rise only to 4 cents over the previous days settlement. The trading range would be 5 cents, the daily limit.

Because futures contract delivery is allowed only in Florida, there is less use of futures for hedging by many end users than there otherwise would be.

Orange juice may be traded profitably from both the long and short sides. However, most traders will be wise to avoid short positions in the winter months, when freezes can propel prices upward in limit jumps. They may be even wiser to avoid brokers who would introduce them to futures trading by shorting orange juice futures in the freeze season!

Demand for orange juice tends to be inelastic. In the short run supply also tends to be inelastic; it takes years for newly planted trees to become commercially productive. For this reason a freeze that destroys part of a season's crop can cause prices to leap skyward. Should the freeze damage or kill the trees, prices will tend to stay high for several years, until supply can be expanded.

Orange juice production in the United States is concentrated in Central Florida, with that peninsula producing about 70 percent of the total. The lower Rio Grande valley of Texas, Arizona, and California together account for the balance. The navel varieties grown largely in California are not used for frozen, concentrated orange juice. It is the valencia varieties that are preferred for frozen, concentrated orange juice production because of their high sugar content.

Following World War II frozen, concentrated orange juice became popular, largely because of the efforts of Dr. L. G. MacDowell and his colleagues at the Florida Citrus Commission. They were able to overcome the loss of flavor that had accompanied evaporation to concentrate by restoring the desirable characteristics of appearance and flavor. Ownership of large quantities of frozen, concentrated orange juice presented risks to producers that a futures market allows to be hedged.

Florida producers have been concerned for some years about Brazil's increasing production of frozen, concentrated orange juice, and that of Central

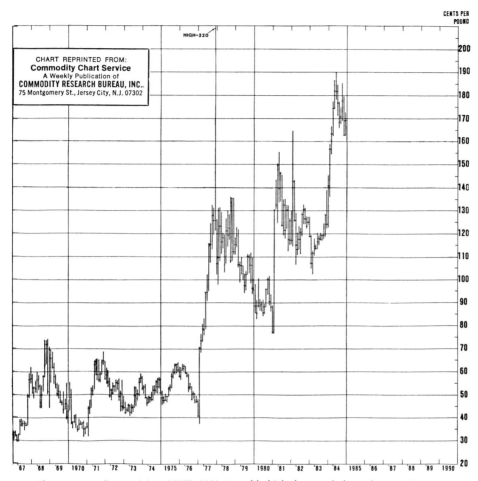

CENTS PER
POUND

CHART REPRINTED FROM:
Commodity Chart Service
A Weekly Publication of
COMMODITY RESEARCH BUREAU, INC.
75 Montgomery St., Jersey City, N.J. 07302

HIGH-220

Figure 15.7.   Orange juice, NYCE, N.Y. (monthly high, low, and close of nearest futures)

America. Freezes in Florida have encouraged this foreign production which competes not only in the United States but in foreign markets important to Florida producers, such as the European nations. If it were not for Brazilian production to fill the gap caused by freeze damage to Florida's crop, prices would have assumed higher levels than they did.

Figure 15-7 contains a history of orange juice futures prices, note the sharp price increases that occurred in several years as the result of freezes.

SUGAR

In ancient times honey was the only sweetener used. However, over the past several hundred years, sugar (more precisely, sucrose) grew to become the dominant sweetener. Although refined sugar has been implicated in dental caries and diabetes, and suspected of contributing to other health problems, its usage continues to be strong. Humans have a collective sweet tooth that demands to be fed.

In the twentieth century the chemical sweeteners saccharine and cyclamate were discovered. However, in recent years health concerns caused cyclamate sweeteners to be banned in the United States, though still allowed in other countries. And saccharine remains under suspicion for its possible link to human health problems. Recently, liquid sweetener derived from corn became an important competitor to sugar, and aspartame joined the ranks of the no- or low-calorie sweeteners.

Sugar is produced in quantity from two unrelated plants, sugar cane and the sugar beet. Cane probably originated in the South Pacific. Columbus brought it to the New World, where the sugar and molasses produced from it became for a time the most important articles of trade. Not only was sugar itself important; so was the related distilled liquid, rum. The sugar beet became important only toward the mid-1800s, though a hundred years earlier beet and cane sugar were shown by a Prussian chemist to be identical.

The rise in importance of the sugar beet began with the British blockade of European shipping during the Napoleonic Wars. Napoleon decreed that some 70,000 acres in France be planted in sugar beets. So quickly did beet production grow, that by 1840 more sugar was produced from this source than from cane. Beet production remained in the lead most of the time until World War I.

Many countries produce significant quantities of sugar. This includes countries that import much of their requirements. In such cases there is generally found some arrangement to protect domestic producers. The United States regulates imports and subsidizes production in several ways. For example, the Agriculture and Food Act of 1981 provided for a minimum loan level of 17 cents a pound for raw sugar produced in the United States. In addition, duties are levied on sugar imported into the United States and quotas are imposed to limit the quantity imported. In 1982 there was, besides an import duty of almost 3 cents per pound, a fee of just over 2 cents a pound. This fee is adjustable, and is set so that it, plus the price of imported sugar, plus transportation charges and import duties, equals the domestic market stabilization price.

Protective trade arrangements may follow former colonial lines or current political alliances. France and England for example, have preferential agreements with former colonies. And, the Soviet Union and Cuba have a trade treaty.

International Sugar Agreement

The International Sugar Agreement (ISA) dates back to 1937. It is the result of attempts by a number of nations to stabilize the price of sugar in world trade. The price stabilization concept calls for (1) accumulation of inven-

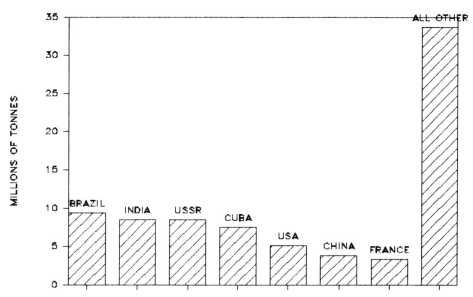

Figure 15.8. World sugar production, 1983–1984. Data Source: Foreign Agricultural Service, U.S.D.A.

tory reserves when supplies are plentiful (and prices tend to be low) combined with export quotas, and (2) release of reserves and dropping of quotas when supplies are scarce. As in all cartel arrangements, success depends on the cooperation of its participants, who must include all the major producers. The ISA and its meetings will likely continue to be important in forming short-run expectations in the futures markets. However, the history of the ISA suggests only limited success in its aim of price stabilization.

Figure 15-8 illustrates the relative rankings of the world's major producers. Unlike some other commodities, no one country is so strongly dominant that it cannot lose its position to one or more challengers with a relatively small shift in production.

Factors Affecting Price

For sugar traded under international agreements, political factors figure as prominently as economic ones, at least in the long run. For world sugar traded outside of the stabilizing influence of international agreements, price tends to respond to supply expectations quickly and sometimes explosively.

Although changes in demand can influence price, such changes tend to occur more or less gradually, and thus are relatively diffused over time. On the other hand, changes in supply, or rather in *expectations* regarding supply, may occur suddenly. These sudden changes can induce rapid price increases in world sugar prices. And, because the world sugar market is small compared to that under trade agreements, the change in supply need not be particularly great to precipitate a sharp run-up in price.

Supplies of sugar are relatively inelastic in the short run. Sugar cane is a perennial grass that grows to 2 inches diameter and 12 feet tall, but it requires about 18 months of growth before harvest, in a warm, moist, tropical, or semitropical climate. Once planted, several cuttings of cane are likely to be carried out even if prices fall. As long as the variable costs of cutting the cane can be covered, it is economical to do so rather than abandon the planting.

Sugar beets grow to 12 inches long and 2 pounds in weight in just a few months in temperate climates. Sugar beets planted in spring are harvested in the fall of the same year in the Northern Hemisphere. Because beets can be brought to production relatively quickly, sharp price increases are likely to be followed by an expansion in planted beet acreage.

Weather and disease can affect sugar production just as they can that of other crops. Hurricanes can devastate cane plantations in and near their path. Rains before or during harvest of sugar beets can adversely affect yields. Late spring weather, drought or cold during the summer months also can adversely affect production of beets.

In recent years conversion of sugar cane into ethanol ("grain" alcohol) for motor fuel, most notably in Brazil, has removed some potential supply from world markets. The extent to which substitution of ethanol for petroleum products will continue is uncertain. It will depend on the relative prices of sugar and petroleum as well as the needs of countries like Brazil to conserve foreign exchange earnings.

Similarly, it is difficult to assess the continuing effects of high fructose (i.e., "fruit" sugar) and glucose corn syrups. These have made inroads in bottled beverages and other processed and prepared foods. However, they pose handling requirements that may limit expansion of their use because they are available only in liquid form. Also, the effects of aspartame and similar low- or no-calorie sweeteners are impossible to assess reliably for the long run. These may grow in importance in the United States and other industrialized countries but few other countries are populated by multitudes concerned strongly with counting calories. And some consumers have become concerned that the high sodium content in some low-calorie beverages may be no better for their health than the sugar contained in traditionally sweetened bottled soft drinks.

Futures Trading

World sugar (No. 11 contract) is traded in New York on the Coffee, Sugar, and Cocoa Exchange. The contract trading unit is for 50 long tons (112,000 pounds) of 96 degree average polarization raw centrifugal cane sugar. Delivery months are January, March, May, July, September, and October. March and October are usually the most active months. Delivery may be made at port in the country of orgin or anchorage in the customary port of export for landlocked countries. Speculators should be aware of this, and the problems they may face if they take delivery. The minimum price fluctuation is 1/100 cent per pound, and the normal daily price limit is 1/2 cent above or below the settlement of the previous trading day. Figure 15-9 contains a price history of the New York No. 11 sugar futures contract.

Domestic sugar (No. 12 contract) is also traded on the New York Coffee, Sugar, Cocoa Exchange. Contract size, price limit and trading months are the same as for the No. 11 contract except that a November contract trades in place of October. Delivery is at designated points within the United States, of American produced raw centrifugal cane sugar, and duty-paid foreign produced sugar of the same grade.

Refined sugar is traded in Chicago on the MCE. The contract is for 40,000 pounds of free-flowing bulk extrafine granulated sugar. Delivery months are January, March, May, July, September, and November. Minimum price fluctuation is 1/100 cent per pound and normal daily price limit is 1/2 cent per pound above or below the previous trading day's settlement price. Delivery is free-on-board origin, freight off Chicago. The bill of lading is used as the delivery instrument.

Raw sugar and white, refined sugar are traded in 50 long ton contracts on the London Sugar Terminal Market. Delivery months are January, March, May, August, and October. Prices are in pounds sterling and delivery port is country of origin.

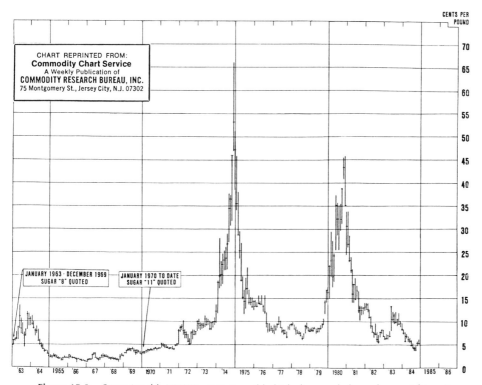

Figure 15.9. Sugar (world, NYCSC, N.Y. (monthly high, low, and close of nearest futures)

On the International Market of White Sugar of Paris a 50 tonne (metric ton) contract of refined sugar is traded. Prices are quoted in French francs. Smaller (10 tonnes raw; 9 tonnes white) sugar contracts are traded on the Tokyo Sugar Exchange.

Notes

[1] Louise L. Wilson, *Catalogue of Cycles: Part I—Economics* (Pittsburgh: Foundation for the Study of Cycles, 1964), p. 17.

[2] Perry J. Kaufman, *Handbook of Futures Markets* (New York: Wiley, 1984): 14–16, 34.

[3] Richard J. Teweles, Charles V. Harlow, and Herbert L. Stone, *The Commodity Futures Game* (New York: McGraw-Hill): 544–546.

[4] Whitney is most famous for the cotton gin. However, he manufactured muskets for the Continental Army in the early 1800s and pioneered the concept of interchangeable parts in manufacturing.

16

Other Physical Commodities

FOREST PRODUCTS

This category includes lumber and plywood. Both respond largely to the same market fundamentals. Those factors, such as interest rates, which affect housing construction affect the prices of both.

Over the years several different lumber contracts have traded. At this writing, a random length lumber contract is actively traded on the Chicago Mercantile Exchange and a Western plywood futures contract has only recently become inactive on the Chicago Board of Trade.

Major factors affecting the price of lumber and plywood are interest rates (and thus new housing starts), weather in producing areas, and labor problems. Strikes in British Columbia by Canadian mill workers can cause sharp price spikes because of the importance of that producing region.

There can develop in lumber what appears to be profitable spread opportunities between different contract months. Traders should be aware, however, that such spreads may not work as planned, even when the implied carrying charge is several times the cost of interest. Unlike most other commodities, lumber can be delivered only at mill site, and there is no provision for the trader to take delivery of a seemingly undervalued contract, store it for several months, then deliver against an expiring long position. Without such arbitrage opportunities, implied carrying charges can become large—as high as 40 percent per annum.

Futures Contracts

Chicago Board of Trade Western plywood contract is for a boxcar of 36 banded units, each of 66 sheets of 4 to 5 ply, 1/2 inch thickness, 4 foot length by 8 food width, exterior glue, with facing veneers of CD grades.

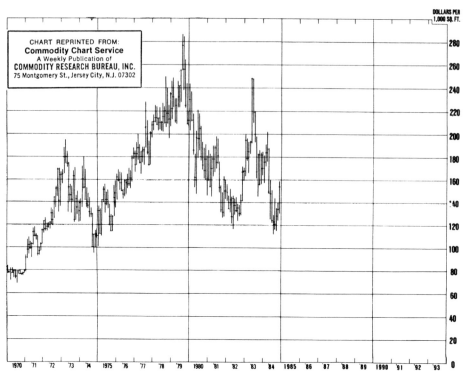

Figure 16.1. Lumber, CME, Chicago (monthly high, low, and close of nearest futures)

Chicago Mercantile Exchange random length lumber contract is for 100,000 board feet. (A board foot is 1 inch thick by 12 inches square.) Deliverable grades are construction and standard No. 1 and No. 2 two by fours of random 8 to 20 foot lengths from mills in the Rocky Mountain and Pacific Coast states of the United States (specifically California, Idaho, Montana, Nevada, Oregon, Washington, and Wyoming) and also Alberta and British Columbia, Canada. The lumber must be wrapped and loaded on flatcars. Among varieties allowed are Hemlock-fir, Alpine fir, Engelmann spruce, and Lodgepole pine. Minimum price tick is 10 cents per 1000 board feet, or $10 per contract. Normal daily price limit is $5 per 1000 board feet, or $500 per contract.

Traders should be aware that strikes by forest and mill workers, especially in British Columbia and the U.S. Pacific Northwest, can cause limit moves that may persist for several days. Subsequent settlement of the labor dispute can then cause prices to fall as precipitately. Figure 16-1 shows a history of CME lumber futures prices.

PETROLEUM PRODUCTS

The Arab oil embargo of 1973 to 1974, and the success of the Organization of Petroleum Exporting Countries created a need for futures trading and an awareness of its benefits. Prior to the embargo, the price of crude oil was low and fluctuations were mild. After the embargo, the prices of various grades of crude increased in level and volatility for almost a decade.

The largest petroleum producing country is the Soviet Union, with an estimated 1983 output of 23 percent of the world total. The United States is second, with 16 percent, Saudi Arabia third with 10 percent, and Mexico fourth with 5 percent. Of the industrialized countries only the United States, the Soviet Union, and the United Kingdom produce sufficient quantities of crude petroleum to rank among the top 15 producers. Figure 16-2 shows relative output of major petroleum producers.

Crude oil is the source of much of the world's energy. Without it there would be no gasoline, diesel or jet fuel, kerosene, naptha, or heating oil except what might be synthesized from coal or other sources at greater cost. Synthetic fuel was produced from coal in Germany during the latter stages of World War II, to try to make up for supplies in crude oil which had been cut off. Today, only South Africa produces synthetic fuels in significant proportion to its total requirements, and is carrying the technology forward.

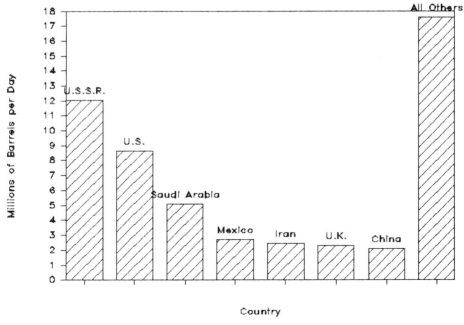

Figure 16.2. World crude oil production, 1983. Data Source: Energy Information Administration.

Most of the world's known reserves of petroleum are found in the Middle East, an area renowned neither for its political stability nor its peacefulness. Production from the Middle East is crucial to world supply. Indeed, without this source, Japan and most of the nations of Europe could not survive as industrial states with current technologies. Even temporary threats to supply from the area can cause sharp price increases, depending on the time of year and stocks in the importing countries. Price decreases are seldom as abrupt as increases, though sharp declines may follow increases that have carried prices higher on rumor than subsequent facts could support.

In the short run, demand and supply are both inelastic, but especially demand. Motorists whose automobiles run on gasoline have no ready alternative; if price goes up they must pay; if supplies are limited, they must wait in line as in the mid-1970s. They will cut down on nonessential driving but, having done that, will have to queue up and pay the going price. Stocks in storage provide a buffer to absorb short run surges in demand. But once this buffer is gone, supplies may not be quickly increased to make up for a large short-fall caused by major producers taking their supplies off the market, as the industrial states found out during the 1973 to 1974 Arab embargo.

Over the intermediate and long run, supplies can be increased as higher prices encourage exploration for new fields, and as technologies are developed for extracting residual petroleum from formerly exhausted fields. Substitutes such as ethanol (grain alcohol) may be produced in quantity from corn without seriously detracting from its use as livestock feed, and "biomass" (renewable nonfood crops and the stalks and leaves of grains and other food crops) may be used as energy sources.

In the intermediate time frame it may be the case that conservation is more important than increased supply. If cars could have their mileage doubled, the effect would be the same as if the supply of gasoline were doubled. Similarly, insulation of homes to use less heating fuel produces the same effect as an increased supply.

Organization of Petroleum Exporting Countries

The factor most responsible for sharply increased crude oil prices in the period following the Arab oil embargo of 1973 to 1974 is clearly the Organization of Petroleum Exporting Countries (OPEC). No other pricing cartel in modern history has been as successful or as much in the public view. Meetings of OPEC remain newsworthy events, even when little is accomplished at them. This is a legacy of the portent for increased petroleum prices associated with the organization's meetings during the 1970s.

Although OPEC met with notable success in increasing nominal crude oil prices in the decade of the 1970s, the *real* price of crude was relatively flat, or even slightly downtrending, from 1974 through 1978. It was the period 1979

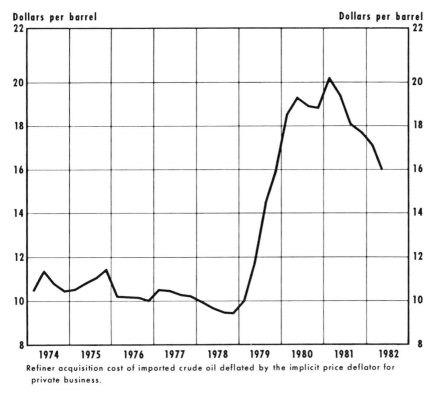

Figure 16.3. Real oil prices (1972 dollars). Source: Federal Reserve Bank of St. Louis, *Review* (November 1982).

through early 1981 that witnessed the largest real dollar increases, as shown in Figure 16-3.

From its peak in early 1981, the real price of crude oil has been on a down trend. Several factors contributed to the turnaround in trend. The sharp increases in price by OPEC precipitated both conservation by consumers and stepped up exploration and production by OPEC member and nonmember countries alike. When the uptrend broke in 1981, the discipline of OPEC wavered. Faced with declining sales, and revenue requirements that had become bloated in the days when it seemed petroleum demand was insensitive to price, OPEC members did not happily abide by production quotas imposed by the organization. And, markedly stepped up output by such notable non-OPEC members as Mexico and the United Kingdom helped to force prices lower.

Futures Trading

A number of different energy futures contracts have been traded. Currently, in the United States, contracts trade on crude oil, leaded and unleaded gasoline, fuel oil, and propane. Crude oil futures are traded on the New York Mercantile Exchange. The contract is for 42,000 gallons (1000 barrels) of light, sweet crude oil. Delivery months are the 12 consecutive months following the current one. Minimum price fluctuation is 0.01 cent/gallon ($4.20/contract) and the normal limit is 2 cents/gallon ($840/contract).

Heating oil (No. 2 grade) futures, leaded gasoline futures, and unleaded gasoline futures also are currently traded on the New York Mercantile Exchange. Propane futures currently trade on the Petroleum Associates of the New York Cotton Exchange.

The New York Mercantile heating oil contract is for 42,000 gallons (1000 barrels) of No. 2 fuel oil. Delivery months are for the 15 consecutive months including the current month. Minimum price tick is 0.01 cent/gallon ($4.20/contract) and normal maximum limit is 2 cents/gallon ($840/contract). A similar contract for 100 metric tons (i.e., tonnes, some 735.7 barrels) trades on the London International Petroleum Exchange. A fuel oil contract introduced on the CBT has not been successful.

Gasoline futures contracts have been introduced by the NYMEX, the CME and the CBT. Currently, only the NYMEX contracts are actively traded. Contract size is 42,000 gallons (1000 barrels). Delivery months are twelve consecutive months not including the current month. Minimum price tick is 0.01 cent/gallon ($4.20/contract) and normal daily limit is 2 cents/gallon ($840/contract).

Liquified propane gas is currently traded on the Petroleum Associates of the New York Cotton Exchange. The contract is for 42,000 gallons (1000 barrels). Delivery months are the 12 consecutive months including the current one. Minimum price tick is 0.01 cent/gallon ($4.20/contract) and the normal daily limit is 2 cents/gallon ($840/contract).

17
Commodity Options

In the United States, options on futures contracts have had a checkered history. In 1936, trading in "privileges" and other options on regulated futures contracts was banned. However, in 1971 commodity options enjoyed a brief but active revival through a loophole in the law. Some 10 international, unregulated commodities could, under the existing law, have options traded. These included silver, copper, platinum, sugar, plywood, cocoa, and coffee.

The discovery and exploitation of the loophole allowing trading in options on unregulated commodities led to rapid growth in options trading. It was estimated that during the first year of trading, 1972, between $200 and $400 million of commodity options were sold.

Lack of regulation, coupled with rapid growth, led quickly to fraud, misrepresentation, and theft as the greedy, incompetent and criminal were attracted to commodity options as middlemen. Even for well-managed and ethical options dealers, the volume of business proved to be too heavy a burden. Accounting systems, cash controls, and audits could not handle the volume of business adequately.

Eventually, the situation led to authorities in several states filing civil, and in some cases criminal, suits against options dealers. Turmoil and confusion resulted, and investor losses mounted along with bankruptcies of options firms. Finally, in 1978 the CFTC outlawed options on exchange traded commodities.

Industry pressure to revive options trading on commodity futures led to limited, experimental trading of options again in 1982, effective October 1, 1982. The CFTC allowed each exchange involved to trade options only on one commodity initially. The options authorized for trading during the test period were on the NYSE Index Futures contract (New York Futures Exchange); Standard & Poors 500 Index Futures contract (Chicago Mercantile Exchange); ValueLine Composite Index (Kansas City Board of Trade); U.S. T-Bond Futures (Chicago Board of Trade); Sugar (No. 11, World Contract—Coffee, Sugar, and Cocoa Exchange); and Gold (Commodity Exchange, Inc.). The motivation for limiting trading to one commodity per exchange was to contain trading in case the regulatory constraints were to prove inadequate to prevent the problems and abuses formerly associated with options on futures in the United States.

The rebirth of futures options did not lead to a rerun of the situation accompanying the initiation of trading in options on unregulated commodities in mid-1971. Trading was sluggish, with little public awareness. Most brokerage offices were not prepared to handle the new options; by mid-1983 few brokers were knowledgeable enough to even key in the proper symbols to obtain price quotes. To what might the relative apathy be attributed? It is safe to identify two factors. First, in 1982 the public was at least vaguely aware of the abuses of the prior decade, and the losses incurred by commodity options traders. Second, in the 1970s the prices of many commodities were especially volatile, and there was a general awareness of the inflation that was propelling prices higher. This attracted many new traders to the commodities markets and to options on futures. In contrast, many commodities were in downtrending, bear markets from October 1, 1982 through much of 1983. Bear markets in futures have never attracted much in the way of public trading enthusiasm.

Despite the slow start of trading in options in the 1980s, by early 1985 the activity in some commodity options had grown appreciably. Among the more successful contracts are those on U.S. T-bonds, the Deutschemark, stock index futures, gold, silver, and soybeans. Other agricultural futures options are still too new for the verdict to be in on whether they will be successful. The latter half of the 1980s will be a period of testing, as the CFTC approves new commodity options. Those options that fulfill real needs can be expected to survive; others will fade from the scene from neglect by the trading public. If inflation finds its second breath, and commodity prices again rise in a climate of increased volatility, significant growth in options trading may be expected to occur.

TYPES OF COMMODITY OPTIONS

There are two fundamental types of options: *call* options and *put* options. A call option entitles the purchaser who holds it to buy a futures contract at a predetermined price regardless of what the market value of the commodity might be at the time the call is excercised. On the other side of the call, the call seller has the obligation to sell a futures contract, to whoever has bought the call, at the predetermined price. This price is termed the *strike price.*

A put option entitles its purchaser to sell a futures contract at a predetermined (strike) price. The holder of the put option therefore fixes the price at which he or she may sell a futures contract. Again, there is another side to the option contract. The seller of the put is obligated to purchase a futures contract from the person who holds the put.

The purchasers of both puts and calls obtain the *right* to excercise them, but not the obligation to do so. On the other hand, the sellers of both types of options incur an obligation. The seller of a call must sell a futures contract if the call is excercised. The seller of a put must buy a futures contract if the put is excercised. Whether or not an option is excercised is at the discretion of the purchaser of the option, the seller has no say in the matter.

Because option purchasers have no obligation, once the broker receives payment for the option, there is no risk associated with nonperformance unless and until the option is excercised. If an option is excercised, then the option holder gives up his or her option for a long (call holder) or a short (put holder) position in the commodity futures. After excercise of an option the erstwhile option purchaser is now like any other commodity customer with a long or a short position. Daily settlement and guarantees by the commodity exchanges themselves make risk of nonperformance on futures contract positions very small. Margin requirements are generally adequate to provide protection in the event a futures contract must be closed out for failure to deposit additional margin if it is called for.

In contrast to the case for option purchasers, the open-ended liability of option sellers presents potential problems and risks relating to possible non-performance in the event a call or put is excercised. Neither calls nor puts will be excercised unless it is to the advantage of the option holder to do so. But, if it is to the advantage of the option holder, it is to the disadvantage of the option seller, who may well be unable or unwilling to perform his or her side of the option contract. In the past such risks were substantial due to the inadequate regulation of options trading.

With the rebirth of commodity options trading in 1982, options are traded on the respective commodity exchanges. Risk from nonperformance has been minimized because the writing of options now requires margin deposits which, just as with futures contract positions, are adjusted daily. With the exchanges regulating trading in options on their respective futures contracts the situation is much different than it was in the mid-1970s. While the risks associated with price fluctuations are no different, the option trader today need not worry that the option he or she purchased, and which is worth much more due to a favorable market, cannot be excercised because of default by the option seller or brokerage house.

OPTION TERMINOLOGY

The *premium* is the price of an option. The futures contract price at which the option purchaser can excercise the option is the *strike price*. The *expiration date* is the last day on which the option may be excercised. An option which is *in-the-money* has a positive *intrinsic value*. For example, a call option with a strike price of 300 would be in-the-money if the market price were 330. In this case the call's intrinsic value is 30 (330–300). Sometimes the option with strike price nearest the market price for the underlying futures contract is referred to as *at-the-money*.

Options have two types of value: intrinsic value and time value. An option must trade at a premium at least as large as the intrinsic value. If it does not, arbitrageurs will quickly purchase the option, excercise it, and simultaneously liquidate the futures contract at a profit as long as transactions costs may be covered. Time value results from the fact that the more time remaining until expiration, the greater the chances of the option increasing in value. Investors are willing to pay more for options with a long time to expiration than for those with little time remaining. Time value may be calculated as the difference between an option's premium and its intrinsic value.

The *option month* refers to the futures contract delivery month, not to the month in which the option itself expires. Thus, a June option on COMEX gold is an option to buy (if a call) or sell (if a put) a June futures contract. The option itself expires after the close of trading on the second Friday of the prior month.

On the first trading day there are a number of strike prices for both calls and puts. For COMEX gold, for example, there are five strike prices for both calls and puts. Additional strike prices are added as the market price of the underlying futures contract moves away from the level it was at on the first option trading day.

The delivery months for which options trade generally cover a span of about a year into the future from the current date. In the case of sugar (No. 11 contract), options are traded on futures for March, July, October, and the first of these months for which futures trading has begun in the next year. For example, in November of any year, options trade on the March, July, and October futures in the following calendar year, plus March of the next year. The COMEX states matters differently for gold: "The trading cycle includes the nearest month from group A plus every month in group B." Group A includes February, June, and October. Group B contains April, August, and December.

Before moving on, there are a few loose ends to be tied up. A seller of options is generally referred to as an option *writer*. An option writer is either covered or naked. A *covered* option writer is one who writes an option against an open futures position: for example, one who has an open long position in T-bond futures and writes a T-bond call; or, one who has an open short position in the NYSE Composite Index futures contract and writes a put.

In the 1970s there was a type of option called a standard double. Such options were a combination put and call for which only one side could be exercised. These no longer exist as distinct options. However, the option trader may construct a substitute by purchasing both a put and a call. Both sides would generally not be exercised because if the price moves so that one option premium rises, the other must necessarily fall. The option with no intrinsic value clearly will not be exercised. An exception might be found in a market in which the price moved far away from the strike price in one direction, with one of the options exercised, and then reversed and moved to the other side of the strike price.

OPTION VALUATION

Call Options

The most widely encountered model for option valuation is that of Black and Scholes.[1] The model rests on the premise that an option premium is a function of the risk-free rate.[2] Assuming that investors have long positions in stocks (or, in our context, commodity futures), then a risk-free position can be established by selling a certain number of options. The number of options to be sold is given by

$$\frac{1}{W_1\,(S,t)} \tag{1}$$

where the denominator is the first partial derivative of the option price with respect to stock (or commodity) price. S denotes the price of the underlying security and t the life of the option. The net portfolio position is risk free because the option price will change by $W_1(S,t)\Delta S$ when the security price changes by ΔS.

The value of $W_1(S,t)$ was calculated by Black and Scholes to be $N(d_1)$, which denotes the cumulative normal probability density function of d_1. Beginning with the value of a risk-free portfolio, hedged with options

$$V_H = SQ_s + WQ_w \tag{2}$$

where Q_s is the number of shares in the risk-free portfolio, and Q_w the number of option contracts. They take the total derivative to obtain the equation

$$W(S,t) = SN(d_1) - e^{-r\tau}XN(d_2) \tag{3}$$

where

$$d_1 = \frac{\ln(S/X) + r}{\sigma\sqrt{\tau}} + \tfrac{1}{2}\sigma\sqrt{\tau} \tag{4}$$

$$d_2 = d_1 - \sigma \sqrt{\tau} \tag{5}$$

$$\tau = \text{time remaining to maturity}$$

$$= t - T$$

$$= \text{time to maturity} - \text{time already elapsed}$$

and

$$X = \text{strike price}$$

A number of important assumptions underly the Black and Scholes option model:

1. Security markets are efficient (in the sense that prices reflect at any moment all information relevant to their value).
2. The underlying security does not provide a dividend return.
3. Short selling is allowed, without restrictions.
4. No transactions costs apply.
5. The option is exercisable only at maturity, that is, a European type option.
6. There is a known and constant rate of interest.
7. Security prices are log-normally distributed. The continuously compounded one-period rates of return are normally distributed and have known constant variance, which is proportional to the square of the security price.

At first it would appear that the assumption that the option is exercisable only at maturity (i.e., a European type option) would destroy the usefulness of the model for American options which may be exercised at any time until they expire. However, this is not a problem for many stocks, nor for commodity futures.

R. C. Merton[3] asserted that for securities paying no dividend, options will not be exercised before the expiration date. The value of an American option must be at least as great as that of a European option because the American option has the same ability as the European with respect to exercise on the expiration date, *plus* the added advantage for the holder to exercise at any given time before that if he or she wishes. Since commodity futures contracts pay no dividends, the Black and Scholes model would seem to be applicable to options on futures contracts.

If one were to plot values of W for a given strike price X, a graph such as Figure 17-1 would be obtained. Note that as the price of the security (or futures contract) moves above the strike price the value of the call option increases and eventually approaches closely the price of the security.

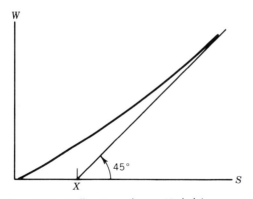

Figure 17.1. Call option value vs. Underlying security.

Put Options

Starting with the premise that the cash requirement for establishing a risk-free position is given by

$$C = V + P - W \tag{6}$$

where

V is the aggregate security value held
P is the put premium
W is the call premium

it can be shown that

$$\frac{W}{V} - \frac{P}{V} = \frac{i}{1 + i} \tag{7}$$

where i is the risk-free rate. When i is small

$$\frac{i}{1 + i} \simeq i \tag{8}$$

From Equation (7) we see that the difference between the relative values of a put and a call is approximately equal to the risk-free rate, i. How is this result obtained? Going back to the equation for the risk-free position, Equation (6), and noting that because it is risk-free the investor should be able to finance his or her holdings at the risk-free rate, we find that the profit obtained is given by

$$\pi = W - \frac{V_i}{1 + i} - P \qquad (9)$$

which should approach zero in a perfect market, due to arbitrage. Taking Equation (9) and setting to zero, then dividing by V to express in relative terms, yields Equation (7).

It should be noted that an equivalent risk-free position could be obtained with a short position in the security, writing a call, and buying a put.

For further discussion and insights into options valuation, the reader is referred to articles by Stoll,[4] Gould and Galai,[5] and to books by Gastineau[6] and by Khoury.[7] Gastineau provides additional models for option valuation, and Khoury provides a very readable summary.

BASIC OPTIONS STRATEGIES

Although the possible combinations of options and futures contracts are seemingly limited only by the imagination and creative talents of investors or speculators, certain fundamental positions and basic combinations may be identified. Armed with this foundation knowledge, one may then modify as required to deal with combinations of options with different strike prices, and so on.

A useful adjunct to the graphic representations that follow is that of *vector* notation.[8] Using column vectors of length 2 (i.e., dimension 2 by 1), one denotes the effect of price movements in the underlying security by $+1$, 0, and -1. The top entry in the vector denotes the effect of a price rise in the underlying security. The bottom entry denotes the effect of a decline in the price of the underlying security. A long position in a commodity futures contract is characterized by the vector $\begin{bmatrix} 1 \\ -1 \end{bmatrix}$. That is, if the stock goes up by one point, the value of an investment in the contract rises by one point; if the value of the contract falls by one point, the value of the investment falls by one point. Similarly, a short position in a commodity futures contract is represented by the vector $\begin{bmatrix} -1 \\ 1 \end{bmatrix}$.

By like reasoning, the position established by buying a call is denoted by $\begin{bmatrix} 1 \\ 0 \end{bmatrix}$ and that of selling a call by $\begin{bmatrix} -1 \\ 0 \end{bmatrix}$. Long a put option is represented by $\begin{bmatrix} 0 \\ 1 \end{bmatrix}$ and short a put option by $\begin{bmatrix} 0 \\ -1 \end{bmatrix}$.

The following examples illustrate fundamental combinations and demonstrate that the investor can create calls from futures and puts or puts from futures and calls. It is also possible to create a synthetic put for securities not having puts traded, through sale of two calls with different strike prices, in combination with a long position in the security.

The reader should note that the vector notation uses 0 and 1 as a convenience. In reality the change in option value depends on its "delta," which is a function of the remaining life of the option, the risk-free interest rate, the price of the underlying instrument in relation to the strike price, and the volatility of the underlying instrument's price. The delta will be close to 1.0 only when the option is in the money and just prior to its expiration. At other times it will be a fraction less than 1.0. Nevertheless, the vector notation is useful for assisting in the analysis of options.

IMPLEMENTING STRATEGIES

In this section the profit and loss potentials of basic options strategies and of certain combinations are examined graphically and with aid of the short-hand vector notation. The strike price is denoted by X, where the context makes clear whether it is a put or call premium, otherwise as P_P for a put, P_C for a call. The price of the underlying futures contract is denoted by F.

For simplicity, transactions costs have been ignored. In practice these may be taken into account by modification of the graphs. Such costs can have a significant effect on the profit-loss potential, particularly for low-premium options. There is considerable variation in transactions costs; brokers work at varying markups from their cost on such trades, and depending on the value of client's business to the firm, and other factors, may charge anywhere from a small markup to a large one.

Write (Sell) a Call

Sale of a call by someone who does not hold an offsetting position in the underlying commodity future is termed by those in the trade writing a naked call, or writing an uncovered call. Figure 17-2 illustrates the profit and loss potential of such a trade. The maximum profit is limited to the premium

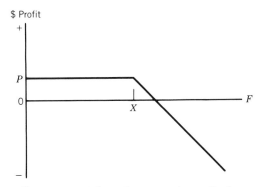

Figure 17.2. Sell a call. Vector: Short call $\left[\begin{smallmatrix} -1 \\ 0 \end{smallmatrix}\right]$.

received. The maximum loss cannot be clearly identified; it is a function of how high the price of the underlying commodity can go, and that can be very high. As long as the futures price F is above the strike price X at expiration, the call will be exercised. This strategy is clearly for one who believes strongly that the futures price will not go higher, but will be steady to somewhat lower.

Buy a Call

This is illustrated in Figure 17-3. One who buys a call clearly must be of the opinion that the price of the underlying futures commodity will go up significantly. It is not enough that the price rise modestly because the premium paid for the call must be recovered in order to just break even. Unless those writing calls are not rational or informed, they will charge premiums large enough to compensate them for the risk they bear vis-à-vis their expected return. This suggests that option premiums will be priced to fairly reflect their profit potential. It implies that the road to riches may not be easily traveled in the realm of options. And, if prices follow a random walk over time, the price of the underlying commodity is as likely to be lower as it is to be higher at expiration of the option.

Sell a Put

This is similar to writing a call but, as shown in Figure 17-4, the profit-loss function is rotated 180 degrees around a vertical axis through the strike price. Again, the maximum gain is equal to the premium, as with writing an uncovered call. Also, the maximum loss is open ended. However, with a put option, a zero price for the underlying commodity provides a theoretical limit, though not a practical one.

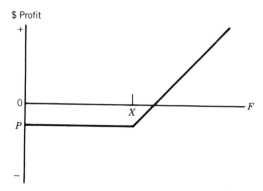

Figure 17.3. Buy a call. Vector: Long call $\begin{bmatrix} 1 \\ 0 \end{bmatrix}$.

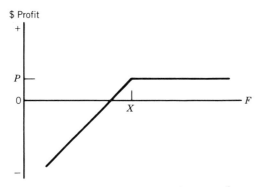

Figure 17.4. Sell a put. Vector: Short put $[\begin{smallmatrix} 0 \\ -1 \end{smallmatrix}]$.

Buy a Put

As with selling a put, there is a parallel to the corresponding trade with a call option. Again, the profit-loss function associated with buying a put is like that obtained by rotating the function for buying a call 180 degrees around a vertical axis through the strike price. The maximum potential loss is limited to the premium paid. The maximum potential gain is theoretically defined by the price of the commodity falling to zero. In practical terms, it will be much less. Figure 17-5 illustrates this trade.

Buy Futures, Write Call

This strategy illustrates the writing of a "synthetic" put, by writing a covered call. If the price rises above the strike price, X, as shown in Figure 17-6, the call will be exercised and the futures contract given up. On the other hand, if the price falls the call will not be exercised and the premium will partially offset the losses.

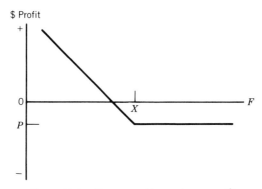

Figure 17.5. Buy a put. Vector: Long put $[\begin{smallmatrix} 0 \\ 1 \end{smallmatrix}]$.

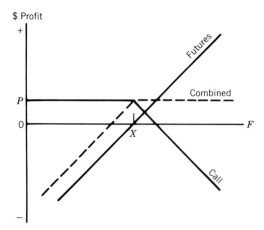

Figure 17.6. Buy futures contract, sell call. Vector: Long futures + Short call = Short put, $\lfloor{}^{1}_{-1}\rfloor$ + $\lfloor{}^{-1}_{0}\rfloor$ = $\lfloor{}^{0}_{-1}\rfloor$.

Sell Futures, Sell Put

This combination, illustrated in Figure 17-7, shows the writing of a "synthetic" call through covered put writing; that is, selling a put that is covered by a short futures position. If the price of the commodity is below the strike price at expiration the put will be exercised and the short futures position offset. A profit equal to the premium results. If the price is above the strike price at expiration, the put will not be exercised and the premium will partially offset the losses on the futures contract.

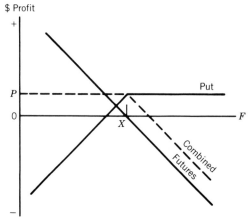

Figure 17.7. Sell futures contract, sell put. Vector: Short futures + Short put = Short call, $\lfloor{}^{-1}_{1}\rfloor$ + $\lfloor{}^{0}_{-1}\rfloor$ = $\lfloor{}^{-1}_{0}\rfloor$.

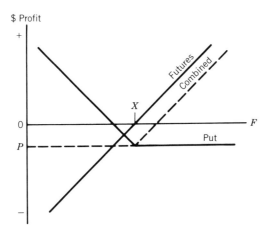

Figure 17.8. Buy futures, buy put. Vector: Long futures + Long put = Long call, $\begin{bmatrix} 1 \\ -1 \end{bmatrix} + \begin{bmatrix} 0 \\ 1 \end{bmatrix} = \begin{bmatrix} 1 \\ 0 \end{bmatrix}$.

Buy Futures, Buy Put

Figure 17-8 illustrates this combination, which results in creation of a "synthetic" long call position. At expiration, a price below the strike price will cause the investor to exercise the put to dispose of his or her futures contract. If the price is above the strike price at expiration, the put will not be exercised. The premium will be lost and will reduce the profit that is made on the futures contract.

Sell Futures, Buy Call

This strategy results in the creation of a "synthetic" long put position, as shown in Figure 17-9. The call will not be exercised at a price below the strike

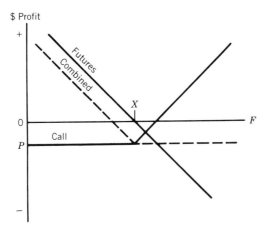

Figure 17.9. Sell futures, buy call. Vector: Short futures + Long call = Long put, $\begin{bmatrix} -1 \\ 1 \end{bmatrix} + \begin{bmatrix} 1 \\ 0 \end{bmatrix} = \begin{bmatrix} 0 \\ 1 \end{bmatrix}$.

price X, and the premium cost will reduce the profit from the futures contract. At a price above X the call will be exercised at expiration so that loss is limited to the cost of the premium.

Write Put, Write Call (Sell Straddle)

Simultaneous writing of a put and a call is termed selling a straddle. Figure 17-10 illustrates the strategy. Note that the premium is the sum of call premium and put premium. The profit-loss vector contains two minus entries for the combination. This means that profit will decline if the price of the futures moves either way. Of course, the premiums provide a buffer; the price of the futures would have to move one way or the other a fairly large distance for a net loss to result. Clearly, at expiration, one or the other, or neither option will be exercised, never both.

This strategy implies that the trader expects the commodity price will change little if any from the strike price.

Buy Put, Buy Call (Buy Straddle)

Simultaneous purchase of both a put and a call results in what is termed buying a straddle. The cost is the sum of the put premium and the call premium. If the price does not change significantly from the strike price, the trader will not recover the full premium cost. However, a large price change in either direction will be profitable. As in the case of selling a straddle, only one option will be exercised at expiration.

This strategy is illustrated in Figure 17-11. It implies that the trader believes a sharp change in price is coming, but doesn't know the direction of the change.

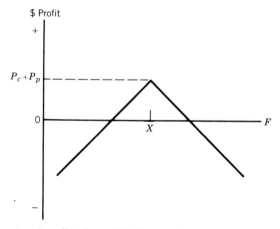

Figure 17.10. Write put, write call (sell straddle). Vector: Short put + Short call, $\begin{bmatrix} 0 \\ -1 \end{bmatrix} + \begin{bmatrix} -1 \\ 0 \end{bmatrix} = \begin{bmatrix} -1 \\ -1 \end{bmatrix}$.

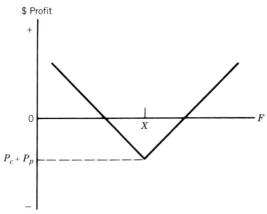

Figure 17.11. Buy put, buy call (buy straddle). Vector: Long put + Long call $[^0_1] + [^1_0] = [^1_1]$.

ADDITIONAL STRATEGIES

In addition to the basic and combined strategies, there are several others which involve options of the same type. These are the "bear call spread," "bear put spread," "bull call spread," "bull put spread," and "neutral calendar spread."

Bear Call Spread

The bear call spread is a combination of long a call with high strike price, short a call with lower strike price. The maximum profit on this combination is equal to the net premium received. The premium paid on the call with the higher strike price will always be less than that paid on the call with the lower strike price. The maximum loss is limited to the difference in the two strike prices, less the net premium received. This is illustrated in Figure 17-12.

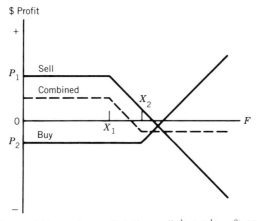

Figure 17.12. Bear call spread. Vector: Long call + Short call $[^1_0] + [^{-1}_0] = [^0_0]$. Maximum profit: $P_1 - P_2$. Maximum loss: $(X_2 - X_1) - (P_1 - P_2)$.

For example, assume a trader expects higher interest rates, and consequently lower bond prices. He notes that the December T-bond futures price is 66-00. He buys a Dec/68 call for a premium of $2000 and sells a Dec/62 call for a premium of $6500. The maximum loss can be no more than $1500. This is the difference in strike prices of $6000 less the net premium of ($6500 − $2000) that is received. The maximum profit possible on the trade is the net premium of $4500 that is received.

Bear Put Spread

A bear put spread is entered by writing a put option with a low strike price and buying a put option on the same commodity future at a higher strike price. This is illustrated in Figure 17-13.

The maximum profit on a bear put spread is equal to the difference in strike prices less the net premium paid. For a put the premium of the option with the higher strike price will always be greater than the premium of the option with the lower strike price.

For example, assume that in late November an investor decides the price of world sugar is likely to fall from its current level of 9.75 cents per pound. She purchases a March put with a strike price of 12.00 cents and pays a premium of 2.20, which in dollar terms is $2464 (=2.20 × $1120). She simultaneously writes a March put with a 10.00 cent strike price for a premium of 0.90 ($1008), for a net premium cost of $1456. The maximum profit she will make is the difference in strike prices (in dollars) of $2240 (12.00 − 10.00), where $1120 is the value of a one cent price change on a contract size of 112,000 pounds, less the net premium received. Thus, the maximum net profit is $784 (=$2240 − $1456). The maximum loss she could incur is given by the difference in premiums, $1456.

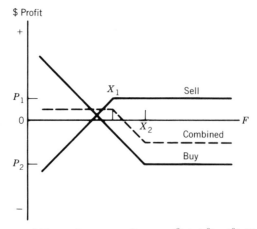

Figure 17.13. Bear put spread. Vector: Long put + Short put $[\begin{smallmatrix} 0 \\ 1 \end{smallmatrix}] + [\begin{smallmatrix} 0 \\ -1 \end{smallmatrix}] = [\begin{smallmatrix} 0 \\ 0 \end{smallmatrix}]$. Maximum profit: $(X_2 − X_1)$ − $(P_1 − P_2)$. Maximum loss: $P_2 − P_1$.

In comparison to the bear call spread, the bear put spread offers a less attractive risk/reward ratio. Assume our trader had instead used a bear call spread. She writes a March call with a 10.00 cent strike price and buys a call with a 12.00 cent strike price, *receiving* a net premium of $1064 (=$1120 (3.05 − 2.10)). Her maximum net profit is now the difference in premiums, $1064, which she begins with. Her maximum net loss is given by the difference in strike price values less the net premium received: $1176 = $2240 − $1064. The bear call spread is clearly superior and dominates the bear put spread for these strike prices and premiums by offering a higher maximum profit ($1064 vs. $784) and lower maximum loss as well ($1176 vs. $1456).

Bull Call Spread

Figure 17-14 depicts the bull call spread. In this trade the investor writes a call for a high strike price and purchases a call on the same commodity future with a lower strike price, in anticipation of higher prices. His maximum gain is the difference in strike prices less the net premium paid. His maximum net loss is the difference in premiums.

Assume, for example, that an investor thinks the price of gold will go up soon. In December he writes an April $420 call for a premium of 4.80 ($480 = $4.80 × 100 oz/contract) and purchases an April $380 call for 19.20 ($1920 = $19.20 × 100). The underlying futures price is $390. The investor's maximum net profit is $(420 − 380) × 100 oz/contract less $(1920 − 480) = $4000 − $1440 = $2560. His maximum loss is the net premium cost of $1440.

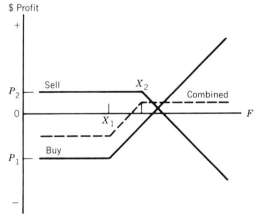

Figure 17.14. Bull call spread. Vector: Long call + Short call $\begin{vmatrix} 1 \\ 0 \end{vmatrix} + \begin{vmatrix} -1 \\ 0 \end{vmatrix} = \begin{vmatrix} 0 \\ 0 \end{vmatrix}$. Maximum profit: $(X_2 − X_1) − (P_2 − P_1)$. Maximum loss: $P_1 − P_2$.

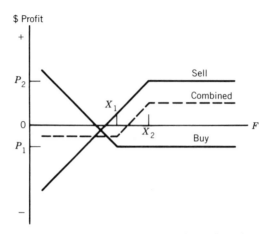

Figure 17.15. Bull put spread. Vector: Long put + Short put $\begin{bmatrix} 0 \\ 1 \end{bmatrix}$ + $\begin{bmatrix} 0 \\ -1 \end{bmatrix}$ = $\begin{bmatrix} 0 \\ 0 \end{bmatrix}$. Maximum profit: $P_2 - P_1$. Maximum loss: $(X_2 - X_1) - (P_2 - P_1)$.

Bull Put Spread

The bull put spread is illustrated in Figure 17-15. In this, the trader writes a put with a high strike price, and buys one with a lower strike price on the same underlying futures. Maximum profit is the net premium received. Maximum loss is the difference in strike prices less the net premium received. The put with the higher strike price will always have a higher premium.

For illustration, assume that the investor in early December decides the stock market will continue to set new record highs in the next few weeks. She writes a NYSE June 104 put for a 6.60 premium ($500 × 6.60 = $3300). She buys a June 96 put for a 2.60 premium ($500 × 2.60 = $1300). The net premium received is $2000 ($500 (6.60 − 2.60)).

The maximum net profit on the trade is the net premium received of $2000. The maximum gain is exactly the same as the maximum loss, a situation obtained by selecting strike prices exactly the same distance above as below the current NYSE index futures "price."

Variations

The examples just discussed assume that both options in a spread would be in the same month. However, in practice there may be good reasons for using different months.

Ratio writing involves writing multiple options against each open futures contract position. The motivation is that most option premiums do not in fact move in lock-step, dollar-for-dollar with the futures price. Thus, one futures contract may serve to cover several options against it. The example COMEX provides is "suppose an investor grants two $340 December gold futures call options at $15 premiums. At the same time he buys December gold futures at $340 an ounce. Since he has collected $30 worth of premium income, the investor is assured of a writing profit as long as the options expire with December gold futures trading somewhere between $310 and $370 an ounce."[9] Thus, a $60 band of profitability has been defined. If the price closes outside that band, net losses will be incurred.

A *neutral calendar spread* is motivated by the observation that options with little time remaining to expiration have faster declines in their premiums than those with longer time remaining. For example, the trader might write a February call and simultaneously purchase an August call in November. As expiration of the February option is approached, its time value (*not* its intrinsic value) approaches zero, while the August option continues to have time value (plus whatever intrinsic value there may be at the given strike price).

It should be noted that with American options the option writer is free to purchase his or her option in the market, thus offsetting the position. Under favorable circumstances, an option writer may be able to write an option several times at a high premium, and offset it at a lower premium if the price of the underlying commodity future falls significantly.

CONCLUSION

Commodity options, after a troubled former incarnation, have been born again. This time the performance and regulation is the responsibility of the various exchanges. The success or failure of trading this time will be a function of the economic role options have to fill, not a matter of public confidence in various individual options dealers of widely varying characteristics.

A number of basic options strategies exist, and these may be combined into a virtually unlimited number of variations.[10] This provides a wide panoply of alternatives to the investor who is capable of, and interested in analyzing option premiums vis-a-vis the underlying futures. The reward to be found in options trading is a profit with potential loss limited in advance to a known maximum.

At the time of this writing, there are two impediments to the commodity option trader: First, most brokers have not studied these options, are not knowledgeable about them, and consequently cannot be of much help to the investor. Second, the volume of trading in some options is insufficient to allow some of the options strategies discussed in this chapter to be successfully applied. Hopefully, as time passes, both these problems will diminish. The problems would appear to be mutually reinforcing. However, it could be argued that if the broker knowledge problem is addressed, trading volume will increase as a result.

Notes

[1] Fischer Black and Myron Scholes, "The Pricing of Options and Corporate Liabilities." *Journal of Political Economy* **81** (May–June 1973): 637–654.

[2] The rate on U.S. Treasury bills is usually used as the risk-free rate.

[3] R. C. Merton, "Theory of Rational Option Pricing." *Bell Journal of Economics and Management Science* **4** (1973): 141–183.

[4] Hans R. Stoll, "The Relationship Between Put and Call Option Prices." *Journal of Finance* **25**, no. 5 (December 1969): 801–829.

[5] J. P. Gould and D. Galai, "Transactions Costs and the Relationship between Put and Call Prices." *Journal of Financial Economics* **1** (1974): 105–129.

[6] Gary Gastineau, *The Stock Options Manual,* 2nd ed. (New York: McGraw-Hill, 1979).

[7] Sarkis Khoury, *Investment Management* (New York: Macmillan, 1983).

[8] For detailed discussion see Nicholas Kane, "The New Options/Futures Markets: Caveat Emptor et Vendor." *The AAII Journal* **9**, no. 3 (April 1982): 5–8 and 11; or Khoury, *Investment Management,* p. 357.

[9] *Options on Comex Gold,* p. 34.

[10] H. Phillip Becker and William H. Degler, "19 Options Strategies and When to Use Them." *Futures* **13**, no. 6 (June 1984): 46–51.

References

1. H. Phillip Becker and William H. Degler, "19 Options Strategies and When to Use Them." *Futures* **13**, no. 6 (June 1984): 46–51.

2. Fischer Black and Myron Scholes, "The Pricing of Options and Corporate Liabilities." *Journal of Political Economy* **81** (May–June 1973): 637–654.

3. R. C. Merton, "Theory of Rational Option Pricing." *Bell Journal of Economics and Management Science* **4** (1973): 141–183.

4. Gary Gastineau, *The Stock Options Manual,* 2nd ed. (New York: McGraw-Hill, 1979).

5. J. P. Gould and D. Galai, "Transactions Costs and the Relationship between Put and Call Prices." *Journal of Financial Economics* **1** (1974): 105–129.

6. Nicholas Kane, "The New Options/Futures Markets: Caveat Emptor et Vendor." *The AAII Journal* **9**, no. 3 (April 1982): 5–8, 11.

7. Sarkis Khoury, *Investment Management* (New York: Macmillan, 1983).

8. Hans R. Stoll, "The Relationship Between Put and Call Option Prices." *Journal of Finance* **24**, no. 5 (December 1969): 801–829.

9. *Understanding Options on Futures* (New York: Coffee, Sugar and Cocoa Exchange, Inc., 1982).

10. *Options on Comex Gold* (Chicago: The Commodity Exchange, Inc.).

11. *Options on Futures: A New Way to Participate in Futures* (Chicago: The Chicago Mercantile Exchange, 1983).

12. *The Option for the Future* (New York: New York Futures Exchange, undated).

13. *Strategies for Buying and Writing Options on Treasury Bond Futures* (Chicago: Chicago Board of Trade, 1982).

14. Kermit C. Zieg and Susannah H. Zieg, *Commodity Options* (Larchmont, NY: Investor's Intelligence, Inc., 1974).

Index